FRIENDS *of the*
Livingston Public Library
Gratefully Acknowledges
the Contribution of

Ashlea and Charles Budzinski

For the 2019-2020 Membership Year

ALSO BY JANET MALCOLM

Forty-One False Starts: Essays on Artists and Writers

Iphigenia in Forest Hills: Anatomy of a Murder Trial

Burdock

Two Lives: Gertrude and Alice

Reading Chekhov: A Critical Journey

The Crime of Sheila McGough

The Silent Woman: Sylvia Plath and Ted Hughes

The Purloined Clinic: Selected Writings

The Journalist and the Murderer

In the Freud Archives

Psychoanalysis: The Impossible Profession

Diana and Nikon: Essays on Photography

NOBODY'S
LOOKING
AT YOU

NOBODY'S LOOKING AT YOU

ESSAYS

JANET MALCOLM

FARRAR, STRAUS AND GIROUX

NEW YORK

Farrar, Straus and Giroux
175 Varick Street, New York 10014

Copyright © 2019 by Janet Malcolm
All rights reserved
Printed in the United States of America
First edition, 2019

The essays in this volume originally appeared in the following
publications: *The New York Review of Books*: "Special Needs,"
"Comedy Central on the Mall" (NYR Daily), "Pandora's Click,"
"Dreams and Anna Karenina," "Socks," "The Master Writer of the
City," "It Happened in Milwaukee," "Sisters, Lovers, Tarts, and
Friends," "'A Very Sadistic Man,'" "Remember the Ladies,"
"'I Should Have Made Him for a Dentist'"; *The New Yorker*:
"Nobody's Looking at You," "Performance Artist," "Three Sisters,"
"The "Émigré," "The Storyteller," "The Art of Testifying," "Women
at War: A Case of Sexual Harassment."

Library of Congress Cataloging-in-Publication Data
Names: Malcolm, Janet, author.
Title: Nobody's looking at you : essays / Janet Malcolm.
Description: First edition. | New York : Farrar, Straus and Giroux,
2019.
Identifiers: LCCN 2018031206 | ISBN 9780374279493 (hardcover)
Classification: LCC AC8.5 .M35 2019 | DDC 814/.54—dc23
LC record available at https://lccn.loc.gov/2018031206

Designed by Jonathan D. Lippincott

Our books may be purchased in bulk for promotional, educational,
or business use. Please contact your local bookseller or the
Macmillan Corporate and Premium Sales Department at
1-800-221-7945, extension 5442, or by e-mail at
MacmillanSpecialMarkets@macmillan.com.

www.fsgbooks.com
www.twitter.com/fsgbooks • www.facebook.com/fsgbooks

1   3   5   7   9   10   8   6   4   2

In memory of Robert Silvers

CONTENTS

PART I

NOBODY'S LOOKING AT YOU

There is a wish shared by women who consider themselves serious that the clothes they wear look as if they were heedlessly flung on rather than anxiously selected. The clothes of Eileen Fisher seem to have been designed to fulfill that wish. Words like "simple" and "tasteful" and colors like black and gray come to mind along with images of women of a certain age and class—professors, editors, psychotherapists, lawyers, administrators—for whom the hiding of vanity is an inner necessity.

The first Eileen Fisher shop opened in 1987, on Ninth Street in the East Village. Today, Eileen Fisher is an enterprise with nearly a thousand employees. The clothes sell in department stores and catalogues as well as in six Eileen Fisher shops in Manhattan and fifty-five throughout the country. Over the years, the clothes have become less plain and more like the clothes in fashion. Some of the older Eileen Fisher customers grouse about these changes. They want the clothes to remain the same, as if anything can. Surely not clothes.

I remember going into the Eileen Fisher shops that were opening around the city in the late 1980s and never buying anything. I was attracted by the austere beauty of

the clothes. They were loose and long and interesting.
There was an atmosphere of early modernism in their
geometric shapes and murky muted colors. You could see
Alma Mahler wearing them around the Bauhaus. But you
could not wear them yourself if you weren't fairly stately.
After a few years, the clothes changed and began to suit
small, thin women as well as tall, substantial ones. But
their original atmosphere remained. I joined a growing
cadre of women who regularly shop at Eileen Fisher and
form a kind of cult of the interestingly plain.

One day in February, I went to talk with Eileen Fisher
at her house, in Irvington, New York, and was immediately struck by her beauty. She does not look like a woman
who is uninterested in her appearance. She looks glamorous and stylish. She is slender and fine-boned. Her straight,
completely white hair is cut in a geometric chin-length
bob. She wears dark-rimmed glasses. Her features are
delicate, and there is a certain fragility about her, an atmosphere of someone who needs protection. And she
came to the interview protected, by two executives in
her company: Hilary Old, the Vice President of Communications, and Monica Rowe, the Director of Public
Relations. I was received in a large, light room that looks
out on the Hudson River and its distant shore (the river
is magnificently wide here) through a picture window. A
lunch of choice dishes—crab cakes, rice salad, a salad of
winter squash and goat cheese—had been laid out on a
long table. Eileen (as I will call her, as one calls Hillary
Hillary) presented herself as someone who is still trying
to overcome an innate awkwardness and shyness and ver-
bal tentativeness. "Speaking and writing have always
been hard for me," she said as her colleagues looked on

fondly and encouragingly, as if at a relative with an endearing quirk.

She apologized for the lunch that clearly needed no apology. But she had planned to serve sushi prepared by her Japanese cook, who had been called away at the last minute. That Eileen Fisher had a Japanese cook did not surprise me; nor did the story she told a few minutes later about a fateful chance encounter with a Japanese designer who became her employer and lover. A sense of Japan hovers over Eileen Fisher's modernism (as it does, when you think about it, over modernism itself).

When the encounter with the Japanese designer took place, in the mid-1970s, she was a young woman from the Chicago suburb of Des Plaines ("Home of McDonald's, Anywhere, U.S.A.," in her description) who had recently graduated from the University of Illinois as a home ec major and had come to New York to become an interior designer. But she wasn't succeeding. "I wasn't good with words," she said. "I wasn't that good with people, either. I couldn't explain my ideas to clients." To support herself, she waited on tables and also took small graphic-design jobs. One day, while at a printing shop to which she had brought a design for stationery, "this Japanese guy was also printing something, and he looked at my design and liked it and said, 'I'm a graphic designer, and I need an assistant. Would you apply for the job?' I applied and he hired me and we ended up getting into a relationship. I moved in with him—that was kind of a mistake—but the working part of it was a great experience. His name was Rei. We went to Japan to work on advertising projects for clients like Kirin beer and a large stationery company and a big chemical company. We needed to present a lot of ideas, to throw in a lot of stuff, so he had me throw in my designs. Then weird things would happen, like they would pick my design. And he would get upset. I think he thought I was this little assistant, I was nice and cute or whatever I was. When they picked my design, it created a problem in our relationship." The relationship did not survive the problem (of her talent), but the lesson of Japan stayed with Eileen: "I got inspired. I saw the kimono. I saw it worn different ways. I saw all those little cotton kimonos and those kimono things they wear in the rice paddies and tie back and little flood pants. I was intrigued by the aesthetic of Japan. The simplicity of it. I was already interested in simplicity from interior design. And Rei was really minimal. But it was the kimono that inspired me. The piece you're wearing is an extension of the kimono."

The piece I was wearing was a heavy, charcoal-gray wool cardigan sweater that I bought at an Eileen Fisher shop six or seven years ago and rarely wear because it is rarely cold enough to wear it. But the day was bitterly cold and raw and windy, and it was not too warm inside to be wearing it. The sweater is a remarkable garment. On the hanger it looks like nothing—it is buttonless and ribbed and boxy—but when worn it becomes almost uncannily flattering. Everyone who wears it looks good in it. Eileen then said something surprising, namely that she had not designed my sweater. Twenty years earlier, she had stopped designing; she had turned this work over to a design team that has been doing it ever since, at first under her supervision and now under that of a lead designer.

"I stored that idea about the kimono," Eileen went on. "After Rei and I split up, I went about my business. I tried to make a living. I did apartments, stationery, small things. I designed a tofu package. But this idea kept haunting me, this clothing thing, the kimono. I was living in Tribeca and had artist friends and designer friends. I was dating a guy who was a sculptor. He was designing jewelry, and he had taken a booth at a boutique show where owners of small clothing stores from around the country come to New York to buy clothes and accessories from small designers. He took me to the show, and I remember looking around and going, 'I could do this.' I had never designed any clothes, but I could picture it, I could see clothes I had designed on the walls."

At the next boutique show, a few months later, Eileen took over the boyfriend's booth. (He had stopped making jewelry but had committed himself to the booth.) She shared it with two other designers, since she couldn't afford the rent for the whole booth. "It was three weeks before the show, and I had no clothes. I had to figure out what to do. I ended up hiring someone to sew for me and make the first patterns."

"You drew the designs?"

"No. I never learned how to draw. I found other garments that were similar, that kind of got me close."

"What do you mean other garments?"

"Things that were in stores. That were similar to what I was thinking."

"You bought these clothes?"

"Yes, and I said to Gail, the woman who was making the patterns, it's kind of like this, but the neck is more like that, and it's a little longer, or it's a little shorter, it's a little wider, it's got a long sleeve or a shorter sleeve or something like that. It was going off of something that existed. Gail sewed the clothes—there were four garments made of linen—and I took them to the boutique show and hung them up. I remember being terrified standing there and waiting for what people would say. But everyone was kind, maybe because I was quiet and shy. I wanted to know what the buyers thought, and they would tell me and I would listen."

Gail had been unimpressed with the designs. "'You have to have an idea, Eileen,' she told me. 'This is a little boring. Put some piping on it or something.'" The psychotherapist Eileen was then seeing was not encouraging, either. "She felt I was making progress with my interior-design business. I was learning to communicate and to express my needs and ask for payment and other things that were hard for me to ask for. She thought that my taking a divergent path was some kind of sabotaging behavior." But several buyers liked Eileen's unadorned garments and ordered them, and at the next boutique show buyers stood in line and wrote orders amounting to forty thousand dollars. This was more than Gail could manage, and a small factory in Queens was found to do the sewing. "We cut the pieces and carried them in garbage bags on the subway to Queens."

Hilary Old and Monica Rowe had been listening quietly while Eileen told this history in answer to my questions. She had not touched her lunch, and, so that she might do so, I questioned her companions about what they did in the company. Rowe, a handsome African-American woman of forty-five with an air of friendly reserve, had only recently joined the company. "I've spent most of my career in corporate communications," she said, mentioning Sephora and Bath and Body Works as companies she had worked for, and speaking admiringly of the "woman-friendly" ethos of Eileen Fisher. Old, who is also forty-five, with a fresh, open face and a manner that is at once confident and modest, has been in the company for eighteen years and rose through the ranks from a job as a saleswoman in the White Plains store. She had majored in women's studies at the University of Colorado and came to the attention of higher-ups in the company when she sent a letter to Eileen in which she expressed her sense of the Eileen Fisher aesthetic as a "totally radical feminist project" and proposed that the company connect itself with women's groups. She was steered toward a job in public relations, working on a newsletter written in Eileen's voice. A year later, she became Eileen's assistant. "I was lucky enough to have that role when the company was going through hard times and had to reimagine and reorganize itself in some profound ways," Old said.

When I asked about the hard times, and how they were surmounted, she and Eileen spoke about the almost magical intervention of a woman named Susan Schor, who arrived as if from Mt. Olympus, though she actually only came from Pace University.

"It began as an effort to give more structure to this almost feminine way of doing things—I didn't know how to run a business," Eileen said. "You're looking at me as if I'm weird or something."

I said I was surprised to hear her say she didn't know how to run a business, since her enterprise was such a manifestly successful one. "Weren't you making a lot of money?"

"Yes. Absolutely."

"That isn't something associated with the feminine."

"To me it was very intuitive. I was always good with numbers. I was good in math."

"So if the company was doing well, why were you dissatisfied? What was lacking?"

Eileen struggled to explain. Evidently, there was both a "need for more structure" and insufficient "joy and well-being." She told the story—now a kind of legendary tale in the company annals—of the male C.E.O. who had been hired during the period of wobbliness and discontent. "It was clear after a few months that this was the wrong path. He was a lovely guy. He would have been the right C.E.O. for our company if a C.E.O. was the right role for our company. But it was the old paradigm of somebody directing the action. I remember after a meeting going, 'I don't think this is going to work.' People would ask me, 'Do we have to listen to him when he tells us what to do?'"

"You yourself don't like to tell people what to do," I said.

"Right, right," Eileen said, and added, "I think it comes out of a family model or something." Earlier, Eileen had spoken of her family with a kind of withering rue. She is the second oldest of seven children, six of them girls. "We sort of raised ourselves," she said. "My mother—I shouldn't describe it like this—but she was a little crazy. My father was an accountant at Allstate Insurance. He was a quiet guy, kind of disengaged."

"So the model for the company was a family without parents."

"Yes. My parents weren't in charge. With my six siblings, we ran the show. We did what we did. My mother put food on the table and cleaned the house, but she never told us what to do. She yelled at us more than anything, but didn't teach us things and didn't really take charge."

The incomparable Susan arrived a few years after the C.E.O. left. "What did Susan actually do?" I asked.

Eileen tried to say, but her reply was like a hermetic text by Judith Butler. She spoke of a "core concept team" and "the leadership forum" and "this kind of concept of facilitating leaders, which is that they're actually doing the work, they're not leading the work, but sort of like the way I've been leading from behind, in a way leading by, you know, letting the group find what's coming up and facilitating that to happen." Once again, she read my face and stopped herself: "You're looking at me like I'm crazy."

I admitted that I had no idea what she was talking about.

Old stepped in but was equally powerless to explain the inexplicable: "What we're trying to do with this different kind of leadership is to have the leader facilitate the process, so you get the team or the craft team in the room together, to ideate together, to generate the ideas together, and then figure out who's going to hold what, who's going to move what forward, so it's less of, it's more about kind of again the holding the space for the team to find."

The talk gradually grew less opaque. But I noticed that whenever the workings of the company came under discussion the language became peculiar and contorted, as if something were being hidden. In fact, the company has nothing to hide. It is remarkably benign and well intentioned. It has a profit-sharing plan for its employees, whereby 29 percent of the profits are given to them. The plan includes the salespeople, who do not work on commission. (Two thousand twelve was an exceptionally profitable year, and every employee received the equivalent of an extra eleven weeks of salary.) The salespeople are expected to wear Eileen Fisher clothes to work, and are given five free garments a month so that they may do so. (The clothes are not cheap; they are priced in the "luxury" category, to which brands such as Ralph Lauren and DKNY belong.)

Along with being generous to its own employees, the company tries to help the workers in the Chinese factories where most of the Eileen Fisher clothes are now made; there is a Director of Social Consciousness, who oversees the inspection of those factories. In addition, there is a Director of Sustainability, who is in charge of environmental exemplariness. The company tries to be as green as it can without losing its shirt. For example, 50 percent of the cotton it uses comes from organic farms that do not use pesticides, and nontoxic dyes are preferred if not always insisted on. Eileen takes justifiable pride in her company's good works and good intentions, and its esprit.

However, when Susan Schor arrived at the company, in 1999, it was slipping away from Eileen. In 1988, she had married David Zwiebel, who owned two dress shops in upstate New York and was one of the early buyers of Eileen Fisher designs. After they married, Zwiebel joined Eileen at the company. She credits him with a "watershed moment": the opening of an Eileen Fisher shop on Madison Avenue at Fifty-Fourth Street. "David found that location and really pushed for it," she said. Before the opening of the Madison Avenue shop, department stores had hesitated to take Eileen Fisher designs; now they saw the point of doing so. Today, department stores represent 70 percent of the company's business. In the late nineties, the marriage ended, and Zwiebel left the company. "That was a hard time," Eileen recalled. "Everything was mixed up. It sort of reminded me of that situation with the Japanese boyfriend. Why do we repeat the same things?" After the separation, Eileen spent less time at the company in order to be with her children, Zack and Sasha, then eight and four.

On her return to the office full-time, a few years later, "Eileen no longer felt at home in her own company," Susan Schor said when I spoke with her at the company's headquarters, at 111 Fifth Avenue. "It had become more corporate, more hierarchical, less collaborative, less caring. There was more unhappiness, I'd say. People weren't kind enough to each other. Deadlines were more important than the process that led to the deadlines."

Schor is a handsome, vivacious, articulate woman of sixty-seven. She was teaching courses on "leadership skills" and "interpersonal skills" at the Pace business school when she and Eileen met, at a birthday party, and felt an immediate rapport. (Schor was wearing Eileen Fisher clothes.) Eileen confided her worries about the company and "some questions she had about her own leadership." She invited Schor to visit the company and observe its workings. Schor immediately recognized the power vacuum created by Eileen's inability to say a cross word to anyone. "It became clear to me that the company needed someone with my background," Schor said, "though it wasn't going to be me, because I loved being a tenured faculty member at Pace." In the end, Schor overcame her reluctance and took on the task she was so well equipped to perform, of getting a C.E.O.'s grip on the company while appearing to be doing nothing of the sort. Where the male C.E.O. had failed, the female professor of the legerdemain of leadership succeeded. Although Schor spoke regular English, and gave the air of being completely forthcoming, she was almost as elusive as Eileen and Old and Rowe had been when I tried to find out what, exactly, she had done to "bring in a very caring, feminine style of leadership that valued people working together, that valued cooperation rather than competition, that made room for having a full life." All that Schor could tell me was that "it was not a happy place when I came," and now it is "a pretty happy organization that keeps getting happier and happier."

At the end of the Irvington lunch, which had been scheduled to dovetail with another appointment, Eileen looked at her watch and proposed that I stay a few minutes longer so I wouldn't have to wait for my train on the chilly outdoor platform—the train was due in fifteen minutes and the station was only five minutes away. "Do you want to see the living room?" she asked. Old, Rowe, and I followed her into a spacious room with a kitchen at one end and beige sofas and armchairs and side tables with books and magazines and attractive objects on them at the other. Two cats curled up on cushions completed the picture of pleasing domestic comfort.

I noticed a third cat on the outside of one of the French doors that lined a wall—standing on its hind legs, its paws eagerly pressed against the glass—and asked if I should let him in. "Oh, no, please don't do that!" Eileen said. She explained that this cat was never let into the house.

He was the bad cat. He had once lived in the house with the other cats, but he had fought with the second male cat and peed all over the floor and when the housekeeper threatened to quit he was expelled from the house and now lived outdoors. He was begging not to come in from the cold, Eileen said, but to be fed. When I asked how he survived the bitter winter weather, she said, "He goes under the house. He's fine. The vet said he's the healthiest of my cats."

When I returned to Eileen's house a few weeks later—this time after lunch—Old and Rowe were on handmaiden duty again, but the interview took place in a different room. A meeting was going on in the room where we had eaten, and I was led to an upstairs room, lined with racks of Eileen Fisher clothes, all in gray, black, and white. Eileen, again, looked beautiful and elegant in a black ensemble of trousers and scoop-neck sweater. "This is what I call my studio," she said of the room, explaining that it had once been her office but now served as an extra meeting room and as a place where she tried on clothes. The racks of gray and black and white clothes—Eileen wears no other palette—were "the things I'm playing with," candidates for "my little closet where I keep the clothes I wear every day." They were also the source of clothes for the public appearances that she now makes more frequently and with less dread. She has gone to China and to meetings of the Clinton Global Initiative. But she is still, she says, "finding my voice."

In the studio, she spoke of another influence on her design that had almost the significance of the Japanese one: her Catholic-school uniform. "When I came to New

York and had to get dressed to look like a designer—whatever that meant—I felt troubled by finding things to wear. So when I started designing clothes I drew on the uniform experience, on the idea that you can just throw that thing on every morning and don't have to think about it."

The school experience itself had been less edifying. "I was fairly traumatized by the Catholic schools I went to," she said. "I think it is part of my silence thing, of just always feeling it is safer to say nothing than to figure out what you think and what you want to say. It was always risky to speak at school."

"Was there punishment?" I asked.

"There was criticism. There was yelling. They would humiliate you and embarrass you."

Eileen asked if I would like to drop in on the meeting downstairs. I would have preferred to continue the conversation about Catholic schools, but with uncharacteristic firmness she said, "I know this will interest you," and led the way down the stairs.

In the lunchroom, the long table had been pushed against a wall, and ten or twelve women wearing Eileen Fisher clothes were sitting on chairs arranged in a circle. They spoke in the same coded language that Eileen and Old fell into when they talked about the company. I recognized some of the terms ("facilitating leaders") and noted some new ones ("delegation with transparency," "agenda building"), feeling the same impatient incomprehension. What were they talking about? The meeting ended when an elegant older woman held up two bronze bells connected by a cord and rang them. "I ring the bells to remind us of timelessness," she said. Then an object, a sort of gilded gourd, was passed from hand to hand.

Each woman said something as she received it. "I feel lighter," one woman said. "I feel humbled and honored," the woman who had rung the bells said. Her name, I later learned, was Ann Linnea, and she is the author, with Christina Baldwin, of a book called *The Circle Way: A Leader in Every Chair* (2010). The book proposes that organizations conduct their business in circles. You sit around in a circle. This eliminates hierarchies. Everyone is equal. To focus the mind, there is a three-part ritual of a "start point," "check in," and "check out." When the book debuted, the Eileen Fisher company was already conducting its meetings in circles, with its own specially designed bells to mark the beginning and the end. "It was in the air," Eileen said of the ritual. "But *The Circle Way* helped us to refine and more deeply integrate it."

Back upstairs, I asked two questions I had been somewhat nervously planning to ask. The first—yes, you guessed it—was about the cat. In the weeks between my visits to Irvington, there had been a spell of exceptionally icy, windy weather, and I had thought of him miserably huddled under the house in the low temperatures. Had she relented and let him in? No, there had been no reason to do so. "He has been outside for three years now. He is the healthiest of my cats," she said again, and added, "The first year he was outside was really hard. It was painful. Every time it would snow or rain I would feel terrible. One freezing-cold day, I thought, Oh, my poor cat, and picked him up. I was going to hug him a little and warm him up—but he was so warm, I couldn't believe it. On another freezing day, I let him into a stone entryway. I thought

I would just let him be there, and he kind of walked around a bit and then he stood by the door so that I would let him back out."

I asked my second question: Why were Old and Rowe present during my interviews with Eileen? Eileen promptly answered, "I assume that the reason you are interested in interviewing me goes beyond me. I sort of stand for a whole company, and I want to make sure that people are honored and that I don't say anything that offends anyone or that hurts anyone."

"But the piece is about you," I said.

"I know the idea for the company came through me in some way, but it's beyond me. I planted the first seed, and now I look around and there's this amazing garden. But I'm just an ordinary person. It's only because I created this company and these clothes that I'm interesting."

Old said smoothly, "Monica and I figure that a lot of conversation will come up about other aspects of the company and other people you may want to meet, and, being ears in the room, we can help make that happen in an easy kind of way. So that's partly our motivation. It's wanting to support whatever your process might be."

"My story is about Eileen," I said. "That Eileen Fisher is a real person—"

"—who puts her cat outside," Eileen cut in, as we all laughed, perhaps a little too loudly and heartily. I found myself babbling about the ethical dilemmas of journalism, about the risk subjects take when they let journalists into their houses and the pangs journalists feel when they write their betraying narratives, and saw Eileen and her colleagues looking at me as I had looked at them when they talked about their company—as if I were saying something weird. We were in different businesses with different vocabularies.

I turned to Eileen. "When you say 'It's not about me' and that you're not interesting, that's a very modest way of talking about yourself."

"I grew up Catholic," she said. "You know, the 'Nobody's looking at you' thing."

"That's part of Catholicism?"

"That's what my mother said all the time. 'Nobody's looking at you.' So for me—in Catholic school, around my mother—it was just safer to be invisible."

Old, with her characteristic accommodating intelligence, said, "Would it be helpful to you, to both of you maybe, to have some time without other people in the room?" I was not surprised when Eileen told me a few weeks later that Old had been promoted and was now one of the four highest-ranking executives of this company of a thousand employees that soft-pedals its hierarchy and doesn't use the word "executive."

I met with Eileen a few more times: once at my apartment, without Old and Rowe, and with no appreciable difference in the character of our conversation; then at the company's corporate headquarters, on Fifth Avenue; and, finally, in Irvington, at a celebration in an Eileen Fisher store at the river's edge, called the Lab Store, which was reopening after being flooded by Sandy. At the celebration, Eileen was waiting for me at the door in an especially fetching outfit of black harem pants, boots, a charcoal-gray cardigan over a gray asymmetrical top, and a light-gray scarf. (Eileen knows how to wear scarves the way women in Paris know how to wear them and American women almost touchingly don't.) The store was full of people, some sifting through racks of clothes or waiting in line for a dressing room and others conversing, with glasses of champagne in their hands. It was a nice occasion. Eileen made a gracious speech of greeting and introduced a dance performance by students and teachers from a local dance studio. After the performance, people came up to tell her how much they loved her clothes and admired her. A woman with a cane who said she had just turned eighty-five was among them. She was wearing Eileen Fisher clothes from another time, which suited her well—an unobtrusive outfit of slacks, shell top, and jacket of an easy fit. The younger women in the room wearing today's less self-effacing asymmetrical designs didn't always carry them off. It occurred to me that Eileen looks better in her clothes than anyone else. What she selects from her little closet and puts on for the day is a work of design itself. In Manhattan, there are small enclaves where almost every woman looks chic—Madison Avenue in the Seventies and Eighties, for example. Almost everywhere else, if you walk along the street and look at what women are wearing, you have to laugh at the disparity between the effort that goes into shopping for clothes and the effect this effort achieves.

During the dance performance, Eileen pointed out an attractive bearded man standing across the room. This was "the new man in my life," Bill Kegg, who is a leadership coach, a profession that is "sort of like therapy, but he's not a therapist. It's more about moving forward." Eileen has herself been in therapy for more than thirty years. "It changed my life," she said. "Without the thera-

NOBODY'S LOOKING AT YOU

pist I had many years ago, there's no way I could have started this business. She didn't say, 'Don't do that,' like my mother did. 'What are you thinking—you can't even sew.' But she questioned. 'What is motivating you? What is it about?' She saved my life. Without her I would be a totally different person." In recent years, Eileen has added yoga, meditation, and what she calls "bodywork stuff" to her repertoire of soul maintenance. She described "this thing called breath work": "You lie on the floor breathing in a specific way, a kind of heavy breathing in that gets you into a sort of dream state. You go through all this stuff and let it go. It's like thirty years of therapy in one hour."

Eileen left the Catholic Church during college, and now attends weekly meetings of the Westchester Buddhist Center (the meetings are held at her offices in Irvington). Four years ago, she went on a weeklong meditation retreat in Colorado with her children, now twenty and twenty-four. When I said I was surprised that she took the children, she said, "The kids loved it. They don't like to talk. They're like me."

Eileen has always been good with money—she says it comes out of her early affinity for math—but she doesn't care about it for its own sake, and she isn't a big spender. "My accountant always says 'Spend more money.' I love my home. I'm comfortable there. But I don't have a lot of needs. Maybe because I grew up the way I did. I like what I like. I travel a little bit. But I had to be talked into traveling first class. I just see myself as ordinary, one of the group. Being treated as special feels a little weird to me. It's something I guess I have to get over at some point." (It could be argued that Eileen has got over it. She tore down the perfectly good house that was on the site of the present one to build a house she liked better, and in many other respects enjoys the privileges of the 1 percent. It should be added that she is a political liberal.)

At the Eileen Fisher headquarters, she and I and Old and Rowe sat in a circle with five other women who had been assembled to talk with me about their functions and had titles such as Facilitating Leader of Design Process and People and Creative, Inspiration, and Research Director. The meeting started with the obligatory ringing of a bell (this one was a flat metal thing encased in wood, and was struck like a gong) and a moment of silence, with eyes closed, like the moment of silent prayer in a Protestant church service. The bell was struck again to end the silence. The women were likable and interesting. Helen Oji had been a painter before she joined the company, Candice Reffe a poet, Rebecca Perrin a dancer. The feeling of camaraderie that often arises when women gather in a group arose from this gathering. At one point, I asked a question: "Eileen said there was a ratio of eighty percent women to twenty percent men in the company. But I don't see any men around here. Where is the twenty percent?" "In Secaucus," someone exclaimed, to hoots of laughter from the rest. There is a warehouse in Secaucus where the men apparently are kept.

Eileen talked about a conference from which she had just returned, of heads of what she called like-minded companies, such as Whole Foods and the Container Store, held at the Esalen retreat, in California. Fifteen men and seven women had been invited, and on the second day one of the men observed that only one woman had spoken during the entire proceedings. "It wasn't me," Eileen said, as the group laughed. She went on, "I thanked him for saying that and said that I had felt frozen and incapable of speech. I know that some of this is me and comes from the way I was brought up. But I also think that men and women talk differently. I don't understand it exactly. Men talk faster. There's more like a debate style. I felt I wouldn't think fast enough."

Eileen took me to the tenth floor of the building, where designers and merchandisers do their work, a vast loft space of calm, complex activity. As we walked through the "amazing garden" that had arisen from the seeds she planted twenty-eight years earlier with her four linen pieces, Eileen would pause before a rack of clothes to touch a sleeve or take the fabric between her fingers, making appreciative murmurs, as someone on a garden tour might make standing before an especially handsome specimen. There was nothing in her manner to suggest that she was anything but a pleased tourist.

A few weeks later, I returned to 111 Fifth Avenue to take a closer look at the tenth floor. My guide this time was Monica Rowe, who took me down a long central corridor lined with racks of sample garments and flanked on both sides by large partitioned spaces with windows, where designers sat at computers or drafting tables or in discussion groups around conference tables. These spaces—with one conspicuous exception—were in keeping with what one thinks of as the Eileen Fisher aesthetic of elegant plainness. The exception, called the "trend and color studio," was like a mocking rebuttal of this aesthetic. The room was full of brightly colored images and objects, among them reproductions of master paintings (Bruegel's *Harvesters* was one, and Vermeer's *Girl with a Pearl Earring* another), a mobile of pictures of birds of brilliant plumage, bins of jumbled fabrics such as you might riffle through in a thrift shop, innumerable small things you might find in the home of a hoarder of small things, baskets overflowing with sparkling ribbons and lace, and a huge ball made of orange cotton strips wound around each other that Chris Costan, the ruler of this domain of color and excess, had found in a market in India.

Costan is a small, pretty woman who is also a painter, and who repudiates the Eileen Fisher aesthetic as decisively in her person as in her surrounding. Her outfit on the day of my visit—a short, puffily pleated beige cotton skirt worn with a horizontally striped pinkish-beige-and-black jersey top and black tights—was clearly not of Eileen Fisher provenance, and her jet-black hair was arranged in one of the most complicated hairstyles I have ever seen, involving a long braid over one shoulder, a high pompadour rising from the forehead, and an assortment of fancy combs and clips appended at irregular intervals to the braid and to the back of the head.

Costan's title is Color Designer, and her job is to create a palette for the clothing line for each season. She draws inspiration, she says, from the fabrics and pictures and tchotchkes she collects, as well as, though to a lesser degree, from books that forecast color trends in fashion. Her palettes are represented on "swatch charts"—sheets of paper on which tiny squares of colored fabric are pasted—that are shown to the designers and merchandisers, who may or may not accept them in their entirety.

When I asked Costan if she thought of herself as a rebellious force in the company, she said, "Yes, I totally see myself that way. I like what's unusual and unexpected and different. I look for colors I find cool at the moment. I'm interested in trends. I create a story. I come from a discipline where everything means something. I'm not sure everyone around here cares. But I'm also a good girl. I fit in with the culture of the company. They've allowed me a lot of latitude because they like what I do. I feel appreciated—though sometimes I get annoyed." A recent source of annoyance was the rejection of one of the colors she proposed—the "wildly trendy" color called cosmetic or skin tone—which happened to be the color that in my ignorance I called pinkish beige when describing her striped jersey. "I wear Eileen Fisher designs sometimes, and I really like them," she said. "But my style is quirkier. I always want to be different. It's my rebelliousness."

As Rowe led me to another part of the floor, I recalled a passage in an Eileen Fisher brochure entitled "Simply—to Be Ourselves":

> The underlying philosophy of our design—no constraints, freedom of expression—extends to the company itself, which is run in a loosely structured manner that allows for an open exchange of ideas. Every employee is encouraged to give input to any area, no matter their position or expertise. The individual is valued for the total picture of who they are and what they can contribute.

I also thought of something Eileen had said about today's company and its leadership: "I don't feel like I need to be there anymore. I feel like they're my full-grown adult children and they do an amazing job and they don't need me." Rowe, who was wearing Kelly-green trousers ("No, they're from my own clothes," she said when I asked if they were of Eileen Fisher design), paused before a short rack of garments with a sign on it reading:

EILEEN'S SAMPLES
DO NOT TOUCH

These were the clothes for Mom's closet, in the obligatory black and gray and white, and as we stood before them, the image of Eileen, in all her delicacy and beauty, wafted out of them like an old, expensive scent.

The New Yorker, 2013

PERFORMANCE ARTIST

What is one to think of the clothes the twenty-nine-year-old pianist Yuja Wang wears when she performs—extremely short and tight dresses that ride up as she plays, so that she has to tug at them when she has a free hand, or clinging backless gowns that give an impression of near-nakedness (accompanied in all cases by four-inch-high stiletto heels)? In 2011, Mark Swed, the music critic of the *Los Angeles Times*, referring to the short and tight orange dress Yuja wore when she played Rachmaninoff's Third Piano Concerto at the Hollywood Bowl, wrote that "had there been any less of it, the Bowl might have been forced to restrict admission to any music lover under 18 not accompanied by an adult." Two years later, the *New Criterion* critic Jay Nordlinger characterized the "shorter-than-short red dress, barely covering her rear" that Yuja wore for a Carnegie Hall recital as "stripper-wear." Never has the relationship between what we see at a concert and what we hear come under such perplexing scrutiny. Is the seeing part a distraction (Glenn Gould thought it was) or is it—can it be—a heightening of the musical experience?

During the intermission of a recital at Carnegie Hall

in May, Yuja changed from the relatively conventional long gold sequinned gown she had worn for the first half, two Brahms Ballades and Schumann's *Kreisleriana*, into something more characteristically outré. For the second half, Beethoven's extremely long and difficult Sonata no. 29 in B-flat, known as the *Hammerklavier*, she wore a dress that was neither short nor long but both: a dark-blue-green number, also sequinned, with a long train on one side—the side not facing the audience—and nothing on the other, so that her right thigh and leg were completely exposed.

As she performed, the thigh, splayed by the weight of the torso and the action of the toe working the pedal, looked startlingly large, almost fat, though Yuja is a very slender woman. Her back was bare, thin straps crossing it. She looked like a dominatrix or a lion tamer's assistant. She had come to tame the beast of a piece, this half-naked woman in sadistic high heels. Take that, and that, Beethoven!

A few months before the performance, I asked Yuja why, out of all Beethoven's sonatas, she had selected the *Hammerklavier*, and she said that she had done it out of defiance. She wanted to prove that she could play the most difficult of Beethoven's sonatas. I said that I was probably not alone in finding the sonata hard, almost unpleasant, to listen to, and several days later she sent me a link to a video of a lecture about the *Hammerklavier* by the Hungarian-born pianist András Schiff. Schiff speaks in the slow, self-savoring way in which many Eastern European men speak, to let you know how interesting and amusing everything they say is—except in his case it is.

Schiff characterized the work as "the greatest" and

"most monumental" of Beethoven's sonatas, "a work that everybody respects and reveres but very few people love." Schiff's object was to communicate his own "deep love for this piece," and he began by talking about Beethoven's metronome markings, which are "incredibly fast" and are ignored by most pianists, who play the piece slowly and ponderously. The piece "is not pretty," but it is not "heavy-handed . . . not made of lead." Schiff mocked the pianists who protract the long third movement to show that "we are very deep and profound. . . . You can have lunch and dinner and breakfast, and we are still sitting here." Schiff went on to say, "If you play this piece at Beethoven's tempi, then it's not ponderous anymore. . . . It is not a piece in marble. . . . It is incredibly human and alive."

At Carnegie, Yuja did not play the piece quite at Beethoven's tempi—these days, few pianists do apart from Schiff—but I found myself responding to it as I had not responded to recordings by the great Maurizio Pollini and Mitsuko Uchida. I had not been able to get past the music's unprettiness. But now I was electrified. The forty- or fifty-minute-long piece (depending on how ponderously or not ponderously you play it) seemed almost too short.

A communication from another audience member, the pianist Shai Wosner, helpfully explained the inexplicable: why a piece that is about struggle and difficulty should have given the pleasure it gave in Yuja's interpretation. "There is hardly any passage in it that is truly comfortable to the hand," he wrote, along with "a certain harmonic tension that runs pretty much throughout the piece between B-flat major and B minor, Beethoven's 'dark, forbidden' key." He went on:

With all the Beethovenian struggle, this piece is also a very "cleanly" conceived sonata, more faithful to the Classical sonata model than any of Beethoven's other late Sonatas. So what I loved about Yuja's performance was how this other aspect of the piece came across . . . her effortless approach brought out the brilliant, clear structure of Hammerklavier and highlighted it from another angle. Like a great monument that's not made of stone but of light-reflecting glass.

Anthony Tommasini, reviewing the performance in the *Times*, wrote, "Ms. Wang's virtuosity goes well beyond uncanny facility. . . . She wondrously brought out intricate details, inner voices and harmonic colorings. The first movement had élan and daring. The scherzo skipped along with mischievousness and rhythmic bite." Neither Tommasini nor Wosner mentioned Yuja's dress, but I wondered about its impact on their experience. I know that what I saw was intertwined with what I heard. Looking at her in that remarkable getup was part of the musical experience. But what part?

Yuja had played the *Hammerklavier* a week or so earlier in Santa Barbara, and Mark Swed had again not failed to notice what she wore. This time, perhaps not altogether seriously, he attributed her choice of costume to altruism. Six days earlier, Murray Perahia, who is sixty-nine, had played the *Hammerklavier* nearby, in Los Angeles. "Hers is a 40-year age advantage," Swed wrote, so "as if to level the field technically, she came out onto the stage . . . tightly squeezed into a red orange gown and wearing platform heels so high that she could barely walk." Swed praised both performances. "Perahia's understanding, feeling and urgency produce a 'Hammer-klavier' for the ages," while Wang, "with a flick of her dazzling fingers on the keys, sends an electric current through the 'Hammerklavier' that makes it modern music, Beethoven for the 21st century." And, while Perahia "emerged from his ordeal exhausted, hardly able to walk offstage" (in spite of his flat-heeled shoes), Wang "in the manner of the greatest virtuosos of yore . . . made this great effort seem almost effortless and was ready for three amazing encores."

In New York, as it happened, Perahia had once again played the *Hammerklavier* a few days before Yuja did and again had had the starch taken out of him. Tommasini returned to Perahia's performance in his review of Yuja's (he had enthusiastically reviewed the Perahia on May 9) and held up the older pianist's exhaustion as a sort of necessary tribute to the piece's profundity and monumentality. "This was not a probing or profound Hammerklavier," he said of Yuja's interpretation, as if suddenly remembering himself and wishing that his praise of her had been more grudging. I could hear András Schiff laughing to himself. *We are very deep and profound. . . . You can have lunch and dinner and breakfast, and we are still sitting here.*

Tommasini ended his review by complaining about the five encores that Yuja played, each one making the *Hammerklavier* recede "further from memory." I have to say that I agreed with him. I had heard these encores before. Yuja habitually wheels them out at performances. They include Vladimir Horowitz's amusing high-speed *Carmen* Fantasy and an equally funny arrangement by various hands of the Alla Turca movement of Mozart's Sonata no. 11 in A Major. The audience, as Tommasini felt obliged to report, went mad with delight. When I first heard Yuja play these encores, I went mad with delight, too. But this time I wished she had left us with an unmediated memory of her *Hammerklavier*. The roars that went up after the encores were greater than those after the *Hammerklavier*. This seemed wrong. But in the split between the concert proper and the encores we may read the split in Yuja herself—her persona as a confident musical genius and as an uncertain young woman making her way through the maze of a treacherous marketplace.

She was born in Beijing to a mother who was a dancer and a father who was a percussionist. She is vague about her emergence as a prodigy. She likes to tell interviewers that her mother wanted her to be a dancer, but that she was lazy and chose the piano because she could sit down. She was performing publicly by the age of six, and entering competitions from which she always emerged with the first prize. When she was nine, her parents enrolled her in the Beijing conservatory, and when she was fourteen, they sent her to a conservatory in Calgary, Canada, where she learned English. From there she went to the Curtis Institute, in Philadelphia, whose head, the pianist Gary Graffman, immediately recognized her quality and took her on as his student, something he did only with the most outstanding talents, such as Lang Lang. Yuja hasn't lived in China since.

About a year ago, I began meeting with Yuja in the Sky Lounge, on the top floor of the building she lives in on Riverside Boulevard, in the West Sixties—a common space with a view of the Hudson River and the New Jersey shoreline, whose privileged-looking armchairs and little tables evoke first- and business-class waiting rooms at airports. When I say "the building she lives in," I am speaking loosely. Yuja tours the world, playing in premier halls, either in solo recitals or with leading orchestras, in London, Paris, St. Petersburg, Edinburgh, Bucharest, Caracas, Tokyo, Kyoto, Beijing, Tel Aviv, Jerusalem, Sydney, Amsterdam, Florence, Barcelona, and San Francisco, among other cities, and spends only a few weeks, between more than a hundred scheduled performances, in the apartment, a studio she bought in 2014.

When you walk into the apartment—which is small and dark—the first thing you see is a royal-blue nylon sheet suspended from the ceiling like a shower curtain and drawn around a lumpish object that turns out to be a Steinway grand piano. The curtain is there to muffle the piano's sound, to accommodate a neighbor for whom the practicing of a world-class pianist is not the thrill it would be for you and me. The rest of the apartment has the atmosphere of a college dormitory room, with its obligatory unpacked suitcase on the floor and haphazard strewings of books and papers and objects. There may be a few stuffed animals on the bed or maybe only a sense of them—I am not sure because I was at the apartment only once. Yuja prefers to see interviewers in the Sky Lounge. When I proposed visiting the apartment again— this time with a notebook—she politely demurred. It was too much of a mess, or the cleaning woman hadn't come.

Yuja speaks in fluent—more than fluent—English, punctuated by laughter that gives one to understand that what she is saying is not to be taken too seriously, and that she is not a pompous or pretentious person. Occasionally, there is the slightest trace of an accent (vaguely French) and a lapse into the present tense.

We talked about her life as a child prodigy. "Oh, yes, I'm a real prodigy," she said. "They still call me wunderkind. I remember when I went to the conservatory for the first time. All the other kids were looking at me like—by then I was already a child star—like I am another species in a zoo. Oh, my God, she's here."

"You seem so unspoiled," I said. "Were you more spoiled then? Or were you unspoiled even then?"

"I think unspoiled came later," Yuja said.

She recalled something I didn't and still don't completely understand about the effect that playing Mozart had on her as a child. She said that performing his Twelve Variations in C Major ("Twinkle, Twinkle, Little Star") permitted her to feel for the first time what it was like to have stage fright. She was eight or nine.

"I was always quiet before a concert, while the other kids were so nervous. They talk, some are very noisy. I don't understand. Why are you nervous? *Until* the first time I played Mozart. I was not nervous until I was onstage. Then I felt I was in a completely different time and space. My fingers just played. And I thought there is a difference between practicing at home and playing onstage."

I asked if she could explain further what had happened to her when she performed the Variations.

"Maybe intuitively I was struck by the beauty, by the symmetry, by how like something inherent in nature it is. Before, I was, Oh, Mozart is so boring."

When I told her of my feeling of awe at the superhuman feat that is a concert performance, she said, "For me that's normal—like talking." She has the erroneous idea that writing a book is a similarly remarkable achievement. She became a serious reader in her teens. Among the books she recently read are Virginia Woolf's *The Waves* and Immanuel Kant's *Critique of Pure Reason*. When I commented on the high-mindedness of her reading, she quickly said, "No, I'm always reading something trashy, too."

I asked about her home life in China. "Did your parents immediately realize that you were different from other children?"

"I don't know. They're very naïve people. Extremely conventional and traditional. Very Communist. If you read Dostoevsky or Tolstoy, you will understand what kind of people they are. Just simple, extremely kind. My dad was really talented, and my mom also. They are extremely artistic—or autistic," she said, with a peal of laughter. "Their environment never allowed them to develop to their full potential."

"Is this what you mean by 'very Communist'?"

"Yeah. Because you have to go to Party meetings and talk about how to do well for society. Twenty-year plan. Five-year plan. You work for the common welfare rather than for the individual. Working for the individual is almost synonymous with being selfish. Which is not how I feel. I feel lucky that I came out when I was fourteen." Yuja's mother came for her graduation from Curtis and for her Carnegie Hall debut; otherwise, Yuja sees her parents only when she performs in Beijing. She speaks of them in an affectionate but veiled way, always stressing their kindness.

When I asked Yuja to elaborate on her sense of the political differences between China and America, she paused before answering. After a while, listening to her, I realized that she was talking about an entirely different subject. I decided to persist. "I asked you about politics, and you have been talking about music," I said.

"You noticed?" she said, laughing.

My visit to Yuja's apartment had taken place after this conversation. It was around four on a hot August afternoon, and Yuja was dressed in denim shorts, very short ones, and a tank top. We had tickets to a five o'clock concert of advanced contemporary music at Alice Tully Hall, and Yuja was debating whether to change for it. She rummaged through the suitcase on the floor and extracted two garments—strapless black-and-white minidresses made of a stretch fabric, called bandage dresses by their French designer, Hervé Léger, because that's how they fit, and characterized by Yuja as "modern and edgy" as well as practical, because they don't have to be ironed and lie nice and flat in a suitcase—and asked my opinion. Should she wear one of them or stay in the shorts? I asked what the issue was—was she interested in comfort or in how she looked? She stared at me as if I were crazy. What weird world was I living in where comfort could even be thought of? She wiggled into one of the bandage dresses, added her high heels, and we walked the three blocks to Lincoln Center at a brisk clip.

In February of this year, on four successive nights at Geffen Hall, Yuja played Mozart's Piano Concerto no. 9 in E-flat Major, the *Jeunehomme*—written when Mozart was barely twenty-one and considered his first masterpiece—with the New York Philharmonic, under the Swiss conductor Charles Dutoit. This was a departure for Yuja. Her career has been built on her playing of the Russian Romantics, the "red-blooded" and "hot-blooded" composers, as she calls them, Tchaikovsky, Rachmaninoff, Prokofiev, for whose "passionate, emotional" pieces her short flame-red dresses seem to have been made. For a while, there was a picture of Yuja in front of Carnegie Hall in the flame-red dress she had worn at a recital in May 2013, her arms raised high in the air in a gesture of culminating abandon. It stopped passersby. Now she was entering a new phase of engagement with Mozart and the nineteenth-century German classical composers. The picture of her in front of Geffen Hall was unremarkable.

A day before the first concert of the series at Geffen, I attended an open rehearsal at the hall. The Mozart concerto was on the first half of the program, to be followed by Respighi's orchestral pieces *Roman Festivals, Fountains of Rome*, and *Pines of Rome*. The Respighi pieces were being rehearsed first, and when I arrived at the hall, around noon, much Respighi remained to be played. Yuja was waiting in the small room upstairs where soloists change clothes and receive visitors. She showed me a closet where the three dresses, designed by Roberto Cavalli, she would wear at the concerts were hanging. I took an immediate dislike to one of the garments—a short pink dress with black swirling lines on its gathered skirt and bodice. It was neither ultra-short and tight nor long and clinging. It was a kind of girlish summer dress. I did not like the idea of Yuja wearing it onstage. The two other dresses were a glamorous dark-blue long gown and a short, also concert-worthy dress.

Yuja curled up on a sofa—she was wearing tight-fitting black leather trousers—and laughingly recalled a newspaper headline she had seen during a tour: "'Twenty-Eight-Year-Old Wunderkind.' Isn't that an oxymoron?" she said. I had arrived early at Lincoln Center and stopped into a café for a sandwich, though not so early that there was time to eat the whole large overstuffed thing. When I offered Yuja the half sandwich the waiter had wrapped, she accepted. Predictably, she opened the sandwich and ate the chicken, then the tomato, then the lettuce, and then—unpredictably—the bread.

Dutoit, a tall man of seventy-nine, appeared with his fourth wife, Chantal Juillet. After husband and wife hugged Yuja, Dutoit stood back to look with elaborate mock lecherousness at her tight trousers. Dutoit and Yuja go back a long way. The infamous habit of Dutoit's second wife, Martha Argerich, of canceling concerts at the last minute had given Yuja one of her early breaks. Argerich was one of the stars Yuja replaced while she was still a student at Curtis; Radu Lupu, Yefim Bronfman, Evgeny Kissin, and Murray Perahia were others. ("With Martha it was like, 'I'm tired . . . do you want to play with the Boston Symphony for me?' And I'm like 'Of course!—Wrong question!'" Yuja told an interviewer for the Australian magazine *Limelight*.) Yuja's ability both to learn fast and to turn the disgruntlement of audiences into amazed delight did not go unnoticed. "By the end of the final movement"—of Tchaikovsky's Piano Concerto no. 1—"the audience stood and roared," the *Philadelphia Inquirer* critic David Patrick Stearns wrote in a review of the concert at which Yuja replaced Argerich.

After some cheerful banter, Dutoit left to rehearse the final Respighi, and Yuja excused herself to warm up in a large adjacent room that had a piano. She preferred that I not go into the large room with her but didn't object to my staying in the small room, where I could hear her play phrases over and over and feel that I was uselessly eavesdropping on coded artistic secrets.

At the concert proper, the following night, Yuja wore

the glamorous dark-blue gown, and played with delicacy and beauty. She and Dutoit and the orchestra were in elating rapport. The first cadenza produced one of those you-could-hear-a-pin-drop hushes in the sold-out hall. She had gone very quiet, and the audience followed as if mesmerized. No one coughed.

"Who can play Mozart the way she did?" Graffman said afterward. "It was so natural, in such good taste. Not that she was doing anything. That's just the way it came out. Who can do that and also play the Horowitz *Carmen* Fantasy?" In *The New Criterion*, Nordlinger wrote, "Mozart ends with a rondo—and it should be fast, exuberant, and fun. It was. Wang ripped the notes out of the keyboard, as much as played them. At one point, I almost laughed out loud. That's how funny she was, and how funny Mozart is."

Yuja must have liked reading this. She had once talked about how funny Mozart is: "Mozart is like a party animal. I find I play him better when I am hung over or drunk." At the same time, she saw Mozart's music as "noble, tragic, like a great Greek play. The human emotion is there but with a lot of godliness in it." On the second night, my heart sank when Yuja walked onstage in the pink dress. Was it my imagination or was her playing less inspired than it had been the night before?

Meeting Yuja in the Sky Lounge a few weeks later on a rainy day, I told her of this impression, and she did not contradict it. "Because of that dress, the little pink one, because it's so different from everything I've ever worn, I didn't really feel myself, and maybe that came through. I liked the pink dress because it was different. Sometimes, the difference might become the style of my next season. It could be what's going to come. Or it could be

something to discard. You don't know until you try it."
She added, "They wanted to put in social media that I
was dressed by the designer Roberto Cavalli."

"Were you feeling something related to the dress
while playing?"

"No, not while playing. Just when I walked onstage.
This was a cute little pink dress, and I thought, It's not
me. It's about a young girl. Just the opposite of the nude
dress."

In 2014, when an interviewer from the London *Tele-
graph* asked Yuja about "her fondness for riskily short,
clingy dresses," she gave a flippant reply: "I am 26 years
old, so I dress for 26. I can dress in long skirts when I am
40." But in fact Yuja's penchant for the riskily short and
clingy has less to do with allegiance to the dress code of
her generation than with an awareness of her own "super-
smallness," as she calls it. She knows that small, tight
clothes bring out her beauty and large, loose garments
don't. But she is not just a woman who knows how to
dress. She is a woman who is constantly experiment-
ing with how to dress when she is playing on a concert
stage. She is keenly aware—as many soloists affect not
to be—that she is being looked at as well as listened to.
Reviewing the Carnegie Hall recital Yuja played in
May 2013, Zachary Woolfe wrote in the *Times,* "I confess that while perhaps 90 percent of my attention was on
her precise yet exuberant playing, a crucial 10 was on her
skintight flame-colored dress." Woolfe went on to brilliantly anatomize the experience of simultaneously listening to and looking at Yuja: "Her alluring, surprising
clothes don't just echo the allure and surprise of her musi-
cianship, though they certainly do that. More crucial,
the tiny dresses and spiky heels draw your focus to how

petite Ms. Wang is, how stark the contrast between her body and the forcefulness she achieves at her instrument. That contrast creates drama. It turns a recital into a performance." When Yuja played the *Jeunehomme* in the girlish pink dress, that contrast was absent. The sense of a body set in urgent motion by musical imperatives requires that the body not be distractingly clothed. With her usually bared thighs, chest, and back demurely covered by the black-splotched pink fabric, this sense was lost.

Yuja's customary self-presentation as a kind of stripped-down car is, of course, only one way of appearing onstage to artistic advantage. When Maurizio Pollini plays in some nondescript suit, his body-aliveness is no less present for us. Martha Argerich's widow's-weeds black gowns heighten the beauty and mystery of her playing. Plainness is never a mistake on a concert stage. For the two remaining Mozart performances, Yuja, realizing her misstep, returned to the designer she regularly uses.

The "nude dress" was a long gown (in recent years, long gowns have been admitted into Yuja's concert-clothes closet, but they have to be slinky) made of body-stocking fabric with sparkling encrustations at bosom and stomach and a long swishing skirt. Yuja wore this fabulously gorgeous costume at the third concert—which had the electricity of the first one—and felt comfortable and happy in its defiant sexiness and her feeling of nakedness.

I looked out the window of the Sky Lounge and saw the New Jersey shoreline disappearing in a gray mist. Yuja herself was in a dark mood. She had recently returned from a European tour and was exhausted and dispirited.

In Munich and Paris, she had played the Mozart piano concerto with Valery Gergiev and the Vienna Philharmonic, and the reception had been only okay. A blog about the Paris concert saying "Yuja Wang disappoints" had stayed with her. She paraphrased its words: "'She didn't have emotion. She's not yet mature enough to play Mozart.'" She went on, "With Rachmaninoff, Prokofiev, Tchaikovsky I can blow them away. 'So amazing, so impressive!' But I went for the surprise, for the unexpected. I ask myself, Am I playing for the applauding, for the standing up, or am I playing because I really like something in the music and I just want to play?"

She talked in the same dark vein about her personal life. She spoke of the "too many people" she meets on tour: "Who are your real friends? I naturally give my love and friendship, but once the tour is over are they really your friends? What's always there, of course, is music. The other things come and go—except maybe your parents." She laughed. "And Gary."

Gary Graffman, who is eighty-seven and now retired as the head of Curtis, and his wife, Naomi, who is eighty-eight, are Yuja's best friends in New York and perhaps in the world. Graffman, you may recall, is the distinguished pianist whose career was disrupted in the late 1970s, when he lost the use of his right hand. When I visited the Graffmans in their apartment at the Osborne, on West Fifty-Seventh Street, they spoke of Yuja as of a beloved granddaughter of whom they are so proud they can hardly stand it. When I asked Graffman how she compared with the other prodigies at Curtis, he said, "She was remarkable among remarkable students. She didn't play like a prodigy. She played like a finished artist." Naomi recalled that when Yuja first arrived at Curtis, Gary asked her to take the new student to lunch, and she dutifully did so. "By the time lunch was over, I thought she has to be at least thirty-five or forty," Naomi said. "She was speaking so intelligently about so many things." Yuja was fifteen and a half.

As Yuja had been a musical wunderkind at six, at twenty-nine she is a kind of existential prodigy, already undergoing the crisis that ordinary people undergo in midlife. "I've been doing this for twenty-nine years. Do I want to go on doing it, or is there something else waiting for me?" She spoke of her sense of alienation from people who don't have to constantly and relentlessly study music and practice, of feeling like an outsider, sometimes even "I don't like to say but almost like a prisoner. I haven't ever enjoyed my free time. It's always like I am challenging myself. I must be a little masochistic." She would see people walking in the park on a beautiful day and long to join them. But by the time she had untied herself from the mast of her art it was midnight, and there was no one to join her in a walk in the park.

At the "millennials' parties" she had attended on the last two nights of the Mozart concerts (their purpose was to encourage young people to go to concerts), she had wearily answered questions from a stage. "I would have enjoyed these parties five years ago," she said. "I still enjoyed them. They were fun. Nice people. I had lots of drinks. But I get the same questions again and again. It's like water goes into the same spot. And then I become a little unpleasant. And then I feel guilty that I was unpleasant. They ask me things like"—she began speaking in a mocking singsong voice—"'Are you single?' 'How do you memorize your pieces?' 'How do you pedal with your heels?' 'Who do you buy your dresses from?' 'Why do you wear short dresses?' 'Why do you wear long dresses?' 'Why do you have short hair?' 'Do you like traveling?' 'Why don't you play more Prokofiev?' 'Why do you play Mozart?'"

The room had darkened, and everything on the river was disappearing. When I drew Yuja's attention to the apparition of the sublime in the window, she was looking at her phone. "I'm just checking," she said. "I'm not being impolite." Yuja treats her phone the way almost every young (and not so young) person today treats it—as a transitional object. She and I have corresponded by email (largely about chocolate), and her messages are filled with emoticons and LOL-like abbreviations. In deference to my age, she does not text me.

When I commented on her melancholy, she denied—and then acknowledged—it: "It's a very depressing thought. Just touring and playing—the same things or different things. But in society people don't allow you to be sad or depressed. It's like a bad thing. It's why I'm antisocial. I feel this negative energy. 'She just complains a lot.' Excuse me, that's part of what I do. You feel all these things. As a musician, you probably feel them more intensely. But society wants me to be happy. My parents. They are the most unintrusive parents. 'I don't care what you do—just be happy.'" She made an *urrrgghh* sound and laughed.

Yuja has made changes in her professional life that she is not sure have solved the problems of doubt and restlessness by which they were impelled. Last year, she abruptly left her manager, Earl Blackburn, of the large Opus 3 Artists agency, with whom she had been since she was sixteen, and joined Mark Newbanks, whose London-based agency, Fidelio Arts, has only three other clients—but what clients!—the conductors Gustavo Dudamel, Lionel Bringuier, and Esa-Pekka Salonen. Although Yuja doesn't speak of it in such terms, the change of managers has the atmosphere of the dissolution of a marriage: a young wife leaves the dull, older husband for an exciting younger man. Naomi Graffman spoke of Blackburn's extraordinary devotion to Yuja: "He coddled her as no one had ever been coddled before. Every little thing she wanted or needed, he did it for her. He would brush her teeth for her if she wanted." The younger man is different. He does not take Yuja's clothes to the cleaners; recently, he did not offer to pick up a Russian visa for her, as Blackburn would have done. "She was furious," Gary said. "Never having had experience with anybody else, she thought that was what managers did." I happened to have heard about the Russian visa from Yuja. She had not mentioned Newbanks, just the fact of this and other annoying little errands she had to run, followed by the playful question "Shall I hire a boyfriend or an assistant?"

I proposed a boyfriend/assistant. Earlier, she had spoken of the obstacle her touring schedule put in the way of lasting romance. The boyfriend/assistant—i.e., a muse—would always be in the next seat on the plane. "No," she said, "guys won't do that. It's okay for a woman to do that. It's harder for guys to get rid of their egos, to be even a little bit subservient." She added, "Of course, I want guys who are successful. Which means that they have their own work, that they're busy—and that I am the one who visits them."

I asked if her romances were with artists of her caliber.

"Not of my caliber," she said without hesitation (and the obligatory peal of laughter). "I never meet people of my caliber who are available."

She talked of the older and old people with whom she feels happy and comfortable (the conductor Michael Tilson Thomas is a kind of runner-up to Gary Graffman in the lovable-mentor sweepstakes): "people who have their whole life behind them"—as opposed to the young with their oppressive burden of futurity. Another older friend, Emanuel Ax, invited her for Thanksgiving last year, and she accepted, but in the end did not go, preferring to "be home and snuggle up and watch Netflix."

She spoke of leaving Earl Blackburn not regretfully, exactly, but with a kind of cold wisdom about the possible pointlessness of the gesture that people three times her age don't often achieve. "There was nothing wrong with the old manager. He really built my career. He was really caring. But I was, like, if I don't make a change, I'll never make a change. I'm bad at confrontation. So I just did it out of the blue. But nothing much has changed. It's a little better here and there. But it's still the same circus."

When I met for coffee with Newbanks—a suave, slender, elegantly dressed man of forty-eight, a former cellist—he told me that his aim as Yuja's manager was to cut back on her engagements and "put air" in her schedule. "She had three days free when I met her—that's impossible." Another goal was to steer her toward experimentation with repertoire, and one of these experiments has already taken place—in March, Yuja played for three nights with the New York Philharmonic in Messiaen's *Turangalîla-Symphonie*, conducted by Salonen. *Turangalîla* is a thrilling, mad, loud piece that features two solo instruments, the piano and the ondes martenot, an early electronic instrument that makes unearthly wavering sounds not easy to hear over the orchestral pandemonium. Yuja's playing was brilliantly audible. She played from a score, and on the night I attended did her own page turning, which lent a certain suspense to the proceedings. The pages flew at a rate of about one every thirty seconds. Would they lie flat? Page turners usually give a little firm pat to the page they have just turned to make sure it will stay in place. Later, Yuja told me that she had put adhesive on the pages to ensure that they would stay in place.

Newbanks said that it is customary for management to take 20 percent of a soloist's fee and 15 percent of a conductor's fee. I asked him, as I had asked Yuja, what her fee was, and, like her, he wouldn't tell me. "No one in the business talks about it," he said. The business evidently exacts a vow of omertà from its members. Newbanks laughingly (perhaps a little nervously) said that Yuja had alerted him to my unseemly interest in money. When I put the futile question to her, she had answered, "I don't usually like to talk about fees," and added, with uncharacteristic humorlessness, "I feel it is degrading to art to measure it with money."

As patches of blue and orange appeared in the sky of the Sky Lounge, Yuja's internal bad weather seemed to lift as well. She recalled her time in Europe with Gergiev: "He is amazing. This is the first time I am playing Mozart with him, and I was curious how he would do it. I did

Russian stuff with him before—the energy for the Russian stuff was unbelievable. And he had the same energy for Mozart, which is scary, because it's overwhelming for Mozart. But it put us into a good place. He has that. Claudio"—the conductor Claudio Abbado—"had that. Claudio is like intense listening. It makes you feel so scrutinizingly uncomfortable. And that place of uncomfortableness is exactly where you want to be every time you are onstage. Because that makes you play better, and that is when you are growing. Feeling comfortable is always like okay, I'll do the thing again. Been there done that."

Yuja reveres Abbado, who died in 2014. When, in the interview for *Limelight*, she was asked what it was like to play under Abbado, she spoke of how "obscure and mysterious" the experience was. During rehearsals, "he didn't say a word—to me at least. And then in the concert, everything just came out. You don't really know what happens with the gestures or the energy field. . . . He made everyone play his or her best . . . without any words."

She spoke of her new repertoire: "It makes me happy playing *Hammerklavier* rather than playing Rach Three another twenty times. I used to only play pieces I was comfortable with and good at, Rachmaninoff, Prokofiev, Tchaikovsky. Now I propose music I won't be comfortable with. This is the only way to get out of my skin, out of myself, and to learn." She added, laughing, "But once in a while I crave those Russians. My heart is crying, *Where are they?*"

A week or so after Yuja's *Hammerklavier* concert, the photograph that accompanies this piece* was taken at

*As it appeared in *The New Yorker* of September 5, 2016.

the new Steinway piano showroom, on Sixth Avenue at Forty-Third Street. When I arrived at the showroom, around noon, Yuja, wearing one of her bandage dresses, was sitting on a table, facing a mirror, as a hair-and-makeup man from Paris applied mascara to her eyelashes. She was patient and compliant and practiced. She had done this before. There are many beautiful portraits of Yuja floating around the print and Internet worlds. After greeting me, she began lighting into Tommasini for his comment about her encores. "If instead of feeling exhausted I feel exhilarated, and want to make people happy by giving them a gift, why not do it?" she said. "It feels like home to play those familiar pieces. People play encores after much more sublime pieces. Why can't you do it after climbing Mt. Everest? Stupid conservative doctrine."

We were on a below-street-level floor, filled with pianos. The photographer, Pari Dukovic, and his three assistants were placing lights and screens around one of them. They had been there since eight-thirty in the morning (catering and hair and makeup had followed at eleven-thirty). Several of Yuja's concert dresses were strewn around an alcove serving as a dressing room, among them the blue-green dominatrix gown she had worn to play the *Hammerklavier.* This was the dress finally chosen for the portrait. The hair-and-makeup man, with whom Yuja had established laughing rapport, revised something in her hairdo at her request. "My cheeks are too fat," she said as she looked in the mirror. She ate a few forkfuls from a plate of salad that her friend Carlos Avila, a pianist who teaches at Juilliard, brought her from the catering table. Then she slipped into the blue-green dress and stepped into stiletto heels, and the photo shoot began. Yuja went to the designated piano, and Dukovic—a handsome young man, with a warm and charming manner—began circling around it, snapping pictures with a handheld camera, as she played bits and pieces of repertoire. At first, she played tentatively and quietly, starting a piece and trailing off—and then she worked her way into a horrible and wonderful pastiche of Rachmaninoff, Chopin, Beethoven, Mozart, Gershwin, Horowitz, Tchaikovsky, all mushed together, playing louder and louder and faster and faster, banging with mischievous demonic force, as Dukovic continued his circling and snapping, like the photographer in the famous orgasmic scene in *Blowup.* Yuja ended with a parodic crescendo as Dukovic shouted, "I love you!" and she burst into laughter.

The arresting photograph that was chosen out of the hundreds, possibly thousands, of pictures Dukovic took of Yuja at the piano and, later, in the first-floor showroom, posed full figure in front of a piano with its lid up, represents her as no concertgoer has ever seen her. The wild disorder of the hair has never been seen in a concert hall. (Yuja's hair tends to stay in place throughout even the most rousing of her performances.) And the foreshortened, oversized hand is an obvious deviation from the consensus we call reality. Will Yuja cringe when she looks at the photograph? Or will she see it as expressive of her impudent, defiant nature and find in it, almost hear in it, an echo of her incomparable musicality?

The New Yorker, 2016

THREE SISTERS

One day in late December, I was sitting at a small table on the fifth floor of the Argosy Bookshop, on East Fifty-Ninth Street, with the three beautiful sisters—Judith Lowry, Naomi Hample, and Adina Cohen—who own and run the business, which they inherited from their father, Louis Cohen, in 1991. Now in their seventies, the sisters have been at the Argosy—which sells autographs, maps, prints, and paintings, as well as old and rare books—since their early twenties. As each one graduated from college, she came to the bookshop, and found the work so congenial and was so good at it that when Cohen died the transition was seamless.

The sisters have distinct personalities. Judith has a firstborn's quiet augustness; she is tall and elegant and could be taken for a college president. Naomi has the second child's ease and confidence; she is merry and vivacious and the family raconteur. Adina, arguably the most beautiful of the beautiful sisters, radiates some of the wistfulness of the baby of the family who can never catch up, though in fact she is the equal of her sisters in every facet of the family business.

The room we were sitting in was Judith's domain. She

is an authority on English and American first editions, and a large collection of them is housed here, the most valuable in a locked case and others on open shelves. On the floor above, Naomi tends a large collection of autographs, letters, and historical documents. But both spend at least two-thirds of the working day on the ground floor, in the bookshop proper, where the life of the enterprise is lodged.

The daughters were very fond of their father—they refer to him as Lou—and have a repertoire of stories about his adventures in the antiquarian book trade that illustrate his cleverness and boldness. Adina told an anecdote from the days of cutthroat competition for books among dealers:

"One day, Lou went to an apartment whose owner was selling his library. There was another book dealer already there, and Lou saw the book dealer point to him and heard him say to the owner, in Yiddish, 'I'll top whatever he offers you.' My father had blue eyes and the dealer assumed he wasn't Jewish. Lou went up to the owner and said—in Yiddish—'And I'll top that.'"

Naomi recalled another instance of Cohen's quick wit. It was during the Depression, and he had sent out penny postcards to people in the *Social Register* asking if they had books to dispose of. Many did. "Once, he went to a house in Tuxedo Park, and a very society type of woman came to the door and said, 'And you are Mr.'"— she paused meaningfully—"'Cohen?' And he—knowing what was coming, namely that 'I would not sell my books to the likes of you'—said, 'Yes, I am Mr. Cullen—C-U-L-L-E-N.' He got the books."

Naomi then began a long story about a book-buying

expedition she had accompanied her father on when she was ten. "It's a very vivid memory. A Dr. Hart, who lived in Bridgeport, Connecticut, came into the store and said he had a houseful of books to sell—all medical."

Judith said, "I think you're wrong that it was all medical books. He had every subject, from animal studies to—"

"No, it was a medical library," Naomi said. "There may have been other subjects. But it was a medical library."

"I don't think so," Judith said.

"I don't know," Adina said. "I was only four."

"Well, it doesn't matter," Judith said.

"So we drove to Bridgeport—"

"You went with him?" Judith said.

"I did go."

"When you were ten years old?"

"Absolutely. It was one of the big moments of my childhood."

"I didn't go," Judith said, "though I certainly know the story."

"Well," Naomi went on, "the house was on the main street of Bridgeport and it was full of books. The stairs were lined with books. There were aisles of bookcases in every room and piles of books everywhere. No one lived there. Dr. Hart had been pushed out of the house by the books and lived somewhere else. There was no way you could assess this library, so Lou pulled a price out of his head, a lowish price, because it was just a nightmare. And Dr. Hart was so relieved that someone was actually interested in the books that he said yes. But he said you have to take them all. Lou said all right and we made many trips there—we only had a station wagon then—and I remember Lou would go through the books and say, 'I'll take this one, I'll take that one,' and when he came to a book he didn't want he threw it out the window."

"No," Judith said. "He couldn't have thrown books out the window."

"Judy—"

"I have told this story myself many times and—"

"But I was there."

"Memory is a strange thing. What happened was that—"

Naomi glared at Judith. "I can't believe that you are telling me what my experience was."

Any reader who has a sibling or siblings will recognize this exchange and its tone. The invisible cord that binds siblings together is wrapped in an insulation of asperity. Sisters, perhaps more than brothers, unendingly irritate one another and scrap with one another. And yet, until this moment—during all the hours over a period of several weeks that I had spent at the Argosy observing its workings—I had seen nothing but an almost preternatural amity flowing between the sisters. They seemed to be of one mind about how the business is to be run and how its functions are to be performed. The spat that had just taken place ended the way spats between cats from the same litter do—it dissolved into nothing. The dust of rivalrous feeling that memory had stirred up settled. Naomi, with a gesture of friendly irony, turned over the telling of the story of Dr. Hart's library to Judith.

Judith said, "After Lou had taken half the books out of the house, something terrible happened. Dr. Hart had an offer on the house and he accepted it. He said to Lou,

'You have got to get these books out of here in a month'—
which was impossible. So Lou matched the offer and
bought the house. Then he could take his time removing
the books. Eventually, he sold the house."

In 1953, Cohen took what proved to be his most decisive
step for the bookstore. He bought the building on Fifty-
Ninth Street that the Argosy now occupies—a nondescript six-story commercial building with a bar on the
ground floor and a lampshade business and dance studio
above. At the time, the Argosy was one door down, in a
town house that was part of a row of brownstones in which
Cohen and other booksellers were renting space for their
shops. In 1963, as if on cue, a developer bought up the
brownstones and tore them down, in order to build a
forty-story skyscraper. As Cohen's fellow booksellers dis-
persed like ants hysterically fleeing a wantonly destroyed
nest, he serenely moved his bookstore into the refuge next
door, where it remains a picturesque anomaly on a street
of sleek tall buildings and shops such as Williams-Sonoma,
Banana Republic, and Sherry-Lehmann Wine and Spirits. The developer tried to buy Cohen's building, but Cohen turned him down. The developer kept raising his
price, and Cohen kept turning him down. Everyone has
his price, the developer believed, but Cohen had no price.
"Everything Lou did was for the business," Naomi said.
"When he bought the building, he was not thinking real
estate. He was not thinking about turning a profit. He
only wanted to protect the business." The daughters, who
have had repeated offers for the building over the years,
feel the same way. "We're safe here," Naomi said. "I can't

even imagine the panic of the people who are renting in New York. What will next month bring?"

Next month, as it happens, or the next few months, will bring, if not panic, serious unpleasantness to the Argosy. The bookshop is not the only anomaly on the block. Next door, on its east side, there is a squat, unusually ugly four-story brick building with a fast-food shop on the ground floor, a business that rents tuxedos and does "expert tailoring and alterations" on the second, and Dawn Electrolysis on the third. Over the years, the owner resolutely refused all offers from developers, but finally was unable to resist forty-nine million dollars. So the squat building will be demolished, and a thirty-story structure will rise in its place. The sisters—who were approached in vain by the developer, as their father had been in 1963—retain their feeling of virtuous safety, even as they brace themselves for the time of blasting and jackhammering and the loss of business when the cranes arrive and the sidewalk is made inaccessible.

Louis Cohen was the seventh child of a Lower East Side immigrant family, whose childhood was darkened and harshened by a catastrophic event that occurred in 1903, when he was in his mother's womb. In an unpublished autobiography, written late in life, Cohen reconstructed the event:

> My father was the owner of a small neighborhood bakery   He was a kindly man and would personally carry bread to destitute families in walk up tenements. On one of his errands of mercy, with

his basket on his shoulder, he presented a good target. Some hoodlums threw snowballs-iceballs from across the street. He was hurt, put his basket down, and went after one of them. It seemed to be a signal for his cronies to join and attack him. He was badly beaten. Soon thereafter his vision became impaired. His optic nerve was affected. He went from doctor to doctor; they could do nothing for him. He became blind.

He was soon homebound, and lost all desire to live. The family, I was told, had to keep all knives, scissors and sharp things out of his reach. They feared he was looking for an opportunity. I was born in the midst of this sad situation. . . . My mother, with her seven children in addition to her other duties, had to supervise the bakery. My father gave me all of his attention. He fed me, changed me, toilet-trained me. I was told I clung to him instinctively. My need for him brought him out of his depression.

Cohen goes on to recall some of his sufferings at the hands of his older siblings and to give the impression that his mother was not especially tenderhearted. But the ill-starred child grew up to be a cheerful, lovable, and successful man. He found his vocation after graduating from high school, in a job as a clerk at an antiquarian bookstore called the Madison Bookstore, where, in Naomi's words, "he fell in love with books." She went on, "Every time he had a nickel or dime he would buy one or two books and take them home and tell his blind father, 'I just bought this book of Dickens's and it's green and it cost ten cents.' This happened over and over until the little tenement apartment was overflowing with books."

In 1925, Cohen borrowed five hundred dollars from an uncle and opened his own bookstore, on Fourth Avenue (then the heart of the city's secondhand-book business), filling it with the books he had accumulated. In his autobiography, he explains how he chose the name Argosy. First, he wanted a name that started with the letter *A*, "as it might appear foremost on any list of bookstores." That crass criterion done with, "I ran through some reference books, and selected 'Argosy' as my choice, as it had romance attached to it. It symbolized treasure and rarities carried by old Spanish galleons."

"He was a smart businessman, and everybody liked him," Naomi said. "He was very pleasant and easy to deal with and he flourished."

"He was very kind," Adina said.

When Cohen moved his bookstore into its new home on Fifty-Ninth Street, he hired an architectural firm called Kramer & Kramer to renovate what had been a rather dismal bar, which someone set fire to on the eve of its closing. The architects transformed the gutted bar into a room of great charm, a vision of cultivation and gentility as filtered through a mid-twentieth-century aesthetic. Along the walls, they installed handcrafted bookcases and suspended green-shaded lamps, casting a warm light, over racks for displaying small old prints. Above the bookcases, on a background of green baize, they hung oil paintings of a harmless, vaguely nineteenth-century character—cows grazing in sylvan landscapes and portraits and still lifes. At the rear of the shop, they built a mezzanine for the display of leather-bound books by classic authors. Outside the store's entrance, to give passersby a foretaste of the pleasures within, they built an arcade with a lighted ceiling, burnished wood paneling, glass cases for the display of antique prints, and a square mahogany table to accommodate bargain-priced books.

This description of the shop and the arcade is based not on old photographs but on recent visits. Both are unchanged. The only conspicuous anachronisms are the computers that sit on some of the small tables scattered about the bookshop—tables that were there in the sixties and prove it by their sagging skirts of brown corduroy, which conceal boxes and shopping bags shoved beneath them. One of these tables, known as "the green table," for its dark-green leather top, was the table at which Lou sat, and today Adina can often be found at it, behind several high piles of books, onto whose first pages she is penciling prices. Across the room, there is a sort of nook where Judith usually sits in front of a computer, looking at online listings of American and English first editions. Judith's forty-five-year-old son, Ben Lowry, who started working at the bookshop fifteen years ago and is now a partner, sits at a desk near Adina. Neil Furman, an amiable, self-effacing associate, who is forty-seven, and who has also worked at the bookshop for fifteen years, and Emily Pettigrew, a young, recently hired assistant, sit at desks beneath the mezzanine. (Neil waves away the expertise he has acquired over the years: "I'm good at faking it.") The room is quiet, almost hushed. Cardboard cartons filled with books—the spoils of the book-buying expeditions the sisters regularly make to the houses and apartments of (in most cases) the recently deceased—sit on the floor. When they are emptied, they are replaced by filled ones, stored on upper floors and in a warehouse in

Brooklyn. They are the pivot on which the activity of the bookshop turns, and its lifeblood.

The antiquarian book business is a funny business. The people it caters to are not exactly non-readers, but they do not buy books just to read them, or even, in some cases, to read them at all. They are interested primarily in things surrounding books: their bindings, covers, paper, typefaces, age, condition, whether they are first editions, if they are signed by the author and if he or she is famous rather than the obscure schlub it is the destiny of most writers to remain or become. An example of a desirable book at the high end of the spectrum might be a well-preserved limited first edition of *Ulysses*. A lesser rarity is a signed copy of Ayn Rand's *The Fountainhead*. The Argosy deals in both the most expensive rarities (it currently offers a copy of the abovementioned *Ulysses* for sixty-five thousand dollars) and the lesser rarities, along with mere secondhand books at various levels of value. The Internet has been a stimulus for this trade. It has made it easier for collectors to collect; they can find rare books more readily than they could when only dealers' catalogues were available. Thus, even though fewer people come to the shop itself today, sales have actually increased.

But there is a melancholy that the sisters feel with particular sharpness at Christmastime. The bookstore used to be crowded with shoppers then. "We were usually too busy to talk to anyone," Judith said. When I visited the shop during the week before Christmas, the sisters had something of the crestfallen air of the hosts of an unsuccessful party, who brighten when a guest comes in and subside into glumness as the evening wears on and the room remains unfilled. One day, I sat with Adina at the cash register as spurts of arriving customers alternated with lulls when the shop was almost empty. A man came in and asked for a copy of *The Lady of the Lake* to give his mother—and one was found, a nice old illustrated edition for a hundred and twenty-five dollars. Another man wanted a photography book for a hundred to a hundred and fifty dollars to give his boss, and Richard Avedon's oversized book of inky pictures, called *An Autobiography*, was produced—and purchased for two hundred dollars. A middle-aged woman bought a history book with a handsome binding as a gift for a teacher for eighty dollars. A woman in her twenties bought a fifteen-dollar botanical print she had found in a rack. A couple approached the counter clutching books they had found on the bargain table outside the store. The greatest sale of the day was to a youngish millionaire who owns a factory in the Czech Republic and comes in every year to buy Christmas gifts for friends. He bought five rare books, for a total of eleven thousand dollars, among them a sixteenth-century architectural text and another copy of the Avedon *Autobiography*, which was worth several thousand dollars, because of the photographer's careless scrawl on its first page.

Late in the day, an elderly man entered the shop and asked for Naomi, who had helped him buy a gift the previous Christmas. He was looking for a print with a Steinway piano in it to give to a friend who worked at Steinway. The man had forgotten what Naomi remembered—that his last year's gift was a print with a Steinway piano in it. Was this the same friend? The man said yes, and reluctantly agreed that a different print was in order. But he wanted it to be Steinway-related, and Naomi suggested that he and she go up to the print gallery, on the second floor, and see what there was—perhaps a picture of the Steinway factory in Astoria.

The print gallery is the result of another of Lou Cohen's impulse buys. In the early 1950s, he bought the Harry Stone gallery of American primitive art, on Madison Avenue, whose owner, a friend, was ill and could no longer run it. As Naomi tells it, "Lou bought the gallery but didn't know what to do with it. He knew it was great. So he called my mother at home and said, 'I have a job for you.' My mother, who was a retired public-school teacher, said, 'No, I don't know anything about paintings and prints.' He said, 'You're going to learn.' She did learn." (In Judith's version, "Lou called my mother and said, 'Can you come downtown?' And she said, 'My hair is in curlers, can it wait?'") Over the years, under the mother's skillful stewardship, the gallery thrived, and prints and maps rather than paintings became its dominant forms. It is now run by an attractive and enthusiastic young woman named Laura Ten Eyck, a Canadian printmaker and sculptor who came to New York in the nineties to do graduate work at N.Y.U. and found herself in need of a job.

Laura recalls an interview with the sisters, who were looking for someone to assist their mother in the gallery. She was intimidated by them. "They sat there. They were so elegant, so intellectual. I had never met anybody like them before. Judith asked me, 'Do you like older people?' 'Well, I have a grandmother.'" This was evidently the right answer. An interview with the mother, Ruth, who was known as Miss Shevin (her maiden name, which she used when she taught school, and kept), came next. "She was so chic," Laura said. "She was in her late eighties, wearing a Chanel suit. She looked at me and only asked one thing—'Where are you from?' When I answered, she signaled the sisters that I was all right." Laura had planned to leave after a year but has stayed for fifteen years. Miss Shevin taught her the print-and-map business, and she in turn was a tactful protective presence for Miss Shevin as she navigated the treacherous shoals of advanced old age. Miss Shevin worked at the Argosy until she was ninety-six and died two years later.

Laura showed me a tiny room off a corridor that had been Miss Shevin's private space, and which has been preserved, because no one could bear to dismantle it. Its walls are densely covered with small paintings and drawings, some of extremely high quality. A bookcase is tightly filled with old books, some rare and many on horticulture. (When Cohen bought a vacation house, in Croton Harmon, Miss Shevin, with her characteristic quickness, became an expert gardener.) A Persian carpet, a cot covered with a blue-and-white Indian spread, where Miss Shevin napped, and a plain wooden desk at which she wrote letters and which she would clear for lunch—brought from home and eaten with her husband—complete the furnishings of the little room, which so clearly evokes its owner and the time she lived in.

I accompanied Naomi and the man with the Steinway friend to the print gallery, and watched as Laura unhurriedly leafed through folders in which an image of the Steinway factory in Astoria might appear, but didn't. The man agreed on other possible subjects for his gift, and when Laura produced a number of folders filled with early-twentieth-century street maps of Queens,

Naomi and I left them to their search and returned to the main floor.

Something bad had happened in our absence. Adina and Ben grimly reported that a signed copy of J. M. Coetzee's *Disgrace*, worth four hundred dollars, had just been sold— had had to be sold—for the "$1" written on its flyleaf. "We don't know where the guy found the book," Ben said. "You or Judith must have done this," Adina said to Naomi. Her accusation hung in the air for a moment and evaporated in the next. Naomi did not rise to the bait, she did not defend herself, there was no argument, there could be no argument. After the initial shock and impulse to blame someone for the error, there was complete, un-spoken agreement among Adina, Ben, and Naomi (Judith had left for the day) that peace must be maintained. I had been afforded a glimpse into the workings of the mechanism by which the Argosy maintains its remark-able homeostasis. When I questioned Ben about the inci-dent, he said, "We try not to mess up. But we handle books very quickly. The little drama you overheard— someone got a great deal. He was very lucky. Someone was going too fast—we don't quite know what hap-pened. But it happens. And it's not a big deal."

Unlike his mother and his aunts, who always come to work stylishly dressed, Ben wears casual clothes and has a manner that is at once laid-back and mildly ironic. He is tall and slender, and has curly black hair. "I'm the young whippersnapper," he said when I asked him about his life at the bookshop. "I'm a partner, but I'm the junior partner. And it's my mother, so it's a little bit of a dance. You can't scream at your boss. You can sort of scream at your mother. And it goes both ways. I'm sure I irritate her at times. Not as an employee but as a son. It's challenging. But it's fun. It adds a whole layer of complexity to this job."

Ben did not come to the bookstore straight from college. He spent eleven years in Colorado as "a ski person—I won't say bum." Finally, he said, he grew bored, and he returned to New York at the time of Ruth Shevin's final illness, when "the girls were thinking about the next generation—the third generation—and it was up to myself, not so much to my brother, Nicholas, who was occupied elsewhere, and to Zack, to see if we could keep this thing going." Zack is Naomi's son, who works in his mother's autographs-and-letters department. Nicholas is the president of Swann Auction Galleries, founded by Louis Cohen's nephew Benjamin Swann (né Schwamenfeld) in 1941 and purchased by his father, George Lowry, in 1969. He also hesitated before joining the family business. After college, he spent four years in Prague, where he taught English and, among other ventures, wrote a restaurant guide and ran a take-out sandwich business.

I asked Ben if he had known his grandfather. "Yes, I knew him very well," Ben replied. "He was very peaceful, soft-spoken, but decisive. He was the heart of this place, and then when the girls took over, when they started to take control from him, he was resistant to some of the modern newfangled stuff they were suggesting. Now they may be somewhat resistant to me."

"What do you do that's different from what your mother and aunts do?"

"Not so very much. When I first came, I said, 'I'll work on your online presence. That will be my foot in the door, and we'll see how that goes and how I like it and how you like me.'" Ben still does a lot of work on the website that he established for the Argosy, and on the orders that come in through it, but he has also become knowledgeable about the book business, as his mother and aunts did, simply by being at the bookstore every day and by going out on book-buying expeditions.

When the sisters speak of book-buying expeditions, they grow excited. The acquisition of books is the activity that lies at the center of their enterprise. It is to them what trials are to litigators, operations are to surgeons. This is where their knowledge and talent are tested. "It's the kind of knowledge it has taken us decades to be comfortable with," Naomi said. "You must know the values of books inside out. You must be able to look at a bookshelf and recognize the one good book on it. There are still libraries we could walk into and not know what to do with." She spoke of a library of six thousand books she had just bought. "I couldn't resist. There were enough valuable books to make buying the whole library worthwhile." The Argosy can buy whole libraries because it has the storage space to do so. This gives it an advantage over dealers who have room only for valuable books. (Today, the Strand Bookstore is the Argosy's only serious local competitor for whole libraries.) After winnowing out the first editions and rare and otherwise desirable books, the chaff is sent to the cellar or put out in the arcade, either on the central table, where there is an array of books for ten dollars or three dollars or five dollars on changing subjects (art, cooking, history, biography, mysteries, say), or in a pair of bookcases in back marked "Sale $1."

I asked Naomi if I could accompany her and her

sisters on a book-buying trip, and she said yes. But the next day Judith, in her big sister's wisdom, vetoed the idea and persuaded Naomi and Adina of its unwiseness. "We don't know how you could understand how we decide so quickly," Naomi said when she told me of the change of heart. She added that they don't want to make public what they pay for a library. However, perhaps to soften the refusal, the sisters allowed me to come along on two expeditions that they evidently felt would not expose their expertise to misjudgment or betray any secrets of the trade. One was to a hoarder's apartment, where they bought some posters and a few books out of kindness and pity for the deranged woman who lived there. The other was to the Riverdale apartment of a woman who had been an avant-garde dancer in the 1920s and had died at the age of a hundred and three. Naomi and I drove to Riverdale to see the small library she had left, which the person dismantling the apartment described as filled with rare art books. We entered a place of chaos and sad dirtiness. Naomi saw at a glance that she did not want to buy the dancer's library and told the dismantler so. She said she would pay a hundred and fifty dollars for ten or fifteen books she would select and carry away in a couple of shopping bags, and the offer was accepted. Among her sharp-eyed choices were a book of Leonardo da Vinci's drawings, a volume of Nabokov's stories, and a copy of *The Catcher in the Rye*.

Nicholas Lowry's choice of Prague as the destination for his flight from the nest probably gave his parents less pause than Ben's choice of Vail did, and may have been overdetermined. "My husband is Czech," Judith told me during a talk in her fifth-floor room. "He came to this country in 1941, at the age of nine, by way of France and then Portugal. His father had a business that made thermometers and thermos bottles. His mother's family business made rubber gloves, baby-bottle nipples, and condoms. They were the biggest condom sellers in Europe.

"When George's parents came to America, they decided they shouldn't be Jewish, because it wasn't a good thing to be. They had had to convert to Catholicism in order to leave Portugal, and didn't practice any religion after they arrived here. And, just as some children can't ask their parents about sex, George and his brother felt that they couldn't ask their parents about religion. So when I was dating George—I assumed he was Jewish, he looked Jewish, his friends were Jewish—he came to my house one day and saw Hanukkah candles and said, 'What's that?' 'Those are Hanukkah candles,' I said. 'Aren't you Jewish?' And he said, 'Well, yes, I mean no, I mean I think part of me is Jewish.' 'Well, which part do you think?' He said, 'Well, my mother, my father, I'm not sure.' I said, 'Why don't you ask them?' So he did, and, of course, they were both Jewish." Judith added that George, in his innocence, told the rabbi who married them that he wanted to convert. "The rabbi said, 'You don't have to. You're Jewish.'"

After "the little drama" of the Coetzee book, Naomi went over to the books sitting in piles along a ledge beneath a bookcase, which it is her chosen task to evaluate and place within the bookshop. "Who shall live and who shall die," she said merrily as she picked up a copy of a novel by E. L. Doctorow, looked at it for a moment, and sent it to its death in the basement, where books that are considered of no special value—ordinary secondhand books—are sold. The books that Naomi was judging were what she called books for reading, as opposed to books for collecting. The books for collecting had already been marked for such destinations as the fifth-floor first-editions room, or a room on the fourth floor called the 900 Room, where rare old books are kept, or the fifth-floor Americana room, or the shelves of fancy leather-bound books on the mezzanine.

The books on the ledge that escape the fate of the Doctorow novel will go into one of the bookcases on the ground floor that carry labels such as "Children's Books," "Poetry," "Philosophy," "Gardening," and "Select Reading." The last named is a large miscellany of works of fiction and nonfiction, arranged in alphabetical order, of which Naomi is the curator. The criteria by which she determines who shall drown and who shall go to "Select Reading" are partly but not wholly determined by the literary worth of the text and by the condition of the book; the author's rising or falling reputation will often tip the balance. "There are not enough requests for Iris Murdoch," Naomi said as she sent a nice copy of *A Severed Head* to the basement. "Not many people ask for Coover"; "Barth is not asked for enough"; "No one asks for Mary Lee Settle"; and "No one has ever asked for Voinovich" were other of her comments about the refusés. Among those who made the cut that day were T. S. Eliot (*The Cocktail Party*), Dickens (*Hard Times*), Truman Capote (*Other Voices, Other Rooms* and *The Grass Harp*), Philip Roth (*Portnoy's Complaint*), and Hemingway (*Death in the Afternoon*).

All three sisters had made a point of saying how much they liked their jobs. "I can't tell you how much we love being here every single day," Naomi said. "I cannot wait to get to work." As I stood with her at the ledge, watching her at her task of assessment—sometimes even offering an opinion when she hesitated—I caught some of her pleasure and excitement. The work of the bookshop is indeed agreeable work. You could even say that it isn't real work. It has none of the monotony and difficulty and anxiety of work. The cartons of books are like boxes of chocolates. Each book is a treat to be savored. That the treats are the end product of what most writers consider an arduous if not downright torturous activity perhaps only adds to their deliciousness. Each book that comes into the shop raises the interesting question of where it should go and what it is worth. The sisters serenely draw on their knowledge and taste ("Sometimes we throw Hitler things in the garbage," Naomi said) to determine the answers. They are proud of their success in carrying on the family business and aware of the mystique that attaches to the old-book trade. Children who inherit slaughterhouses or factories that manufacture incontinence products may not feel as blessed.

One day, Judith showed me an email from a girl in China—"a simple Chinese girl in her final year of senior high," as she called herself—who "started to have a dream of working in a bookstore" when she was very young. "Books make me feel safe," she wrote. "Staying in somewhere with books" was what she wanted to do. But it isn't only simple Chinese girls who want to stay in somewhere with books. Bookshops have an almost universal appeal. What constitutes this appeal is hard to pin down. When you enter an art gallery or an antique shop, you see what you hope will surprise and delight you, but a bookstore does not show what it is selling. The books are like closed clamshells. It is from the collective impression, from the sight of many books wedged together on many shelves, that the mysterious good feeling comes. Is there something that leaks out of the closed books, some subliminal message about culture and aspiration? The association of books with humanistic ideals is deeply entrenched in the public imagination, and finds its way into the rueful articles that regularly appear about the closing of bookshops in cities throughout the world, whose own subliminal message is that books are a kind of last bastion against barbarity.

This association is taken to the height of absurdity when decorators come into bookshops and buy books by the yard for the apartments of their barbaric clients. The three sisters are properly contemptuous of but grateful for this trade. There is a back room at the Argosy where books for decorators are kept, some arranged by color. All-white libraries are apparently in vogue today among decorators of advanced taste. When Naomi was going through the books on the ledge, she pounced on a book by Milan Kundera whose white cover made it a candidate for the all-white shelf. Sets of no great value but bound in impressive-looking leather and gilt are earmarked for the less advanced decorators. However, as Naomi wryly reported, when Ralph Lauren's subalterns come to the Argosy to buy old leather-bound books for his fantasy aristocratic interiors, they avoid the sets of classic authors in mint condition that a parvenu would choose. For his imaginary old-shoe libraries, Lauren seeks tattered, scuffed, broken-spined copies of books by obscure writers, and finds them in the Argosy's basement in a section titled "Old Bindings, $10." I stopped in at the Ralph Lauren store at Seventy-Second Street and Madison Avenue to see how his shabby-chic library looked in situ, but a new fantasy—something sleek and metallic—had evidently taken hold of Lauren's imagination, and there wasn't a book to be seen in the entire store.

In a conversation at the 2010 PEN World Voices Festival, Patti Smith told the novelist Jonathan Lethem about her lifelong love of old books. "Even as a child I would go to rummage sales or church bazaars and pick out books for pennies, for a quarter. I got a first-edition Dickens with a green velvet cover, with a tissue guard, with a gravure of Dickens. You could get things like that. It has never gone away, my love of the book. The paper, the font, the cloth covers." Lethem then asked Smith, "And did you work at rare bookshops at one point?" She replied:

> I only worked at one: Argosy Book Store, in 1967. Though I falsified my credentials as a book restorer. The old fellow who ran Argosy was very touched by me and he tried to train me, but I spilled rabbit glue all over a nineteenth-century Bible. He said it was not really rare, though; it was just a trainer Bible. Still, he had to let me go.

Richard Rosenblatt, who is the Argosy's current restorer, was trained by a successor of Patti Smith's named Grace Owen and by "the old fellow" himself, twenty-eight years ago, when he was thirty-five. Restoring is Rosenblatt's secondary profession. His first calling is art: he is a realist painter, primarily of landscapes, whose work sells—steadily—through galleries on Cape Cod and in Garrison, New York. He works four days a week at the Argosy, in an anteroom of the print gallery, seated at a long table, and wearing a spectacularly dirty apron but giving the impression of a neat, well-put-together person. Behind him are shelves of books with broken spines and loose pages and torn covers. His tools are bookbinder's glue, a metal instrument called a micro-spatula, a tongue-depressor-like implement called a bone folder, an X-Acto knife, rice paper, book cloth, acid-free tissue, and quantities of rubber bands, which he says are key to the operation. The sisters and Ben bring him damaged books that they consider valuable, and he repairs them—"mending gently," as he calls it, with a minimum of intrusion and the easy decisiveness of the achieved craftsman.

Perhaps the biggest disappointment of the holiday season, the most anxiously awaited guest who did not show up, was Bill Clinton, who frequently came to the Argosy during the weeks before Christmas to buy expensive gifts for friends. But this year he had been called away to the funeral of Nelson Mandela at the time of his expected visit, and now, after a false report that put everyone at the shop into a state of heightened adolescent excitement, it became clear that he would not appear. Many years ago, Adina, at a birthday dinner for Averell Harriman—to which she had been brought by a Washington lawyer she was going out with—had been seated next to Clinton, whom she had never heard of, since he was then only an Arkansas politician though already the world's most indecently charming man. The next day, Adina and Clinton met again, at another function, and—as she wonderingly reported—he remembered every word she had said at dinner. When Clinton became president, Adina sent him a historical document she thought he might like. He began coming to the bookstore after the end of his presidency. When he and Hillary moved to Chappaqua, he applied to the sisters for help after a flood in the basement ruined most of the books they had temporarily stored there. The Argosy succeeded in restoring or replacing all but a few.

On New Year's Eve day, a young man came into the Argosy with four boxes of books that the sisters immediately bought from him. The books all bore the bookplate of the lawyer-novelist Louis Auchincloss, who died in 2010, and whose library was known to have been sold. The young man had a strange story about a room with a sliding door that had been overlooked at the time of the sale, from which the books came. The sisters didn't examine the story too closely. A quick glance had told them that these were books they wanted, and they offered a price. He accepted, and Judith wrote him a check. A sense of Lou Cohen hovered in the air. "To prepare my daughters for a bookselling career, I conducted classes in the bookstore by going over new acquisitions with them," he wrote in his autobiography. "I would take center position and comment on each book as I handled it. Later each of the girls took turns pricing the books, with me on the sidelines watching and only occasionally correcting. They have often corrected me, and justifiably."

A great many of the books in the four boxes were by

Henry James and Edith Wharton, in old though not rare nineteenth- and early-twentieth-century editions. Many had penciled writings on the flyleaves and blank back pages. In his copy of *The Wings of the Dove*, Auchincloss left a record of his novelist's aliveness to the lesson of the master:

> Points of View Book 1 Kate
> Book 2 Densher
> 3 susie's
> 5 Millies
> But see p. 194, for a shift back to Kate's

Another annotated volume was an 1882 edition of Henry Adams's novel *Democracy*, which had been published anonymously and had given rise to a great deal of speculation about its authorship. Henry James had evidently been one of the speculators. Auchincloss noted on the flyleaf:

> P 209 H James spotted the term "mock lace" and said only an Englishman would have used it. An American would have said "imitation lace." But, of course, Adams had lived for years in England.

On a back page of Wharton's *The Custom of the Country*, Auchincloss wrote, "P. 37 'When the kissing had to stop' is actually a line from Browning's 'A Toccata of Galuppi's.'" In *Madame de Treymes*, he noted that "Fanny has been 'improved' like Chad Newsome," and "the Boykinses seem to stem from the Tristrams in HJ's The American."

The sisters evaluated the Auchincloss books and

dispatched them to various destinations in the bookshop. Judith took a poetry collection called *A Masque of Poets*, which included one of the few poems that Emily Dickinson published in her lifetime, the well-known "Success," to the first-editions room. A number of the James and Wharton novels went to "Select Reading," among them a specially attractive two-volume edition of *The Golden Bowl*, published in 1927. I considered buying the set (for sixty dollars) but hesitated too long. The book was gone when I went to look at it again. Among the books in the four boxes that were not written by James or Wharton was a little book, from 1884, called *Bibliothèque de la reine Marie-Antoinette*, whose flyleaf thrillingly bore the faded signature of Edmond de Goncourt. But the book wasn't worth much, Naomi told me: "He isn't asked for."

Auchincloss was a longtime customer of the bookstore, and, Naomi fondly recalled, he would always check "Selected Reading" to see if one of his novels had been admitted into its elite ranks. He was very happy, she said, when this finally happened. He continues to be represented in "Select Reading" by one of his novels—and in the basement's fiction section by eighteen of them.

Naomi's son Zack is the only child of her marriage to the late Stuart E. Hample, who made a career of being funny in many genres: children's books, plays, cartoons, comic strips, and performances. He died in 2009, at the age of eighty-four. Zack, a friendly and cheerful man of thirty-six, has been working in his mother's top-floor aerie for the past two years, cataloguing her collection of autographs, documents, and letters for the Argosy website. But he is at his post full-time only during the months of the year when baseball isn't being played. During the baseball season, he is a ball hawk. A ball hawk, as defined by Paul Dickson's baseball dictionary, is (1) "an especially fast and adept outfielder; one who covers a lot of ground," and (2) "a person who collects as souvenirs balls that are hit outside a ballpark." Zack is not a ballplayer; it is the second definition that applies to him, though it doesn't begin to express the magnitude of his collection, or the excess of his zeal. In twenty-five years, he has caught more than seven thousand baseballs hit or thrown into the stands at major-league ball games, the majority during batting practice, but many during the game proper. He is by far the world's leading ball hawk of the second kind. He traces his obsession to early childhood, when he watched baseball on television and saw the fans who caught foul balls or home runs "celebrating as if this was the best thing that ever happened to them." He went on, "Little kids are impressionable, and that stuck in my mind, though I know that a lot of little kids see fans catching balls on TV and they don't go on to become insane about it."

Zack brings to cataloguing the same qualities that he brings to ball hawking. He is currently obsessed with eliminating every one of what he calls "the ugly abbreviations" that were standard in the days of laconic printed catalogues but are not needed on the wordy Internet. Thus, for example, "TEG" becomes "top edge gilt" in Zack's relentless restorations of full words to the online listings. He is also revising descriptions of the items that were affected by Hurricane Sandy. Hurricane Sandy? At Fifty-Ninth Street and Lexington Avenue? When Naomi said "We are safe here," she was not factoring in the role that the freakishly accidental plays in almost every life.

During the hurricane, a long row of bricks at the level of the thirty-second floor came loose from the skyscraper next door—the one that replaced the brownstones—and came crashing down, some into the street, and others onto the Argosy's roof, where they made a hole, so that water gushed into the sixth-floor autograph room and then seeped down into the fifth-floor first-editions room, and even reached the fourth-floor shipping department. A great many of Naomi's valuable documents and autographs were either damaged or completely ruined, and many of Judith's first editions were lost beyond repair. "Insurance paid for that," Zack said. "But it's weird. We all feel like, yeah, we're getting the money for a book it might have taken ten years to sell and so in a way we got the money quicker—and yet it was so unsatisfying and depressing." By the time of my visits to the Argosy, the yearlong work of restoration of the fourth, fifth, and sixth floors was completed, and no trace of the damage remained. In fact, in some respects, the rooms had profited from the disaster; when their moldering and curling linoleums were removed, for example, beautiful wood floors came into view that nobody suspected were there.

Early in our talk, a messenger had come in and handed Zack a letter, which he glanced at and put aside. Now he picked it up and said, "I think this is a piece of hate mail. I recognize the handwriting. In 2009, I had an unfortunate experience with a fan at Yankee Stadium. I caught a lot of balls during batting practice, and some guy in the stands took exception. He said something rude, and what I should have done was just walk away. But for some reason I chose to engage, and it just escalated and got ugly.

Now this guy sends me hate mail. Of all the things in the world that are horrible and cause suffering to other people, you wouldn't think that catching baseballs was one of them."

In the middle of January, the three sisters and I had another conversation around the table in the first-editions room. Naomi recalled that her father always had his nose in a book dealer's catalogue, studying the "points" by which rare editions could be recognized and distinguished from editions of lesser value. Judith cited a classic "point." On page 205 of a true first edition of *The Great Gatsby*, a typesetter's error turns Fitzgerald's "sickantired" into "sick in tired." "If someone comes in and says he has a first edition of *The Great Gatsby*, you turn to page 205 and if it says 'sickantired' you say, 'Well, yes, it's the first edition, but the second issue, and therefore isn't worth as much,'" Judith said. Then, once again, as if some higher force compelled them to do so, Judith and Naomi fell into squabbling about the past. I had remarked on the way Lou seemed to do everything right. "Or were there some mistakes?"

"If there were mistakes," Judith said, "they were not big ones."

"Well," Adina said, "when he bought the building next to him, he could have bought the whole block for those prices."

"He bought what he needed," Judith said.

"He was paying the mortgage for decades," Naomi said.

"He never had a mortgage," Judith said.

"*What?*" Naomi said. "I remember the day he paid it off."

"He never had a mortgage."

"He didn't have the money to buy a building."

"It was cheap. This building cost a hundred thousand dollars."

"I don't know where you got that number from. It was a hundred and fifty-three thousand."

"I was going to say a hundred and fifty-five thousand."

"There's no way he could have paid that kind of money. He had a very small operation. He didn't have a hundred and fifty-three thousand dollars."

"I happen to know there was no mortgage."

"I happen to know there was."

The fight went on—and then, as before, abruptly ended, without resolution and with no blood drawn.

Adina brought up, not for the first time, a gesture made by her older sisters that felt like a caress. "After I was here maybe a year, my sisters spoke with my father and said, 'We think that Adina should be earning the same salary we are.' Because I'd never catch up otherwise. I'd be a hundred and they'd be a hundred and two. It made us very friendly and very warm."

"We really get along," Naomi said. "But more since our father died. When he was alive, we were always vying for his attention and compliments, and there wasn't enough of either to go around. He was very chintzy with his compliments. It was embarrassing for him to say a nice word. It would be emoting to say, 'You did a good job.' So we were always trying to pry a compliment out of him. But after he died we really stuck together. We have always been equals here. There is no struggle for power—because there is no power to have."

"We are foremost interested in the welfare of the Argosy," Judith said. "We have that as a goal, so we usually agree."

"It's not hard," Adina said.

I asked them to describe themselves.

"We have different personalities and we have a lot of different outside interests," Judith said. "We don't see a lot of each other after work. We have different friends and we do different things."

"We have different strengths," Naomi said. "Judy is a fantastic letter writer. Adina is fantastic with customers. She has patience. She is good at finding gifts for people. She is very neat. I am a slob. But we're kind of interchangeable in the jobs of the bookshop. We all love to be at the front desk."

"What were you like as kids?"

"I was quiet," Judith said. "Naomi was very active. My mother described how we started to walk. I almost never fell down because I would figure out how far it is from here to there. Naomi never walked. She started running before she could walk and she fell down all the time, but she picked herself up. I was careful and quiet."

"I was the baby," Adina said.

The talk turned to the curriculum of the New York public schools the sisters (and I) had attended in the 1940s. Judith recalled the home ec class in which pupils first sewed white cotton aprons and hats and then learned to cook parsley potatoes while wearing them. She recited a verse she had learned in the class, and never managed to forget, about the art of washing dishes:

Rinse the shining crystal
Then the silver bright

Delicate cups and saucers
We shall wash all right
Next the china dishes
Bowls and platters too
Last the pots and pans
And then we're through.

We talked about what life was like in New York during our girlhoods. Natives like us are a rare breed. We smile to ourselves at the people who come here from Ohio or Missouri and, within a year or two of their arrival, consider themselves echt New Yorkers. But they are! It is the avid people from somewhere else who fan the city's extravagant flame as they scale its hierarchies of finance, commerce, and art. We indigenes with our proprietary airs are all very well, but we don't count in the New York scheme of things, just as the Argosy doesn't. The demolition of the squat building next door and the construction of its thirty-story replacement will soon begin. When that is completed, the Argosy will stand alone on the block of massive structures, like a wildflower that has found a bit of soil in a crack in the pavement. Godspeed, wonderful bookshop, on your journey into the uncertain future.

The New Yorker, 2014

THE ÉMIGRÉ

In the spring of 1939, the father of the historian Peter Gay had a fateful premonition. As Gay writes in his memoir, *My German Question: Growing Up in Nazi Berlin*, he and his parents were booked on a ship called the *St. Louis*, scheduled to leave Hamburg, Germany, for Havana, Cuba, on May 13. But something told the father to switch to a ship called the *Iberia*, leaving for Havana two weeks earlier. On May 27, a fortnight after the Gays (or Fröhlichs, as they were then known) safely reached Havana, the *St. Louis* arrived and was overtaken by a ghastly tragedy. Nine hundred and seven Jewish refugees on board never set foot on Cuban soil. The Cuban government, with inexplicable callousness and arbitrariness, revoked their landing permits and barred them from leaving the ship. The *St. Louis* circled the Caribbean, seeking asylum for its passengers, but no country, including our own, would take them. The ship finally returned to Europe, where four countries—Belgium, France, Holland, and England—accepted a quarter of the passengers each. The 287 refugees who went to England were the fortunate ones. Of those who went to Belgium, France, and Holland, only around forty survived the Nazi occupation. Gay remembers standing in the harbor of Havana and watching the tragedy unfold. "It was thanks to [him] that we were looking at the St. Louis rather than traveling on it," he writes of his prescient father, and adds, "Would I have survived if we too had been passengers on that ill-fated ship, to end up an American citizen, an American family man, an American professor? The simple figures tell the story: the odds would have been against it."

Among the other fortunate passengers on the *Iberia* was a nineteen-year-old Hungarian Jew named George Jellinek, whose father, too, had been prescient, though, as it turned out, not prescient enough. Jellinek senior, who owned a restaurant in Budapest, felt the necessity of getting his son out of Hungary as war appeared inevitable and conscription in the Hungarian army probable, but did not foresee the unimaginable. Jellinek's parents stayed in Hungary and perished in the Holocaust. His sister, Eva, who also stayed, survived by means of false papers.

Jellinek eventually reached New York—Cuba was only a way station for refugees waiting to be admitted to America—and became part of an emigration whose impact on postwar American culture has yet to be fully chronicled. If he is not among this emigration's most imposing figures, he is surely one of its most genial spirits. For thirty-six years, his hour-long radio program, *The Vocal Scene*, has given extraordinary pleasure to large numbers of listeners, and when it goes off the air, at the end of the year, its like will surely not be heard again.

Devotees of the program tend to be older people. I listened to *The Vocal Scene* on WQXR many years ago and began listening to it again after happening upon it one evening last April. It acted on me like a madeleine. It powerfully evoked my childhood in the 1940s, when there was no television and families sat around in the evening listening to the radio—in the case of my family, to classical music. I could scarcely believe that Jellinek was still alive—he must be in his hundreds. Later, I discovered that my memory of listening to Jellinek when I was a child in the forties was a false one; *The Vocal Scene* did not begin until 1969. But such is the period flavor of the program, such is its atmosphere of anachronism, that my mistake is understandable.

"Hello, this is George Jellinek," says a voice at the outset of *The Vocal Scene*. This voice is at least as integral to the pleasure of the program as are those of the opera singers that fill the hour with gorgeous sound. It is a voice with a slight hoarseness and a pronounced foreign accent. It is a voice also inflected by cheerfulness, kindliness, intelligence, and slight hamminess. The program on the night I rediscovered *The Vocal Scene* was entitled "Eight Ways to Sing an Aria," and began with this Jellinek commentary:

In the third act of Gounod's *Faust*, the rejuvenated Faust comes to Marguerite's house. He is already fascinated by the girl, and Mephisto has already awaked in him a physical desire for her. But the music Gounod wrote for this scene is almost entirely devoid of sensuality. The tone is almost worshipful in the aria "Salut, demeure chaste et pure" (I greet you, chaste and pure dwelling). We may know the outcome of Faust's visit, but at this juncture the tenor should not sound like a seducer. He should project a passion

restrained by a sense of spirituality that trans-
forms Marguerite's garden into something like a
shrine. . . . We are about to hear this aria performed by eight different tenors ranging over
sixty years of recorded history. This may seem
like a reckless venture on my part, but I feel confident that you will find this hour neither dull
nor monotonous.

Jellinek's confidence was not misplaced. "Salut, demeure chaste et pure" is one of French opera's most rav-
ishing arias. One does not have to see the opera's setting
of a dark garden; one hears it in the music's lush sweetness. After listening to the aria once, one wants to hear it
again; after eight times, one is satisfied but not sated. The
eight tenors—César Vezzani (singing on a 1931 recording), Georges Thill (1930), Helge Roswaenge (1928),
Jussi Björling (1949), Beniamino Gigli (1931), Plácido
Domingo (1979), Richard Leech (1991), and Ivan Koz-
lovsky (1949)—gave eight conspicuously distinct inter-
pretations. Some sang in French, and others in German,
Italian, or, in one case, Russian. A little drama was pro-
vided by the high C that comes near the aria's end. How
would the tenors dispatch it? Like baseball players at
bat, they swung at the C. Some of them hit it out of the
park; others didn't. "His high C is impressive," Jellinek
said of Vezzani, but added, "That high C should not be
judged in isolation. It is contained within a long legato
phrase, 'où se devine la présence,' and Vezzani, like most
tenors, takes a breath before 'la présence' in order to be
able to negotiate that high C. No serious damage is done,
but the legato arc is broken." Björling earned Jellinek's

praise for taking "that entire crucial phrase . . . on one unbroken breath." At the same time, Björling's French "is only passable."

When I visited Jellinek at his home, in Hastings-on-Hudson, a few weeks later, I had to revise my image of him as a frail, very old man with a deeply lined Central European face and a shabby ill-fitting suit. In actuality, Jellinek is a sturdy, vigorous man of eighty-four, with a full, handsome face and the air of someone who knows that his suit is well cut. Moreover, he does not seem particularly foreign, nor does his accent seem as pronounced as it does when it comes from his disembodied voice. When we size each other up, our eyes evidently trump our ears; the actual Jellinek comes across as a fairly, if not entirely, regular American.

I come from a refugee family myself, and some of what has always drawn me to *The Vocal Scene* is my association of Jellinek with the New York émigré community to which my parents belonged during and after the Second World War. One of the striking characteristics of this community was its achievement—you could even say its overachievement—of mastering English. These émigrés made it their business to speak and write English that was not only grammatically correct but idiomatic beyond the requirements of ordinary usage. The pride that my father and his fellow émigrés took in their ability to stroll through the language as if it were a field of wildflowers from which they could gather choice specimens—of stale standard expressions and faded slang—is touchingly evoked by Jellinek's radio commentaries. His accent only magnifies the predictability of the language he writes in—which, of course, is the language that all but the poets among us use. Just a few degrees separate Jellinek's English from that of the native-born. However, those degrees give it its character and flavor and place it in a time that is not our own.

Jellinek and his wife, Hedy, a retired economist, live in a two-bedroom apartment with a view of the Hudson in an unpretentious brick apartment building near the shore. Like Jellinek's commentaries, the Jellinek apartment gave me a feeling of déjà vu. It is furnished with the mixture of fifties American modern furniture and upholstery and late-nineteenth- and early-twentieth-century European pictures and objects that constituted the homes of the émigrés I used to know. The Old World relics at the Jellineks'—photographs of Austro-Hungarian grandparents and great-grandparents in ornate gold frames, old prints and drawings, vases and bowls of European crystal and porcelain—derive almost entirely from Hedy's side of the family. She and her parents left Nazi Vienna in 1938. Among the very few traces in the Jellinek apartment of George's prewar life is an oval studio photograph of him as a boy in short pants with a violin tucked under his arm and a wonderful, schmaltzily serious look on his six-year-old face.

As Hedy served tea and pastries at a long table in a dining alcove, George spoke of his early life. Hedy confined herself to the role of hostess and supportive spouse, disclosing almost nothing about herself, and occasionally allowing a sense of tartness to emerge. George said he had studied the violin for eleven years, but never practiced enough to become a virtuoso performer. He came to op-

era late—he saw his first opera, *La Traviata*, at the age of
sixteen. "I was a typical chamber-music snob," he said.
"We chamber-music people looked down on opera. It
seemed like just a lot of noise and gestures, while chamber
music was pure and refined. But, when opera hit, it hit
me with a vengeance. I had no exit strategy." Jellinek's
father's restaurant was near the Budapest opera house,
and George went to the opera almost every night. The
opera season in Budapest ran from September to June,
and George attended a hundred and fifty performances
during each of his last two years in Hungary.

"I was rather deficient in my knowledge of French opera," Jellinek said, and when he went on to attribute this
deficiency to the Francophobia by which Hungary was
gripped between the world wars, I felt yet another stir of
childhood memory. I remembered the condescending
way my Czech parents used to talk about Hungarians.
Though not in the same league with the seriously bad
Germans, Hungarians were regarded as inferior and somewhat absurd in our household. We used to sing a song
that went:

Nem sere fe pekete
Gulásem se nacpete.

The first line is nonsense, a kind of parody Hungarian. The second line is Czech and means: "With goulash
you will stuff yourselves." When I reported these deplor-
able memories to Jellinek, he remembered, in turn, his
own anti-Czech feelings. He recalled vile things that
his teachers said about the (I always thought) innocuous
second president of Czechoslovakia, Edvard Benes. All

this enmity and jingoism, of course, came out of the alliances of the First World War and its aftermath. Hungary, which had fought alongside Germany, was carved up by the victorious French and English. Its most deeply resented loss was the vast region of Transylvania, given to Romania; the newly formed Czechoslovak Republic was given the smaller region of Slovakia but was only slightly less resented. As a consequence, Jellinek said, "the Hungarian government saw to it that we did not play the music of Enescu, we did not play the music of Smetana, we did not play the music of Dvorák."

After the Holocaust shattered the delusion of assimilation to which German and Central European Jews had clung until it was too late, a surviving Jew could hardly be expected to feel much of the old nationalistic pride. And yet I have to confess to the twinge of disappointment I felt when I learned that Jellinek, though his name is Czech, isn't Czech; and Jellinek himself continues to helplessly identify with his native culture. When he accepted an award from the American Hungarian Foundation in 1986, he felt it imperative to insert a bitter note: "I don't know what would have become of me in Hungary, because my native land rejected me, and my parents—who had held out bright hopes for me—were destroyed during those few years when Hungary brought disgrace to its heroic thousand-year history." But he went on to express his gratitude "for what my Hungarian heritage gave me: a terrific fundamental education, a basic understanding of history, an interest in languages, an immersion in a wonderful literature that is unfortunately unknown to much of the world, and the beginnings of my musical education. . . . And not the least of this Hungarian heritage is the recognition that, as a son of a small nation, speaking a language that is foreign to most of humanity, in order to succeed, one simply must try harder."

Jellinek's career in America is a kind of textbook example of trying harder. After he arrived in America from Cuba in the fall of 1941, he worked as a waiter in the Catskills and then—with the Spanish he had picked up in Cuba—became the Spanish correspondent for a New York export firm. He was drafted into the U.S. Army in 1942 and served as a lieutenant in the infantry from 1944 until 1946. He considers his graduation, against all odds, from the tough officer-training school at Fort Benning, Georgia, the triumph of his life. In an article about the Fort Benning experience published in the magazine *On the Air* in 1977, Jellinek recalled walking in the woods practicing the officers' art of barking commands: "Night after night I walked among the trees that darkly towered over me, piercing the nocturnal calm with my ferocious shouts." He went on, "Do I find public speaking difficult? It's a piece of cake to the Benning graduate." At the tea table, one of the few remarks that the reticent Hedy allowed herself was to point out that, of two hundred candidates, George was one of a hundred who did not flunk out at Fort Benning.

Jellinek went overseas and fought in the final battles of the war in Europe; after the armistice, he used the German it was obligatory for every Hungarian to learn to interrogate suspected war criminals. Back in New York, he worked at a succession of jobs in the recorded-music field: first as a salesman at a record store called the Merit Music Shop; then at an organization concerned with music rights called the Society of European Stage Authors and

Composers; then at, of all places, the Muzak Corporation; and, finally, at WQXR, which hired him as its music director. He created *The Vocal Scene* as a corrective to what he felt to be the station's inadequate coverage of operatic music. During these years, Jellinek also wrote two books, *Callas: Portrait of a Prima Donna* (1960) and *History Through the Opera Glass* (1994); reviewed records for *The Saturday Review of Literature*, *Opera News*, and the *Times*, among other publications; appeared on the Metropolitan Opera's Saturday-afternoon broadcasts; taught at N.Y.U.; and built the enormous personal collection of vocal-music records—even more enormous than WQXR's collection—that has been the backbone of *The Vocal Scene*. He and Hedy were married during his second year in America (they had met through a cousin on his first day in New York), and their daughter, Nancy, was born in 1948.

The walls in the Hastings-on-Hudson apartment that are not filled with the relics of Hedy's European past or with shelves of records and CDs are crowded with tributes to Jellinek's achievements in America. There is an honorary degree from Long Island University, an award from N.Y.U. for outstanding teaching, a Grammy, and dozens of inscribed photographs of opera singers and conductors, among them Ezio Pinza, Richard Tucker, Eugene Ormandy, André Kostelanetz, Victoria de los Ángeles, Maria Callas, Marilyn Horne, and Jarmila Novotná.

During the past decade, Jellinek has been winding down his enterprise. In 1984, he retired as WQXR's music director. He has gradually sold or donated more than a thousand of his records, and he has written no new scripts since 2000. What one has been hearing on *The Vocal Scene* is slightly emended repeats of old broad-

casts. Jellinek told me of his decision to permanently re-
tire *The Vocal Scene* at the end of this year, and invited
me to come to WQXR to observe the taping of his farewell program.

The taping was a quiet affair. The broadcast engineer, a
handsome young woman named Juliana Fonda, sat at
a large computerized control panel while Jellinek sat in a
darkened recording booth. Before entering the booth,
Jellinek discussed technical matters with Fonda. They
talked in the calm, settled way of people who have worked
together for a long time and know what to expect of each
other. Jellinek handed her the CDs from which she was
to play excerpts at the proper intervals, and disappeared
into his booth. The program was devoted to music of farewell and began with a duet from the fourth act of Gounod's *Roméo et Juliette*, sung by Angela Gheorghiu and
Roberto Alagna. The duet's trembling sweetness, like
that of "Salut, demeure chaste et pure," takes one about
as far from the present moment as it is possible to get. It
evokes the nineteenth century's impossible romantic
yearnings. It summons images of beaded velvet costumes
and flats depicting ancient parks and forests. That the velvet is threadbare, the beads grimy, and the flats faded
only adds to the music's nostalgic pull. The geographic
accident that put my parents in a part of the Austro-
Hungarian Empire that did not have to peevishly abjure
French culture but, on the contrary, worshipped it makes
me feel the pull especially strongly.

Jellinek next offered Bidú Sayão's rendition of Manon's
farewell to her little table in Act II of Massenet's opera;
followed by Joan Sutherland and Luciano Pavarotti

saying addio to each other in *Rigoletto*; and Mirella Freni and José Carreras singing the finale of *Don Carlo*. I glanced over at Jellinek as he read his commentary, and realized anew how great a part of the pleasure of *The Vocal Scene* is the pleasure of listening to George Jellinek. He is an artful broadcaster, reading with a storyteller's deliberation and an actor's grasp of cadence.

The *Don Carlo* selection ended the first half of the program, and Jellinek stepped out of the booth. "Any mistakes?" he asked Fonda, who shook her head. "That was the easy half," he said. And, indeed, the second half was not a piece of cake. Jellinek was nervous and several times stumbled over words. (Whenever this happened, he would take a deep breath and then repeat the entire phrase so that it could be spliced in later.) He was obviously looking ahead to the last segment of the program. As the strains of Haydn's *Farewell Symphony* rose, he said, "And now it is time for my own personal farewell to you, and it is not easy. . . . As you can imagine, I am leaving *The Vocal Scene* with a heavy heart, and I want to emphasize that no one is forcing me; it is my decision." He went on to speak of "the labor of love" the program had been and to say that those

who know me regard me as a modest person. But my modesty has its limits, and I am not modest enough to deny that I am very proud of what I have accomplished in the past thirty-six years. . . . Every one of my nearly two thousand programs was conceived with a central idea in mind, and your thousands of letters, postcards, and email messages have assured me of your enthusiastic appreciation. I am even immodest enough to believe

that my scholarship and overall experience combined with a personal style left a legacy hard to
duplicate.

When Jellinek stepped out of the booth, Fonda came
toward him and they embraced. Then they got to work
splicing in the corrected stumbles and adjusting the length
of one of the musical selections.

After the work was done, Jellinek and I went to talk
in a conference room. I asked him why he was taking the
program off the air instead of continuing to recycle the old
broadcasts. "I am getting older and my listeners are getting older," he said. "It's time to go."

"But you will be flooded with requests to continue
the broadcasts," I said. Jellinek shook his head. His mood
of immodesty had passed. "I have not done anything that
passes the test of immortality," he said. "Great artists pass
this test. The legacy of a Rubinstein is preserved in his records. I have done nothing like that. I've done a number
of clever programs."

Jellinek ushered me out of the studio, leading the way
through long corridors and holding doors open with
elaborate European courtesy. For the first time, I noticed
that he walked with a slight sway—so slight as to be almost invisible—but one that subtly evoked the stylized
movements of the czardas. I said nothing to him of this
near-subliminal association, and when he reads of it here
he will probably be surprised.

The New Yorker, 2004

THE STORYTELLER

In Rachel Maddow's office at the MSNBC studios, there is a rack on which hang about thirty elegant women's jackets in various shades of black and gray. On almost every weeknight of the year, at around one minute to nine, Maddow yanks one of these jackets off its hanger, puts it on without looking into a mirror, and races to the studio from which she broadcasts her hour-long TV show, sitting at a sleek desk with a glass top. As soon as the show is over, she sheds the jacket and gets back into the sweater or T-shirt she was wearing before. She does not have to shed the lower half of her costume, the skirt and high heels that we don't see because of the desk in front of them but naturally extrapolate from the stylish jacket. The skirt and heels, it turns out, are an illusion. Maddow never changed out of the baggy jeans and sneakers that are her offstage uniform and onstage private joke. Next, she removes her contact lenses and puts on horn-rimmed glasses that hide the bluish eyeshadow a makeup man hastily applied two minutes before the show. She now looks like a tall, gangly tomboy instead of the delicately handsome woman with a stylish boy's bob who appears on the show and is the current sweetheart of liberal cable TV.

Maddow is widely praised for the atmosphere of cheerful civility and accessible braininess that surrounds her stage persona. She is onstage, certainly, and makes no bones about being so. She regularly reminds us of the singularity of her show ("You will hear this nowhere else"; "Very important interview coming up, stay with us"; "Big show coming up tonight"). Like a carnival barker, she leads us on with tantalizing hints about what is inside the tent.

As I write this, I think of something that subliminally puzzles me as I watch the show. Why do I stay and dumbly watch the commercials instead of getting up to finish washing the dishes? By now, I know every one of the commercials as well as I know the national anthem: the Cialis ad with curtains blowing as the lovers phonily embrace, the ad with the guy who has opioid-induced . . . constipation (I love the delicacy-induced pause), the ad for Liberty Mutual Insurance in which the woman jeers at the coverage offered by a rival company: "What are you supposed to do, drive three-quarters of a car?" I sit there mesmerized because Maddow has already mesmerized me. Her performance and those of the actors in the commercials merge into one delicious experience of TV. *The Rachel Maddow Show* is a piece of sleight of hand presented as a cable news show. It is TV entertainment at its finest. It permits liberals to enjoy themselves during what may be the most thoroughly unenjoyable time of their political lives.

Maddow's artistry is most conspicuously displayed in the long monologue—sometimes as long as twenty-four minutes, uninterrupted by commercials—with which her show usually begins. The monologue of January 2, 2017, is an especially vivid example of Maddow's extraordinary storytelling. Its donnée was a *Times* article of December 31, 2016, with the headline "Trump's Indonesia Projects, Still Moving Ahead, Create Potential Conflicts." The story, by Richard C. Paddock, in Jakarta, and Eric Lipton, in Washington, was about the resorts and golf courses that Donald Trump is building in Indonesia and the cast of unsuitable or unsavory characters who have been helping him move the projects along. Among them are Hary Tanoesoedibjo, Trump's business partner, a billionaire with political ambitions that might put him into high office in Jakarta; Setya Novanto, the Speaker of the Indonesian House of Representatives, who had to resign when he was accused of trying to extort four billion dollars from an American mining company; and the billionaire investor Carl Icahn, a major shareholder in that mining company, who had recently been named an adviser to the Trump administration on regulatory matters. It was one of those stories about Trump's mired global business dealings that are themselves marked by Trump's obscurantism, and which tend to mystify and confuse more than clarify—and ultimately to bore. They have too much information and too little.

In Maddow's hands, the *Times* story became a lucid and enthralling set piece. "This story is amazing and it starts with copper," Maddow said at the beginning of the monologue, looking happy. She had already told us that she was glad to be back from her vacation and wasn't disheartened by the election. People had approached her "with concern in their eyes" and asked how she felt about the coming year. "I found myself . . . saying, 'I'm really excited for 2017.' I am! My job is to explain stuff—and, oh my God, is that a good job to have this year!"

Maddow then explained the properties of copper. She showed pictures of the Statue of Liberty, pennies, and wires. She talked about the "massive global appetite" for copper electrical wiring, and about a mining company called Freeport, based in Arizona, which is the world's second-largest producer of copper. One of Freeport's operations is in Indonesia, where it extracts gold and silver, as well as copper, from a mine that covers almost half a million acres. Maddow showed arrestingly beautiful photographs of the mine's crater—which is so huge that it is not just visible from space but "easily visible." She pointed out that the Freeport business in Indonesia is so far-reaching that the company "is the single biggest taxpayer for the whole country. . . . Of all the two hundred and sixty million people in Indonesia, its biggest tax payment every year comes from Arizona."

Why is she telling us this? Maddow anticipates the question. Her acute storyteller's instincts tell her that this is the moment to show her hand. Without any transition, she says, "In our presidential election this past year, do you remember when Indonesia had a weird little cameo role?" Of course we don't remember anything of the sort. Maddow goes on, "It was in the Republican primary. It came up—it was so strange, so unexpected, not just inexplicable but unexplained. . . . It didn't ever make any sense—until now. I love it when a story doesn't make sense for a year and then all of a sudden it does." She is laughing, almost chortling. "It rarely happens when you get it so clearly."

The weird cameo role was played by the then not-yet-disgraced Speaker of the Indonesian House, Setya Novanto. Maddow showed a video of Trump at a press

conference at Trump Tower, which he had called to announce that he would sign a pledge he had originally
refused to sign, promising to support the winning Republican candidate. (All the other Republican candidates had
signed it.) At his side was a short, smiling Asian man.
"Hey, what's this random Indonesian guy doing there?"
Maddow says. The video goes on to show Trump with
his arm around the guy's shoulders, saying, "Hey, ladies
and gentlemen, this is an amazing man. He is, as you
know"—as we know?!—"Speaker of the House of Indonesia. He's here to see me. Setya Novanto, one of the
most powerful men, and a great man, and his whole group
is here to see me today, and we will do great things for
the United States. Is that correct? Do they like me in Indonesia?" The Speaker says, "Yes." "That was such a random moment in the presidential election, right?" Maddow
says. "It was weird at the time, totally inexplicable. Well,
now we get it."

What Maddow has prepared us to get with her geog-
raphy lesson about copper and the mine in Indonesia is
the scandal in which Setya Novanto got caught up, and
by which Trump, because of his continuing business relationship with the amazing Indonesian, is tainted. "That
mining company that operates a giant open-pit mine
that's the largest gold mine in the world and you can
see it from space," Maddow says, showing a picture of the
oversized crater again, and looking enormously pleased
with herself, "one of their executives met in Indonesia
with that same politician who we just saw with Donald
Trump, and he secretly taped him trying to shake down
the mining company for four billion dollars." Freeport's
contract with the Indonesian government runs out in

2021; the company would like to extend it. "The guy who was standing there with Trump, who got introduced at that press conference, that politician was caught on tape telling the mining company that, yeah, he could get them an extension of their contract. In fact, he could get them a twenty-year extension of their contract . . . if they could provide him with a little something." We learn that the tape was played all over Indonesia, and that Setya Novanto was forced to resign as Speaker. In the end, though, he was reinstated, because the tape was ruled inadmissible as evidence.

As Maddow nears the end of her monologue, she mentions the *Times* story from which she got most of her material: "Donald Trump's new real-estate deals, that golf course he wants to build . . . the Indonesian resort deals that brought this politician to Trump Tower in the first place, the Trump Organization has just confirmed to *The New York Times*, those deals are on, those projects are moving forward." The reader who has been following my own lesson in comparative narratology will notice that Maddow has been sparing in her use of the *Times* narrative. Many characters that figure in the *Times* story are missing from Maddow's, most conspicuously Trump's Indonesian business partner Hary Tanoesoedibjo. Apart from the not negligible problem of pronouncing his name, Maddow understands the importance in storytelling of not telling the same story twice. The story of Donald Trump and Setya Novanto is enough. You don't need the additional story of Donald Trump and Hary Tanoesoedibjo to show that Trump's business dealings are problematic; nor do you need quotations from experts on ethics (the *Times* cites Karen Hobart Flynn, the president of Common Cause, and Richard W. Painter, a former White House ethics lawyer) to convince us that they are. By reducing the story to its mythic fundamentals, Maddow creates the illusion of completeness that novels and short stories create. We feel that this is *the* story as we listen to and watch her tell it.

As a kind of ominous confirming coda, Maddow holds up the appointment of Carl Icahn as an adviser on corporate regulations. (He has since resigned.) "This new key member of the federal government for whom they have invented a job . . . is the single largest shareholder in that mining company, whose mines in Indonesia you can see from space," she says. "And now that company will presumably be in an excellent position to do whatever needs to be done to benefit whoever needs to be benefitted. . . . This is apparently what it's going to be like now. Everybody's got to pay attention now."

Every so often, a show of Maddow's fails to please. There was the notorious show of March 14, when Maddow pitched two pages of Trump's 2005 tax return that had come her way—"Breaking news"; "The world is getting its first look"—and was all-around pilloried for producing nothing much except a stir about herself. Someone had leaked the first two pages of Trump's tax form to a financial reporter named David Cay Johnston, who passed them on to Maddow. The pages showed that, in 2005, Trump had made more than a hundred and fifty million dollars and had paid thirty-seven million in taxes. This glimpse only deepened the mystery of the tax returns that Trump has withheld, and had all the signs of being a leak

from the White House intended to demonstrate that the
president was plenty rich and had paid his taxes. The show
was an embarrassment that, interestingly and yet perhaps
unsurprisingly, did not embarrass Maddow. The bad
press that she received from commentators and news-
casters (there was a scathing piece in *Slate* by its television critic, Willa Paskin, titled "Rachel Maddow Turned
a Scoop on Donald Trump's Taxes into a Cynical, Self-
Defeating Spectacle") did her no harm. Nothing seems
to do anyone harm these days. Maddow's ratings only
rose. She saw no reason to apologize or explain. "I really
have no regrets at all," she said when I pressed her for an
admission of miscalculation. "People were mad that it
wasn't more scandalous. But that's not my fault. I did it
right."

This was not the case with the show of October 29,
2014, for which Maddow almost immediately saw reason to apologize. The show began with Maddow placing
on her desk, one by one, a graduated set of ceramic kitchen
cannisters. "Here in our offices at 30 Rockefeller Center,
in our office closet, actually, we have, sort of randomly, a
really hideous complete set of kitchen cannisters," she
said, drawing them to her with an impish smile. "A full
set of mushroom-ornamented, baby-poop-colored, made-
in-China ugly kitchen cannisters. They take up a lot of
space, but I can't get rid of them. We bought these hideous kitchen cannisters when a producer on our staff
stumbled upon them while out shopping and realized—
photographic memory—that these were an exact match
to one of the best campaign-ad props thus far in the
twenty-first century. Look." A picture then appeared on-
screen, showing a woman sitting in front of a display of

the same mushroom-ornamented cannisters that live in the office closet at MSNBC. The woman was Sharron Angle, a Nevada Republican, who had tried to make a political comeback after an unsuccessful attempt to unseat Harry Reid in his Senate race in 2010. "It wasn't so much that Harry Reid won that Senate race in 2010," Maddow said. "It was that Sharron Angle lost that race, because Sharron Angle talked like this." Maddow then showed a series of statements made by Angle, under headings such as "2nd Amendment Remedies":

> I feel that the Second Amendment is the right to keep and bear arms for our citizenry. . . . This is for us when our government becomes tyrannical. . . . And you know, I'm hoping that we're not getting to Second Amendment remedies. I hope the vote will be the cure for the Harry Reid problem.

"I sure hope the vote will be the cure for the Harry Reid problem," Maddow said, with one of her nicest smiles. "Democrats had no business winning that Senate race in Nevada that year. But Sharron Angle threatening that if conservatives didn't get the election results that they wanted they would start shooting in order to get the election results that they wanted—that was enough to spook people who might otherwise have supported her. . . . You just can't run people like that for statewide office." Angle had evidently learned her lesson, and in her new bid for office—for a House seat this time—she used the Mushroom Cannister Remedy to reassure voters and show that "there was nothing to be scared of when it comes to her." They could see that she was just another nice, kitsch-loving Republican lady.

Not so Maddow's next character, Joni Ernst, who was running for the Senate in Iowa and now "turns out to have a Sharron Angle problem. A piece of tape has emerged where Joni Ernst, like Sharron Angle before her, is threatening that she is ready to turn to armed violence against the government if she doesn't get what she wants through the political process." Maddow showed Ernst at a lectern, saying, "I have a beautiful little Smith & Wesson nine-millimeter, and it goes with me virtually everywhere. But I do believe in the right to carry, and I believe in the right to defend myself and my family, whether it's from an intruder or whether it's from the government, should they decide that my rights are no longer important." (In the end, Ernst won her race, without having to shoot anyone.) Maddow closed the segment with: "I would say watch this space, but I know all you're watching right now is these hideous kitchen cannisters."

The next night, an unsmiling Maddow addressed her audience thus: "Okay, so last night I may have crossed the line. I went a little too far and said something that offended some of our viewers, and rightly so. It was not my intention to offend. So we've got a Department of Corrections segment coming up. Anybody who likes to watch this show because you like to yell at me while I'm on the screen, you will like this next thing that I'm going to have to do. Mea culpa on the way." Sitting in front of a sign that read DEPARTMENT OF CORRECTIONS, Maddow recapitulated her narrative of the page Joni Ernst took from Sharron Angle. "Tonight, I have a correction to make about that. I will tell you, though, that this correction has nothing to do with Joni Ernst." In fact, the "correction" was not a correction at all. Maddow had made no factual errors. She had merely betrayed her youth. She had not lived long enough to know that you do not mock people's things any more than you mock their weight or accent or sexual orientation. "Have nothing in your houses that you do not know to be useful, or believe to be beautiful," William Morris wrote in his famous dictum. Morris knew very well what was hideous. But he knew enough about human nature to insert that inspired "believe."

Maddow's disparagement of the mushroom cannisters brought her a torrent of mail. She read aloud from it: "I was insulted that you referred to the cannisters as ugly, as I had bought that set many years ago. I wish I still had my cute, adorable cannisters." "Hey, Rachel, my mother has a set, too—we could use a matching set." "If by hideous you mean the most awesome cannisters of all time then you are correct." More messages appeared on the screen: "*Hideous*??? What ever do you mean?" "Those were my grandma's mushroom cannisters! She had matching pots, s&p, spoon rest, napkin holder and a wall clock."

"I have been aesthetically swayed," Maddow said, setting down the sheaf of letters. "Yes, I once believed that those mushroom cannisters were hideous, in the context of threatening armed violence against government officials, à la Sharron Angle in Nevada and Joni Ernst in Iowa. I also do still kind of think they're hideous here at my office. But in real life, on your shelf, on your kitchen counter, in the recesses of your childhood memories, the Merry Mushroom cannisters your mom bought at Sears in the seventies—which also happened to match your Merry Mushroom curtains—those mushroom cannisters really aren't hideous. They are lovely. So thank you for fact-checking me on this. I sincerely regret what I now believe is an error. I love your mushroom cannisters and your kitchen—I love all of it." She had been hugging the biggest cannister. Now she removed its lid and put it on her head. "Sorry."

Maddow was born forty-four years ago in the small city of Hayward, in the San Francisco Bay Area, and grew up in neighboring Castro Valley. Her brother, David, now on the staff of a bioscience company, was born four years earlier. Her father, Robert, a lawyer, worked as the counsel for the local water company, and her mother, Elaine, had an administrative job in the school district and wrote for a community newspaper. "I had a middle-class, suburban upbringing," Maddow told me. "I graduated from the local high school at seventeen and went to Stanford. I came out soon after I got to college, and that caused a rift—a temporary rift—with my family. It was very hard for them. My mom is very Catholic, and my dad saw how much it hurt my mom. But now my parents and I are close again. They couldn't be more supportive. They're very close to my partner."

Maddow's partner is Susan Mikula, a fifty-nine-year-old artist, with whom she has lived for the past eighteen years. They met in a small town in Massachusetts, in the western part of the state, a few years after Maddow graduated from Stanford. She was writing her thesis for an advanced degree from Oxford, where she had studied as a Rhodes Scholar. (She had also received, as not many applicants do, a Marshall Scholarship.) "I wanted to be in an unhappy living situation to get the thesis done," she said. She supported herself by doing odd jobs, and word of one of these jobs brought her to the door of Mikula, who was looking for someone to do yard work. When Mikula opened the door, a *coup de foudre* followed.

Maddow had been an athlete in high school. Her sports were volleyball, basketball, and swimming. In her senior year, she badly injured her shoulder playing volleyball and was faced with a difficult choice. "I was a good athlete," she told me. "I wouldn't say I was a great athlete, but I was good, and I was scouted by a number of schools for an athletic scholarship. When I hurt my shoulder, I had to decide whether to get it fixed so I could go on being an athlete, or not. To get it fixed meant surgery and rehabilitation and starting college a year late. I decided not to get the shoulder fixed—it works perfectly well in regular life—and to go to college right away. Stanford, which had the best teams in the country in my sports, would not have given me an athletic scholarship anyway.

"Around this time I was realizing I was gay. I was coming out to myself. And, having grown up in this conservative town in the Bay Area with my relatively conservative Catholic parents, I knew this was not a place I wanted to be a gay person in. When I realized I was gay— it's not that I hadn't had inklings—when it finally clicked into place, I was, like, 'Oh! That's it. That's what I am!' There was no ambiguity about it. It was an epiphany. It was the same thing when I met Susan. I know that people don't believe in love at first sight. It was absolutely love at first sight. Bluebirds and comets and stars. It was absolutely a hundred percent clear."

I asked Maddow if coming out to herself was preceded by feelings about a particular woman. She said, "No. It was much more an intellectual thing."

It was a thing that brought her into AIDS activism. The epidemic was then in one of its darkest periods. Maddow worked in hospices and with organizations helping

prisoners who had the disease. "We were taking this overwhelming, maddening, depressing, very sad thing that
my community and my city were going through and fig-
uring out what pieces of it we could bite off and fix, finding winnable fights in something that felt like a morass
and was terrible," she said. This work continued throughout college and graduate school and culminated in her
doctoral thesis, on H.I.V. and AIDS reform in British and
American prisons.

Maddow spoke of her detachment from what she calls
"electoral politics" during the time of her AIDS activism.
She recalled giving money to Harvey Gantt, who was
running against Jesse Helms in the 1990 North Carolina
Senate race, because of Helms's homophobic position on
AIDS. "That was the closest I came to having an electoral-
politics impulse," she said. "I didn't have strong feelings
about Republicans and Democrats. In some ways, I still
don't."

"Even with what the Republican Party has become?"
I asked.

"I'm very interested in the conservative movement
and in what the Republican Party has become," Maddow
said. "I think I am a liberal. I believe that government is
a manifestation of the social contract. It's a way we ought
to work together as our best selves to make things better
for the least among us and improve society as a whole. But
I'm almost more interested in the sociology of conservative and liberal styles, particularly of conservative styles. I
think the conservative movement is fascinating and ar-
cane. The dynamic between the conservative movement
and the Republican Party—of which there is no parallel
on the left—is a really interesting ongoing saga that has
incredibly sharp turns in it. And the people who are

inside this movement are often very bad observers of what is happening. Which is nice for me, because being definitely on the outside gives me a better perspective on it. I happened to have a fascination with crazy right-wing racist politics—and all of a sudden that's relevant. It's my moment."

I think I am a liberal. Why the equivocation? It may derive from the restless politics of Maddow's parents. "When I was growing up, both my parents were centrists. They were Reagan Democrats—Democrats who voted for Reagan," she said. "But during the George W. Bush administration my dad became a motivated liberal. Dick Cheney in particular made my dad into a liberal. My mom less so. But when Schwarzenegger was elected governor in California, in 2003, I remember her saying, 'I feel like I don't have a president, I don't have a governor, and I don't have a Pope.'"

Maddow's entrance into broadcasting began as a lark. While she was writing her thesis and doing her odd jobs in western Massachusetts, she heard about an audition held by a local radio station for someone to announce the morning news. She got the job—understandably. She has a beautiful voice, low in register but with a clarion brightness to it, and beautiful diction. This job led to others, to higher and higher rungs on the ladder of radio broadcasting (the liberal network Air America was her final radio destination, in 2004), and then to work in television news at MSNBC and, ultimately, to her own show, which began airing in 2008.

When I went to observe Maddow doing her broadcast, at MSNBC's headquarters, in Rockefeller Center, I didn't know what to expect, but I was unprepared for the large, eerily silent studio, some of whose props I recognized from watching the show—the desk with the glass top, the garish views of Manhattan skyscrapers. At five minutes to nine, the studio was empty except for me and a young man who had come to bring me earphones. At four minutes to nine, a calm young woman appeared and adjusted the large cameras that faced the desk. At a few seconds before nine, Maddow rushed in and sat down at the desk. She performed her long opening segment. During commercials, she typed furiously on a small computer. Watching her performance at home can be an exhilarating experience. Watching it in the studio was a somewhat flat one. Maddow went through her paces, but they were paces. A few days later, I visited a room—called the control room—a floor below the broadcasting studio, where seven people sit in front of futuristic-looking computers and carry out the work of illustrating Maddow's commentary with photographs, videos, and writings. They all seem to know what they are doing, but they do not seem relaxed. Things can go wrong, and they sometimes do. The wrong illustration can appear, for example, and Maddow has to react to it with practiced grace and humor.

The hour of the show is the culmination for Maddow of a workday that starts at around 12:30 p.m., when she acquaints herself with the day's news. At two o'clock, she meets with her staff of twenty young men and women in a room equipped with a whiteboard and two facing rows of identical small desks. The day that I came to a meeting, Maddow arrived ten minutes after the hour, dressed in jeans and a black sweater. She stood in front of the whiteboard, which displayed a list of possible subjects for the show. An elliptical exchange about the various items followed. Maddow would ask a question, and someone would answer. She was informing herself about the possible stories. By the time of the meeting, "I have a pretty good idea of at least what is in contention for making the show that night. I already have two or three ideas. But by the end of the meeting I've usually changed my mind," she said. "It's a grumpy meeting. A little testy." I noticed none of this at the meeting I attended; I just found it hard to follow.

"Do you start writing your text after the meeting?" I asked.

"No. I start reading. I read far too long after the meeting. I know what will be in the show, but I haven't read enough detail, and I don't start writing until it's too late."

"What time do you start writing?"

"I should start writing at four-thirty. Sometimes I don't start writing until six-thirty."

I told her how impressed I was that she can write her substantial monologue in such a short time.

"It's a bad process. It's impressive in one way, but it's—reckless. It kills my poor staff. They're so supportive and constructive. But it's too much to ask. They need to put in all the visual elements and do the fact-checking and get it into the teleprompter. It's a produced thing and requires everybody to do everything fast. And it's a broken process. If I could just get it done an hour earlier, I think I would put ten years back in the lives of all the people who work with me."

I asked her why she didn't start work earlier in the day. Part of the problem, she told me, is that the news

changes in the course of the day. But she has a more compelling reason for starting work at noon: "I've tried starting at nine. It's not that I have anything so important
going on in my life that I wouldn't trade it to be better at
my job, but it's that you can only have your brain lit up
for that long before it starts to break down and you stop
making sense and stop being creative. What I don't want
to give up is the originality."

She went on, "The thing that defines whether or not
you're good at this work is whether you have something
to say when it's time to say something. Because you're
going to have to say something when that light goes on.
I could roll in at eight o'clock and have my producers tell
me what to say and book seven people for me to chat with
about the news. There are people who have made a very
successful living doing that in this work. I just don't want
to do it that way. I want to have something to say that
people don't already know every single night, every single segment, and that makes it hard to get the process
right, because that's the only thing I care about."

I asked her what she did in the morning hours, before she turned on the light switch for her brain. "I'll go
to the gym, or spend time with Susan, or sometimes,
when the weather is nice, I'll go fishing before I go to
work. I try to do something that is definitely not work,"
she said. The writing of her sobering book, *Drift: The
Unmooring of American Military Power*, published in
2012, was another "not work" activity—as were her interviews with me. She would come to my apartment (she
preferred this to meeting in the furnished sublet that she
and Susan had had to move into after a fire in their own
apartment destroyed most of the interior and many of

their possessions) and we would talk for an hour or an hour and a half. Maddow has given many interviews, several dozen, and when I told her that I had read some of them she was curious about my reaction. I said that everyone said pretty much the same things about her personal life (as I expected to do myself). "Does that surprise you?" I asked.

"No, it is my sense as well," she said. "I have a private life and a private me that is separate and apart from what is on television. I go on television and I do this thing and it's real, it's part of me, but it's not all of me. The rest of me is my own. It's not for everybody else. You sort of pick a slice of your life that you're going to share as your non-TV persona and you give that to people—and they find it more or less interesting."

Maddow has suffered from depression since childhood, and a few years ago she decided to allow this affliction a place in her non-TV persona by speaking about it in interviews. "It was a hard call," she said. "Because it is nobody's business. But it had been helpful to me to learn about the people who were surviving, were leading good lives, even though they were dealing with depression. So I felt it was a bit of a responsibility to pay that back."

The depression comes in cycles. She doesn't know how long a bout of depression will last—it can be one day or three weeks. She takes no medication, but expects that one day she will have to—"I will not have a choice." But she dreads the thought of "a change to the psyche."

"Is there a manic side?" I asked.

"Yes, but much less than when I was young. That has flattened a bit."

"Have you had psychotherapy?"

"No."

"Are you afraid of changes to the psyche it might produce?"

"No. I'm just not interested. I'm happy to talk to you for this profile, because I'm interested in you and in this process. But, in general, talking about myself for an hour—it's not something that I would pay for the privilege of. It just sounds like no fun."

Maddow's TV persona—the well-crafted character that appears on the nightly show—suggests experience in the theater, but Maddow has had none. "I am a bad actor. I can be performative. But I can't play any other character than the one who appears on the show. I can't embody anyone else." To keep herself in character, so to speak, Maddow marks up the text that she will read from a teleprompter with cues for gestures, pauses, smiles, laughs, frowns—all the body language that goes into her performance of the Rachel figure. "My scripts are like hieroglyphics," she said. I asked her if I could see a page or two of these annotated texts. She consented, but then thought better of it.

"Does the name Ben Maddow mean anything to you?" Maddow asked during one of our early interviews. "Yes, it does," I said. In the early eighties, I had read a brilliant book—an illustrated biography of the photographer Edward Weston—by a man of that name. The book gave no information about him to speak of, and I did not seek it out, though I was curious. In the eighties, curiosity about authors was less urgent, perhaps because the New Criticism was still a force to reckon with, or, probably, more to the point, because there was no Google to instantly gratify it. So, when Rachel Maddow became a household name, it didn't summon the name of Weston's biographer. But now that she uttered it, and said he was a distant relative about whom she knew very little, I hastened to press the keys that would tell me who he was. I learned that he died in 1992 and is largely remembered today as a left-wing Hollywood screenwriter, who wrote or collaborated on such classics as *The Asphalt Jungle*, *Intruder in the Dust*, and the documentary *Native Land*, and was blacklisted between 1952 and 1958. After graduating from Columbia, in 1930, he was unemployed for two years and finally found a job as a hospital orderly and then one as an "investigator" for a Roosevelt-era agency called the Emergency Relief Bureau. He found his calling, and learned his trade as a screenwriter, when he joined a fellow-traveling collective called Frontier Films to work on documentarics.

While studying at Columbia, Ben had been a protégé of the poet and critic Mark Van Doren, and began publishing poetry in little magazines. "My poetry was pretty dreadful, so exaggerated," he told Pat McGilligan, the author of *Backstory 2: Interviews with Screenwriters of the 1940s and 1950s*. He adopted the nom de plume David Wolff because, as he told McGilligan, "I didn't want the people at the Bureau to think that somehow I was uppity." In 1940, his long poem "The City," published in *Poetry* under the David Wolff pseudonym, was awarded one of the magazine's major prizes, which later went to, among others, Robert Lowell, Ezra Pound, and W. S. Merwin. Allen Ginsberg said the poem influenced him in the writing of *Howl*. It is long forgotten. It may be one of the most dreadful poems ever written, worthy of inclusion in *The Stuffed Owl: An Anthology of Bad Verse*, a collection that Wyndham Lewis and Charles Lee published, in 1930, to universal delight. It is hard to choose a typical example among the poem's twenty-seven stanzas. They all read sort of like this:

> Black halloween! I walked with the crooked nun;
> Heard the cruel father sob in the empty room;
> and households dining together in daily hatred;
> the posed hysteria, and the idiot calm; and those
> whose love was poisoned with delay, I saw still
>   smile,
> —and felt in myself forever the anguish of
>   understanding.

After six years on the blacklist and working "in the shadows," as it was called, Maddow caved in and named names to the House Un-American Activities Committee. McGilligan reports this reluctantly and sadly. As he had observed when interviewing Ben—and as I had inferred from the Weston biography—Ben was an exceptionally interesting and civilized man. Leafing through my copy of the biography, I am struck anew by its quality of mildly exasperated tenderness toward its subject.

Why am I telling you this? When I told Rachel of my fascination with Ben Maddow and of my feeling that by inserting him into a piece that was supposed to be about her I was imitating her forays into left field, she nodded in agreement. "It's our form of exhibitionism," she said. "Here's what *I'm* interested in. Here's what grabs *me*. I'll pull you along on the same thread I followed. I think it works. As long as people are connected to you as the author, it works." The thread I am pulling is attached to a "family secret" that Rachel casually revealed to me one morning. She said that "Maddow"—with its mild subliminal association of meadows in summer—is a fake name. Not faked by her or her parents but by a nineteenth-century Ellis Island official who bestowed it on a family of Russian Jewish immigrants named Medvyedov, derived from *medvyed*, the Russian word for "bear." One of the few things Rachel has been told about her kinsman Ben is that he chose David Wolff as his pen name because he thought *medvyed* meant "wolf."

Rachel's paternal grandfather, Bernard, came, like Ben, from this renamed family. He grew up in New Jersey, and became a jeweler. Shortly before the Second World War, he married a woman from a Dutch Protestant family named Gertrude Smits. Rachel speculates that Gertrude's parents were "not psyched about Trudy marrying a Jew, so this became a subject that was not discussed in the family. It wasn't exactly a family scandal, but it was close to a family secret that Grandfather was Jewish." Rachel's father, Robert, was brought up as a Protestant. When he and the "very Catholic" Elaine were engaged, he agreed that their children would be brought up in her faith. He converted to Catholicism when Rachel was eight years old.

Maddow recalled that around ten years ago, when she and her brother were home for a holiday, her mother made a formal announcement: "'You know, your grandfather was Jewish.' And David and I were, like, 'Yeah?' My parents thought they were breaking news to us, but my brother and I had known Grandfather was Jewish for a very long time, though we didn't know how we knew." In 1938, when Bernard and Trudy married, anti-

Semitism was still a fact of life in America, like soda fountains in drugstores. Words like "mishegaas" and "shpilkes," which trip from Rachel's tongue in her broadcasts, were never heard in Edward R. Murrow's. The revelation that someone you didn't know was Jewish was Jewish was breaking news of a sort. Today, it is something that is apt to receive a "Yeah?" response. My parenthetical tale of the blacklisted distant relative and the covertly Jewish grandfather—set in motion by Rachel's unguarded question "Does the name Ben Maddow mean anything to you?" and told under the spell of her own meandering narratives—remains incomplete and unsatisfying. My respect for Rachel's powers of storytelling is only redoubled by my sense of the absurdity of attempting to imitate her. She is inimitable.

Maddow's excitement about 2017 has died down. She is as disarming and funny as ever, but sometimes the gaiety seems a little forced. Here and there she is magnificent. In a show on June 30, which could be called "An Essay on Disgust," she lashed out at Donald Trump as she had never done before. The occasion was Trump's distasteful attack on two MSNBC commentators, Joe Scarborough and Mika Brzezinski. Maddow set up her argument by talking about the political tool of distraction. Typically, a politician who wants to divert attention from a subject he prefers the public not be overly interested in will introduce another subject that will act the way a glittering toy acts on a susceptible baby. But Trump, she said, "doesn't just merely distract people, he disgusts people. He breaks the bounds of decency. Breaks the bounds of what people generally agree are the moral rules for engagement in public discourse." The extremity of Trump's offensiveness forces us to take the bait, to "weigh in as being opposed to this vile thing. . . . With a normal politician's normal political distraction, almost all of us will just observe it, right? We're either distracted by it or we're not. This guy's strategy, though, it is really different. It's to sort of tap on the glass of your moral compass—'Is this thing on?' To try to make you feel implicated by your silence." She went on to speak of the damage Trump does with his "nuclear version of a conventional political tactic." She said, "The thing he damages is something he neither owns nor particularly values, in the abstract, at least. The thing he hurts is the presidency and by extension the standing of the United States of America."

Reading the text of the essay is a lesser experience than watching Maddow deliver it on the air. Its logic is a bit insecure, and it is repetitive. But during the broadcast you felt only the force of Maddow's moral conviction. She is no longer a practicing Catholic, but she has a religious temperament. "I grew up in a believing Catholic home and that has stuck with me," she told me. "I believe in God, and I probably consider myself Catholic. And I think that in the most basic sense we have to account for our lives once they are done. I don't have a cartoonist's picture of Heaven that governs my actions, but I do think you have to make a case for yourself." This was part of her answer to a question I asked about a commencement speech that she gave at Smith College, in 2010, in which she characterized the saloon-smashing prohibitionist Carrie Nation as "an American huckster, just promoting herself," who had done the country irreparable harm.

She counseled the students to seek glory—the glory of making selfless ethical choices—not fame. That her own quest for glory has brought fame in its wake may be a paradox that occasionally strikes her, but does not put her into a state of high shpilkes.

The New Yorker, 2017

PART II

THE ART OF TESTIFYING

On the second day of David Souter's appearance before the Senate Judiciary Committee, in September 1990, Gordon Humphrey, a Republican senator from New Hampshire, with something of the manner of a boarding-school headmaster in a satiric novel, asked the nominee, "Do you remember the old television program *Queen for a Day?*"

"Well, it wasn't something that I spent much of my youth watching," Souter said, "but I've heard the term."

Humphrey fussed with papers and went on, "Yes, well, going back to the days of black-and-white TV, let's play 'Senator for a Day.'"

"I still have a black-and-white TV," Souter put in.

"I don't doubt it," Humphrey said, and continued:

I hope you don't watch it much. My theory is that nothing would do more good for this country than for everyone to smash his television set . . . because people would begin—especially parents and children—would begin talking and children would begin doing their homework instead of watching—having their minds filled with rubbish every evening from our wonderful networks.

Humphrey collected himself and went on to propose that Souter put himself in the shoes of a senator interrogating a Supreme Court nominee and asked him what he would be most concerned about. He added that he was asking not so much for his own benefit as for that of "the young people who are tuned in—"

"On television," the voice of a quick-witted Joseph Biden, the chairman of the committee, rang out.

"On television, yes," Humphrey concluded, as Souter smiled puckishly and the audience burst into laughter.

1

During the confirmation hearings for John Roberts last September, old black-and-white movies came to mind unbidden. Watching Roberts on television was like watching one of the radiantly wholesome heroes that Jimmy Stewart, Joel McCrea, and Henry Fonda rendered so incisively in the films of Capra, Lubitsch, and Sturges. They don't make men like that anymore. But Roberts had all their anachronistic attributes: the grace, charm, and humor of a special American sort in which decency and kindness are heavily implicated, and from which sexuality is entirely absent. It was out of the question that such a man be denied a place on the Supreme Court. The plot of the hearing hinged not on whether Roberts would be confirmed but on how the eight Democrats on the committee—Patrick Leahy, of Vermont; Edward Kennedy, of Massachusetts; Joseph Biden, of Delaware; Dianne Feinstein, of California; Russell Feingold, of Wisconsin; Charles Schumer, of New York; Herbert Kohl, of Wisconsin; and Richard Durbin, of Illinois—would perform.

In his opening statement, Roberts offered a baseball analogy to illustrate his notion of judicial seemliness. He likened judges to umpires, who "don't make the rules; they apply them. . . . They make sure everybody plays by the rules, but it is a limited role." He added, "Nobody ever went to a ball game to see the umpire." At the game of Senate confirmation, however, Roberts was precisely the person everybody had come to see: he was the batter to whom eighteen pitchers would pitch. Eight of them would try to strike him out while ten (Arlen Specter, of Pennsylvania; Orrin Hatch, of Utah; Charles Grassley, of Iowa; Jon Kyl, of Arizona; Mike DeWine, of Ohio; Jeff Sessions, of Alabama; Lindsey Graham, of South Carolina; John Cornyn, of Texas; Sam Brownback, of Kansas; and Tom Coburn, of Oklahoma) would ensure that he got on base.

The fastballs that the Democrats hurled were fueled largely by memorandums that Roberts had written as a young attorney in the Reagan administration advising his superiors on how best to undermine civil rights, voting rights, affirmative action, and antidiscrimination legislation. The written record of what Kennedy called "a narrow and cramped, and, perhaps, even a mean-spirited view of the law" was the focus of the Democrats' pointed questioning. The Democrats invited Roberts to disavow the misguided views of his youth—Surely you don't believe such stuff now? they asked him in not so many words. And in not so many words Roberts indicated that he still did. But words were not decisive in this hearing. Roberts's dazzlingly sympathetic persona soared over

the proceedings and enveloped them in its aura. In the
third round of questions, Charles Schumer looked over
his glasses at Roberts and said, "You did speak at length
on many issues and sounded like you were conveying
your views to us, but when one went back and read
the transcript each evening, there was less than met the
ear that afternoon." But in fact it was the eye that created
the illusion.

Roberts had a wonderful way of listening to questions.
His face was exquisitely responsive. The constant play of
expression on his features put one in mind of nineteenth-
century primers of acting in which emotions—pleasure,
agreement, dismay, uncertainty, hope, fear—are illustrated on the face of a model. When it was his turn to
speak, he did so with equal mesmerizing expressiveness.
Whenever he said "With all due respect, Senator"—the
stock phrase signaling disagreement—he looked so genuinely respectful, almost regretful, that one could easily
conclude that he was agreeing with his interlocutor rather
than demurring. During the first round of questions,
Biden flashed his famous insincere smile and said, "This
shouldn't be a game of gotcha." In point of fact, the
Democrats—notably Biden himself—"got" Roberts a
number of times, but no matter what disagreeable things
were said to him he maintained his invincible pleasant-
ness. Biden scored heavily, for example, when he said:

> In 1999 you said in response to a question . . .
> "You know, we've gotten to a point these days
> where we think the only way we can show we're
> serious about a problem is if we pass a federal law,
> whether it's the Violence Against Women Act or

anything else. The fact of the matter is conditions are different in different states, and state laws are more relevant . . . more attuned to different situations in New York as opposed to Minnesota. And that's what the federal system is based upon."

Judge, tell me how a guy beating up his wife in Minnesota is any different condition in New York.

What could Roberts say? He could only flounder, but he floundered so prettily that Biden had to laugh and say "Okay." Schumer, too, repeatedly won debating points but never penetrated Roberts's armor of charm. In the second round of questioning, Schumer offered this inspired set piece:

You agree we should be finding out your philosophy and method of legal reasoning, modesty, stability, but when we try to find out what modesty and stability mean, what your philosophy means, we don't get any answers.

It's as if I asked you: What kind of movies do you like? Tell me two or three good movies. And you say, "I like movies with good acting. I like movies with good directing. I like movies with good cinematography." And I ask you, "No, give me an example of a good movie." You don't name one. I say, "Give me an example of a bad movie." You won't name one. Then I ask you if you like *Casablanca*, and you respond by saying, "Lots of people like *Casablanca*." You tell me it's widely settled that *Casablanca* is one of the great movies.

Arlen Specter, the chairman of the committee, intervened to say that Schumer's time was up, and that there would be a fifteen-minute break. Roberts meekly asked if he could respond before the break, and, when given permission to do so, he said, "First, *Dr. Zhivago* and *North by Northwest*"—bringing down the house. Roberts went on to give an unconvincing defense of his evasiveness, but it was too late—there was too much good feeling wafting through the room like lavender air freshener—for the weakness of his argument to matter. Roberts's performance gave the word "disarming" new meaning. In the end, three Democrats—who had been no less pointed in their questioning than their fellow Democrats—voted to confirm Roberts. "I will vote my hopes and not my fears," Herbert Kohl said, confessing, "I was troubled by parts of Judge Roberts's record, but I was impressed by the man himself." The two other Democrats who voted for Roberts—Patrick Leahy and Russell Feingold—similarly allowed Roberts's persona to lull them into unguarded optimism. Even Democrats who voted against Roberts acknowledged his spectacular winningness.

But no performance can be entirely without flaw, and there was one extraordinary moment when Roberts was taken by surprise and propelled into uncharacteristic, unattractive at-a-lossness. Dianne Feinstein—a thirties-movie character in her own right, with her Mary Astor loveliness, and air of just having arrived with a lot of suitcases—was questioning him. As she later recalled, "When I couldn't get a sense of his judicial philosophy, I attempted to get a sense of his temperament and values, and I asked him about the end-of-life decisions, clearly decisions that are gut-wrenching, difficult, and extremely personal." Feinstein looked at Roberts and said:

I have been through two end-of-life situations, one with my husband, one with my father, both suffering terrible cancers, a lot of pain, enormous debilitation. Let me ask you this question this way: If you were in that situation with someone you deeply love and saw the suffering, who would you want to listen to, your doctor or the government telling you what to do?

Roberts, his brow furrowed with concern and empathy, replied:

Well, Senator, in that situation, obviously, you want to talk and take into account the views and heartfelt concerns of the loved one that you're trying to help in that situation, because you know how they are viewing this. You know what they mean when they're saying things like what their wishes are and their concerns are, and, of course, consulting with their physicians.

Huh? For once, the ear trumped the eye. What was Roberts saying? What had happened to his syntax? Why all those "you"s and "they"s when the answer clearly called for an "I"? As Roberts went on speaking in this unsettling language of avoidance, Feinstein coldly interrupted, "That wasn't my question." "I'm sorry," Roberts said demurely. "I'm trying to see your feelings as a man," Feinstein said. But she wasn't able to sustain the moment.

She fell into the trap of rephrasing her question in a way that allowed Roberts to say, "Well, that's getting into a legal question." Feinstein quickly backed off. "Okay. I won't go there," she said, as the split screen showed Roberts smiling with relief and perhaps a bit of triumph.

The Republican bridesmaids performed their ceremonial function with varying degrees of perfunctoriness. Specter, who had the role of chairman to play as well, played it as a courtly old man. A recent battle with cancer had left him thin and almost without hair. It was hard to see in this diminished figure the dark-haired man who fifteen years earlier had interrogated Anita Hill with such arrogant ruthlessness. No one who watched the Clarence Thomas hearings will forget the look of hatred that Hill directed toward Specter as she parried his assault on her credibility with her weapon of steely truthfulness. Specter no longer inspires hatred, of course, but he remains an obscurely sour figure. Some fundamental unlovableness adheres. It doesn't help that he speaks with excruciating slowness, as if he were a southerner.

Lindsey Graham, who is a southerner, speaks at northern speed, and to highly entertaining effects. When it was his turn to question Roberts, he didn't just stroke him. He cut to the chase:

> You were picked by a conservative president because you have associated yourself with the conservative administrations in the past, advising conservative presidents about conservative policies. And there's another selection to be made, and you're going to get the same type of person. And you can—I'm not even talking to you now— to expect anything else is just not fair. I don't

expect—I didn't expect President Clinton to
pick you.

I'm not even talking to you now. Graham brought to the
surface what is always lying just below it at televised
Supreme Court confirmation hearings: namely, that the
Judiciary Committee members are never merely talking
to the nominee; they are always talking to their constitu-
ents as well.

The confirmation hearing as we know it today evolved
over the past century. In his excellent book *The Selling of
Supreme Court Nominees* (1995), John Anthony Maltese
lays stress on the inescapably political character of the
nomination process. Since the early days of the Republic—
starting with the Borking of George Washington's ap-
pointee for chief justice, John Rutledge—Supreme Court
nominations have been fiercely fought over by rival sena-
torial factions. However, only in the twentieth century
did these fights become public spectacles. A pivotal event,
in Maltese's account, was the passage of the Seventeenth
Amendment, in 1913, which changed the method by
which senators come into office—from appointment by
the state legislature to direct election—and intensified
their activity as jumpy instruments of public will. The
first public confirmation hearing took place in 1916, for
Louis Brandeis (the first Jew to be named to the high
court). Dozens of witnesses, pro and con, flocked to the
hearing, but Brandeis himself did not choose to come.
His advisers felt, Maltese writes, that "to do so would
give the appearance that Brandeis was on trial." Not
until 1925 did a nominee—Harlan Fiske Stone—testify
before the Judiciary Committee, and thirty more years
went by before it became customary, if not obligatory,

for the nominee to testify. Between 1930 and 1955, four nominees testified and fifteen didn't. Since 1955, when the second John Marshall Harlan was nominated, every nominee has testified.

Brandeis's advisers were right: the Supreme Court nominee, sitting alone at a table facing a tribunal of legislators seated above him on a dais, is on trial. But so, of course, are the legislators. Each one knows that when he is up for reelection voters will remember (or someone will remind them of) his words and his demeanor. Graham presently abandoned all pretense of examining Roberts. "Let's talk about righting wrongs here," he said to the folks back home, and went on:

> I think it stinks that somebody can burn the flag and that's called speech. What do you think of that?
>
> Roberts: Well [laughter]. We had the Flag Protection Act after the Supreme Court concluded that it was protected speech.
>
> Graham: Show me where their term "symbolic speech" is in the Constitution.
>
> Roberts: Well, it's not.
>
> Graham: It's not. They just made it up, didn't they? And I think it stinks that a kid can't go to school and say a prayer if he wants to voluntarily. What do you think about that?
>
> Roberts: That's something that's probably inappropriate for me to comment on.
>
> Graham: What do you think Ronald Reagan thought of that?
>
> Roberts: His view was that voluntary school prayer was appropriate.

Graham: I think it's not right for elected officials to be unable to talk about or protect the un-
born. What do you think of that?
Roberts: Well, again, Senator . . .

The fifty-year-old Graham has a gift for comedy—he
delivers his lines as if he were working a nightclub crowd—
and exudes an air of cynicism that right-wing politicians
do not usually permit themselves, and that is very refreshing. The right-wing politician Sam Brownback has a
more conventional style. During his questioning of Roberts, he paused to say that because of *Roe v. Wade* "we
now have forty million fewer children in this country to
bless us with" and that "eighty percent to ninety percent
of children prenatally diagnosed with Down's syndrome
never get here—never get here." Roberts as gracefully declined to engage with the anti-abortion Republicans as
he had declined to engage with the pro-choice Democrats.
He was like the host of a successful and elegant party. Everybody could go home feeling good and good about
himself. No one had spilled his champagne or been rude.
When, four months later, Roberts joined Scalia and
Thomas in their dissent to the majority opinion in *Gon-
zalez v. Oregon*, which upheld the state's law permitting
assisted suicide, no one even seemed to feel betrayed.
Good parties cast lovely long shadows.

2

The Democrats came home from the hearing for Samuel
Alito as if they had been beaten up by a rival gang in a
bar. At the Roberts hearing, they had been vigorous and

assured, sometimes even magnificent, in their defense of liberal values. At the Alito hearing, they were erratic and disoriented, as if suffering from a malaise they had fallen into between the two proceedings. In fact, what they were suffering from was the nominee. In his opening statement, Alito told this story:

> During the previous weeks, an old story about a lawyer who argued a case before the Supreme Court has come to my mind, and I thought I might begin this afternoon by sharing that story. The story goes as follows. This was a lawyer who had never argued a case before the court before. And when the argument began, one of the justices said, How did you get here? Meaning how had his case worked its way up through the court system. But the lawyer was rather nervous and he took the question literally and he said—and this was some years ago—he said, "I came here on the Baltimore and Ohio Railroad."

Throughout the hearing, in answer to almost every question, Alito said, in effect, that he had come here on the Baltimore and Ohio Railroad—and thus defeated every attempt to engage with him in dialogue. Each answer ended the matter then and there. He was like a chauffeur who speaks only when spoken to, and doesn't presume to converse. While Alito listened to questions, his face was expressionless. When giving answers, he spoke in a mild, uninflected voice. His language was ordinary and wooden. His manner was sober and quiet. He was a negligible, neutral presence.

It seemed scarcely believable that, in his fifteen years

on the federal bench, this innocuous man had consistently ruled against other harmless individuals in favor of
powerful institutions, and that these rulings were sometimes so far out of the mainstream consensus that other
conservatives on the court were moved to protest their extremity. Or that in 1985, on an application for a job in
the Reagan Justice Department, he had written, "I am
particularly proud of my contributions in recent cases in
which the government has argued in the Supreme Court
that . . . the Constitution does not protect a right to an
abortion." And, further, that "in college I developed a
deep interest in constitutional law, motivated in large part
by disagreement with Warren Court decisions, particularly in the areas of criminal procedure, the Establishment
Clause, and reapportionment."

If Roberts was a pill the Democrats could agree to swal-
low even before tasting its delicious sugar coating, and Harriet Miers was a pig in a poke that some Democrats were
prepared to buy, Alito was a nominee no Democrat could
accept. But no Democrat could touch him. The impassive
Alito paralyzed the Democrats. Their hopes of block-
ing the nomination by bringing forward two stains on
his character—his membership in a notorious organization called Concerned Alumni of Princeton, which opposed the admission of women and minorities; and his
failure to recuse himself in a case involving the Vanguard
company, in which he had a financial stake—were decisively
dashed. The stains proved too small—the garment remained
presentable.

Twenty years ago, William Rehnquist, at the hearing
for his elevation to Chief Justice, offered a model for how
to parry embarrassing questions about your past. When
asked about reports that as a young poll watcher he had

harassed minority voters, Rehnquist shook his head sadly and said, "No, I don't think that's correct," and when asked about a restrictive clause in the lease to his country house barring "members of the Hebrew race" he said, "I certainly don't recall it." Alito, similarly, didn't recall joining the Concerned Alumni. "I have racked my memory," he said each time he was asked why he had joined. Nor could he explain why he hadn't recused himself in the Vanguard case. The Democrats realized too late that their pursuit of the Concerned Alumni and Vanguard matters was a trap. This time, the Republican bridesmaids didn't merely simper. They hastened to close ranks and attack the Democrats for their cruel badgering of Alito.

Lindsey Graham rose joyfully to the occasion. Rules of seniority placed him late on the program (he was elected to the Senate in 2002) and gave him the material for great shtick. He did a little preliminary routine with Vanguard ("Why would Judge Alito sit down in the corner of a room and say, I think I've got a conflict, but I'm just going to let it go and hear the case anyway?") and moved on to the Concerned Alumni:

> Graham: Now this organization that was mentioned very prominently earlier in the day, did you ever write an article for this organization?
>
> Alito: No, I did not.
>
> Graham: Okay. And some quotes were shown, from people who did write for this organization, that you disavowed. Do you remember that exchange?
>
> Alito: I disavow them. I deplore them. They represent things that I have always stood against and I can't express too strongly . . .

> Graham: If you don't mind the suspicious na-
> ture that I have is that you may be saying that
> because you want to get on the Supreme Court;
> that you're disavowing this now because it doesn't
> look good. And really what I would look at to be-
> lieve you're not—and I'm going to be very honest
> with you—is: How have you lived your life? Are
> you really a closet bigot?

Is Lindsey Graham really a closet liberal? The sense of
double entendre that always faintly hovers over Graham's
speech is almost palpable in this passage. "I'm not any
kind of a bigot, I'm not," Alito said. Graham assured
Alito that he believed him, not because of his good reputation but because of "the way you have lived your life and
the way you and your wife are raising your children." Then
Graham had the audacity to cite—not by name—the
Abramoff scandal as an instance of the kind of guilt by
association that Alito was being subjected to:

> We're going to go through a bit of this ourselves
> as congressmen and senators. People are going
> to take a fact that we got a campaign donation
> from somebody who's found to be a little differ-
> ent than we thought they were—and our political
> opponent's going to say, "Aha, I gotcha!" And
> we're going to say, "Wait a minute. I didn't know
> that. I didn't take the money for that reason." . . .
> We have photos taken with people—and some-
> times you wish you didn't have your photo
> taken. But that doesn't mean that you're a bad
> person because of that association. Judge Alito,
> I am sorry that you've had to go through this.

I am sorry that your family has had to sit here and listen to this.

It was at this moment that Mrs. Alito got up and left the hearing room to have her famous cry. The TV camera barely caught the image of her figure brushing past two seats, and the TV watcher would have attached no significance to the sight. Unlike the forbiddingly beautiful and elegant Mrs. Roberts—who sat motionless during her husband's hearing, with a look of intense, almost anxious concentration on her face—the buxom Mrs. Alito fidgeted and looked around and never seemed to be fully engaged with the proceedings. As it was later reported (around the globe), Mrs. Alito had been so upset by the bad things the Democrats had said about her husband, and so moved by Graham's defense, that she had to leave in tears. But to anyone who had observed Mrs. Alito's demeanor in the days before the incident, Charles Isherwood's comment in the *Times*—"Surely grinding boredom may also have played a part in her scene-stealing eruption and flight from the Senate chamber"—had the ring of truth.

The Alito hearings were indeed grindingly boring. Although subjects of the highest interest were introduced— spying on citizens, torture, abortion, the right to privacy, civil rights, discrimination, executive power—the talk was never interesting, since Alito could never be drawn. Like Roberts, he eluded the Democrats' attempts to pry his judicial philosophy out of him, but, unlike Roberts, he offered no compensatory repartee. He was always just a guy answering questions *very carefully*. Over and over, the Democrats quizzed Alito on his pro-police, pro-

prosecution, and pro-employer opinions. (The legal scholar
Cass Sunstein analyzed forty-five of Alito's dissents in
cases where individual rights and institutions were in
conflict and found that in thirty-eight of them Alito took
the side of the institution.) And over and over—like an
accountant patiently explaining why the figures on a tax
return are correct—Alito spared no dry detail in justifying his reasoning.

As the hearings wore on, and the fight between the
Democratic and Republican committee members took on
heat, Alito became an almost peripheral figure. The charge
that the Democrats were cruelly badgering Alito was in
fact unfounded. They had been a lot tougher on Roberts.
At one point in the Roberts hearing, Joe Biden pushed
Roberts so hard—indeed was so fresh to him—that Specter had to intervene and say, "Let him finish his answer,
Joe." But, when questioning Alito, Joe practically tugged
his forelock. "Presumptuous of me to say this," "You'd
know better than I, Judge," "I don't mean to suggest I'm
correcting you," "I'm not presuming to be as knowledgeable about this as you," "All I'm suggesting is," "You've
been very gracious" are among the examples of Biden's
nervous servility. (In the second round of questioning, in
a gesture of propitiation that can only be called deranged,
Biden put on a Princeton cap.) But the very idea of questioning Alito's probity left the Democrats open to charges
of bullying. Where the fair Roberts had been fair game,
the mousy Alito was out of bounds. Why don't you pick
on someone your own size? By the time the Democrats
realized their tactical error, it was too late to correct it.
That the judge who consistently rules against little guys
should become the confirmation hearing's own little guy

was one of the proceeding's more delicious (and, for the Democrats, bitterest) ironies.

On the Senate floor two weeks later, with Alito no longer there to drain their blood, the eight Democrats spoke their fears with forceful urgency. Kennedy, Leahy, Durbin, and Feinstein were especially eloquent, and Biden behaved himself. Over the days of debate, the flame of filibuster flickered and subsided, and the ten Republicans, smelling victory, showed the losers no mercy. Jeff Sessions, who had been one of the quieter presences in both the Roberts and the Alito hearings, now came to demonic life:

> It is almost amusing as we have gone through the committee process to see them grasp in desperation to find something to complain about with Judge Alito. None of them could agree on what they didn't like. They bounced all over the place mostly. It sounded like they didn't like President Bush. They were having grievances about Abu Ghraib prison, which President Bush had nothing to do with.

Sessions went on:

> They have been hankering for Harriet Miers, which is rather odd, I think. They have suggested somehow that some right-wing cabal caused President Bush to withdraw her nomination. . . . They have complained steadfastly that Judge Alito somehow is a tool of President Bush to defend his national policy and his war on terrorism and that

Judge Alito is going to be a part of his efforts to arrogate powers to the executive branch. Who has been at President Bush's right arm for five years? It's Harriet Miers. . . . She has been involved in every one of these decisions about executive branch powers, National Security Agency wiretaps of Al Qaeda telephone conversations. She has been part of all of that. You think they would have let her come through here? They say: Oh we think she would be a fine nominee. What would they have done to her?

(Sessions had a point. The Democrats' tears for the martyred Harriet Miers had something of the crocodile quality of the Republicans' tears for Mrs. Alito's. The Democrats' outrage over Alito's dissent in the case of *Doe v. Groody* was similarly transparent. The case involved the warrantless strip search of a ten-year-old girl and her mother during a drug bust. Alito sided with the police, who argued that an affidavit gave them the authority to search the mother and daughter. The Democrats treated the incident as if it were the Rape of Nanking.) Other Republicans made other gloating speeches about the hapless Democrats, and, of course, none of it mattered because there would be no filibuster and Alito would be confirmed by the Republican majority in the Senate. John Kerry arrived exhausted from an economic conference in Davos to try to rally the minority troops. Sessions, apparently unaware of Kerry's return, jeered at the "international" filibuster "hatched in Davos, Switzerland, where Senator Kerry now is with those masters of the universe trying to figure out the world economy. Maybe they ought to spend more time trying to get the

oil prices down than worrying about conjuring up a filibuster of a judge as able as Judge Alito."

When it was Biden's turn to speak, he quoted a remark that Alito had made during the hearing that he had
not been alone in finding striking. Biden had been questioning the nominee about his position in a case involving the Family and Medical Leave Act, and had asked
whether he and his fellow judges on the panel had taken
into consideration the fact that pregnant women sometimes need leave for bed rest during the last two months of
pregnancy. Alito replied that, no, they had not considered
that, and added, "We can't know everything about the
real world." The remark leaped out of the gray blur of
Alito's technocratic speech like a confession that can no
longer be withheld. It confirmed what we already knew
about this dour and oddly innocent man.

Perhaps nowhere is the sense of Alito's alienation
more palpable than in his dissent in *Riley v. Taylor* (2001),
the case of a black man who was convicted of murder (and
condemned to die) by an all-white jury, and who had ap-
pealed the verdict on the ground of discrimination. The
appeals court, ruling en banc, accepted the possibility of
discrimination and reversed the conviction. But Alito
couldn't see what the majority saw. He argued that his
colleagues had been wrong to be influenced by the fact
that within a year three other murder cases in the
county had been tried by all-white juries. He wrote:

> "An amateur with a pocket calculator," the major-
> ity writes, can calculate that "there is little chance
> of randomly selecting four consecutive all-white
> juries." Statistics can be very revealing—and
> also terribly misleading in the hands of "an ama-

teur with a pocket calculator." The majority's simplistic analysis treats the prospective jurors who were peremptorily challenged as if they had no relevant characteristics other than race, as if they were in effect black and white marbles in a jar from which the lawyers drew. In reality, however, these individuals had many other characteristics, and without taking those variables into account, it is simply not possible to determine whether the prosecutions' strikes were based on race or something else.

The dangers in the majority's approach can be easily illustrated. Suppose we asked our "amateur with a pocket calculator" whether the American people take right- or left-handedness into account in choosing their presidents. Although only about 10% of the population is left-handed, left-handers have won five of the last six presidential elections. Our "amateur with a calculator" would conclude that "there is little chance of randomly selecting" left-handers in five out of six presidential elections. But does it follow that the voters cast their ballots based on whether a candidate was right- or left-handed?

Judge Dolores K. Sloviter, the author of the majority opinion, dryly replied to Alito, "The dissent has overlooked the obvious fact that there is no provision in the Constitution that protects persons from discrimination based on whether they are right-handed or left-handed. To suggest any comparability to the striking of jurors based on their race is to minimize the history of discrimination against prospective black jurors and black defendants."

The facts that Alito overlooks are, of course, facts that his fellow right-wing ideologues also can't see from the mysterious planet—even farther away than Davos, Switzerland—they inhabit. During the Roberts and Alito hearings, it was almost amusing to hear the nominees ritually denounce discredited Supreme Court decisions, such as *Plessy v. Ferguson* (1896), which refused a Creole named Homer Plessy the right to sit where he wanted on a train, and established the separate-but-equal doctrine; and *Korematsu v. United States*, which countenanced the internment of Americans of Japanese descent during the Second World War. Is there any reason to think that, had he been on the Court when these cases came before it, Alito or Roberts would have opposed the majority? Roberts was much given to affirming his fealty to "the rule of the law." He said, "Somebody asked me . . . 'Are you going to be on the side of the little guy?' And you obviously want to give an immediate answer, but, as you reflect on it, if the Constitution says that the little guy should win, the little guy's going to win in court before me. But if the Constitution says that the big guy should win, well, then the big guy's going to win, because my obligation is to the Constitution." The cases that are the glory of Supreme Court history are the cases where the little guy won; the cases that are its shame are those where he lost. The Constitution doesn't say who should win. Nine people do.

3

Another memorable passage in the David Souter confirmation hearings occurred while he was being questioned

by the Democratic senator from Ohio, Howard Metzenbaum. Metzenbaum asked Souter, as fifteen years later
Feinstein asked Roberts, to give a personal rather than a
legal response to a question about a controversial issue—
abortion, in this case. Metzenbaum described in grue-
some detail cases of illegal abortion from the pre-*Roe*
era, and then said, "My real question to you isn't how you
will rule on *Roe v. Wade* . . . but what does a woman
face, when she has an unwanted pregnancy, a pregnancy that may be the result of rape or incest or failed
contraceptives or ignorance of basic health information?
And I would just like to get your own view and your
own thoughts of that woman's position under these
circumstances."

Souter paused before replying. Then he said, "Senator, your question comes as a surprise to me. I wasn't
expecting that kind of question, and you have made me
think of something that I have not thought about for
twenty-four years." Souter went on to tell a story from his
days at Harvard Law School. He had an appointment as
a resident proctor (a student adviser) in a Harvard College freshman dormitory, and one day a student came to
him for counsel. "He was in pretty rough emotional
shape," Souter recalled,

> and we shut the door and sat down, and he told
> me that his girlfriend was pregnant and he said,
> "She's about to try to have a self-abortion and she
> doesn't know how to do it." He said, "She's afraid
> to tell her parents what has happened and she's
> afraid to go to the health services," and he said,
> "Will you talk to her?" and I did. . . . I will not
> try to say what I told her. But I spent two hours

in a small dormitory bedroom that afternoon, in
that room because that was the most private place
we could get . . . listening to her and trying to
counsel her to approach her problem in a way different from what she was doing, and your question has brought that back to me, and I think the
only thing I can add to that is I know what you
were trying to tell me, because I remember that
afternoon.

As Souter spoke—gravely and slowly (but not too
slowly), with his strong New England accent (he said "lore"
for "law" and "sore" for "saw" and "floor" for "flaw")—
one had the feeling of lights dimming on a set. One of
the characters would soon get up to draw the curtains
and turn on a lamp. This was not the only time in the
Souter hearing that one felt as if one were seeing a well-
wrought play rather than witnessing a piece of left-to-
chance reality. In his opening statement, Souter told the
senators that he was looking forward to "our dialogue,"
and dialogue did indeed take place—often very gripping
dialogue. As Alito had unnerved, you could almost say
unmanned, his questioners, so Souter gave his interlocu-
tors to know that this was a play in which all the roles
had good lines. If Souter—a slight man (his thinness
had a mildly ascetic cast) of enormous, subtle intelligence and a moving absence of self-regard—was the star
turn, he permitted the supporting cast of senators to perform no less brilliantly. Watching tapes of the Souter
hearings makes one feel how things have deteriorated.
But not so fast. When the stately Shavian drama of
the questioning of Souter ended, a new and entirely dif-

ferent drama began. The furies arrived. Molly Yard, the president of NOW; Fay Wattleton, of Planned Parenthood; Eleanor Smeal, of the Fund for the Feminist Majority; Kate Michelman, the executive director of NARAL; and Elizabeth Holtzman, the New York City comptroller, testified against Souter with fierce disdain. They assumed (as Michelman assumed about Alito when she testified against his confirmation in January) that Souter would cast a decisive vote to overturn *Roe v. Wade.* "I tremble for this country if you confirm David Souter," said Molly Yard. "Women's lives are literally on the line." She sneered at Souter's account of the scene in the freshman dorm: "This shows empathy? How do we know but what he may have cold-bloodedly told her she would be a murderer if she ended her pregnancy?"

Souter's record on civil rights, voting rights, gay rights, and victim rights and his bias toward law enforcement was similarly mocked and denounced by the feminists. Had these angry witnesses been able to see into the future, would they have testified as they did? Of course not. And had I *not* known how things turned out with Souter, would I have watched the tape of his confirmation hearing with the same charmed delight? Of course not. We read what we can into reality's impassive face. Alan Simpson, a prescient pro-choice Republican senator from Wyoming, said to Michelman and Wattleton, "I really believe you are making a big mistake on this one. . . . These things are going to come up again. There are going to be other Supreme Court choices when you are really going to need to be in the trenches. This is not one of those cases." He went on to say that Souter was "bright, intelligent, studious, caring, chivalrous, patient, probative, civilized, and a great listener and if that ain't enough for you, I think you are making a real mistake." "I think we have a difference of opinion," Wattleton said. After the furies left, a little parade of law-enforcement officials went by who said that when Souter was attorney general of New Hampshire he had shown the police unfailing courtesy and kindness.

Then came another twist of the plot. Howard Phillips, the chairman of an organization called the Conservative Caucus, took the stand and compared Souter to Adolf Eichmann. After Souter performed his aria of the freshman dorm, Metzenbaum had said that's nice, it shows "you have empathy for the problem." But was there any reason to think that Souter could empathize with *both* sides of the abortion debate? His record showed strong anti-abortion leanings. Was there anything he could show on the "other" side? To which Souter replied that he was a trustee of a hospital in Concord where abortions were performed. Now Phillips accused Souter of being "an accomplice" to "the shedding of innocent blood." "I would say that there is a fundamental distinction between the position of the groups such as NOW and NARAL and Planned Parenthood and so forth which urge a 'no' vote on Judge Souter," Phillips said. "Their position is that they are not absolutely certain that Judge Souter is going to be with them to their satisfaction. I, on the other hand, am absolutely certain on the basis of the record that Justice Souter does have a permissive view toward abortion." (Phillips went on to say that he was "troubled by his answers to other questions," above all by "one he gave to Senator Thurmond at the very beginning of the hearings, when he said that the power of the law comes from the people. I don't believe that. I believe it comes from God.")

After the debacle of the Alito hearing, Joseph Biden said that confirmation hearings should be abolished. (During the Roberts hearing, he had already remarked, "These hearings have become sort of a Kabuki dance" and "I am moving to the view that I'm not sure these hearings are the proper way to determine how to vote for a judge.") Biden is not the first to make such a proposal. In 1988, in response to the noisy Bork hearings, a Twentieth Century Fund Task Force on Judicial Selection recommended that the confirmation process be restored to a quieter former mode, whereby the nominee was judged solely on his written record and on the testimony of legal experts. These recommendations were ignored, as we know. As John Anthony Maltese points out, they were posited on the dubious idea of

> a golden age when Supreme Court nominees were not required to testify, when the factious whims of public opinion were ignored by senators, when the legal qualifications of nominees were considered without the taint of political motivation, and when senators deliberated behind closed doors rather than posturing in the glare of television lights. The problem is that the apolitical nature of that golden age is largely fictitious.

Maltese's book is devoted to the political fights by which Supreme Court nominations are by their very

nature dogged. Another book could be written about
Supreme Court nominations since television lights first
glared at them, in 1981, when Sandra Day O'Connor
appeared before the Judiciary Committee. The televised
hearings have not been uniformly edifying—the Alito
hearing may be the least instructive of the lot—but
each has its atmosphere and, so to speak, plot. The hearing for the nomination of Ruth Bader Ginsburg had the
atmosphere of a garden party held to fete a beloved aunt
about to embark on a wonderful journey. Ted Kennedy,
who usually sits at confirmation hearings looking as if he
had a toothache, was charming and funny. The Republicans were polite and deferential. During the recent hearings, the Republicans repeatedly boasted of their gracious
acceptance of Ginsburg in contrast to the Democrats'
sulky resistance to Roberts and Alito. Lindsey Graham
was particularly mordant in his description of Ginsburg
as an A.C.L.U. Commie whom, nevertheless, the Republicans manfully swallowed because Clinton had won
the election. So why don't the Democrats manfully swal-
low Bush's appointees? Why are they being such poor
sports? "Elections matter," Graham said. As the Democrats might have retorted—but didn't think or know to do
until Senate debate on Alito was under way—Ginsburg
had not been thrust on the Republicans the way Roberts
and Alito had been thrust on the Democrats. She had
been preapproved by Orrin Hatch. Hatch recalls the circumstances in his book *Square Peg: Confessions of a Citizen Senator.* He writes that when Byron White resigned
from the Court, Bill Clinton called him to ask how his
secretary of the interior, Bruce Babbitt, would go over
as a nominee. Hatch, then chairman of the Judiciary

Committee, told Clinton that Babbitt was too liberal and would be hard to confirm, and gave him two names as alternatives: Ginsburg and Stephen Breyer. (In a footnote, Hatch writes that Ginsburg's record as a federal appeals court judge was "very similar to that of another subsequent Supreme Court Justice, Antonin Scalia.")

The Thomas hearings, in contrast, with their incredible final act, had a dark character—though it wasn't until Jane Mayer and Jill Abramson published their tour de force of reporting, *Strange Justice: The Selling of Clarence Thomas*, that we understood just how dark. Thomas's "high-tech lynching" speech, in which he denied Anita Hill's accusations with moving vehemence, was one of the great performances of its time. But Mayer and Abramson's research—their interviews with confidants of Hill's who corroborated her account and with schoolmates of Thomas's who recalled his crude sexual humor and regular attendance at pornographic movies—makes it all but impossible to believe that the zealot who sits in Thurgood Marshall's place on the high court didn't say those crassly dirty things to Anita Hill. Even more disturbing is the book's account of how the far right, the lesson of Bork fresh in its memory, stopped at nothing to get this nominee on the Court.

Since Bork, nominees have played their cards close to their chests. Bork could conceivably have saved his nomination by not constantly showing his losing hand, but more likely the combination of powerful organized opposition on the left and the Democratic majority in the Senate was always enough to defeat it. By the time of Thomas, the right had mobilized, and has never again failed a stricken nominee. The so-I-lied convention, established by Thomas (who told the senators that he believed in a constitutional right to privacy and when safely on the Court said that, well, actually, he didn't), along with the mantra of "If I talk about recent Supreme Court cases, the sky will fall," has been firmly in place since the Thomas hearings. Biden's misgivings about the hearings are justified: when they are over we know no more about the nominee's judicial philosophy than we did before they started. But they yield another kind of knowledge: a portrait of the nominee emerges from them that may be as telling as any articulation of his judicial philosophy. When Alan Simpson asked David Souter whether he would be able to remove his personal feelings from his judgments, Souter said, "We always ask, we constantly ask ourselves, Senator, whether we can do that. We have no guarantee of success, but we know that the best chance of success comes from being conscious of the fact that we will be tempted to do otherwise." Neither Alito nor Roberts showed himself capable of such fineness of mind. In the light of Souter's testimony before the Judiciary Committee, his opinions on the high court should not have been surprising. And, in the light of theirs, Roberts's and Alito's probably will not be, either.

Biden also left out what may be the most compelling reason of all for the continued life of confirmation hearings: the intimate glimpse they give us of eighteen of our legislators. Which ones we love and which ones we hate is determined by our partisanship, of course. But as we watch them playing their big-league game we may sometimes forget to root, and just sit transfixed by their remarkable athleticism.

SPECIAL NEEDS

The nine-part docuseries *Sarah Palin's Alaska*, shown late last year on the cable channel TLC, has the atmosphere of a cold war propaganda film. It shows the Palin family during the summer of 2010, making happy trips to one pristine Alaskan wilderness area after another—fishing, hunting, kayaking, dogsledding, rock climbing—and taking repeated little swipes at the left. During a visit with her dad to a store in Anchorage named Chimo Guns, where she is buying a rifle for a camping trip in bear country, Palin remarks:

> Out and about in Alaska's wilds it's more common than not to see somebody having some kind of weapon on their person, in fact it's probably as commonplace as if you're walking down in New York City and you see somebody with a BlackBerry on their hip.

New York, of course, is code for all the things that Palin-style populism is against. I don't have to tell my fellow Commies what these things are.

Not long ago Paul Krugman neatly distinguished

between our two political sides. One side, he wrote in the *Times*,

> considers the modern welfare state—a private-enterprise economy, but one in which society's winners are taxed to pay for a social safety net—morally superior to the capitalism red in tooth and claw we had before the New Deal. It's only right, this side believes, for the affluent to help the less fortunate.

The other side

> believes that people have a right to keep what they earn, and that taxing them to support others, no matter how needy, amounts to theft. That's what lies behind the modern right's fondness for violent rhetoric: many activists on the right really do see taxes and regulation as tyrannical impositions on their liberty.*

The Palins travel in small planes into the tooth-and-claw wilderness to enact their allegory of unspoiled capitalism. Palin, who is both narrator and star of the series, performs arduous and sometimes even dangerous feats of outdoorsmanship to demonstrate the conservative virtue of self-reliance. In the episode in which she struggles for a foothold on a vertiginously steep glacier at the foot of Mt. McKinley in eerily beautiful and vast Denali National Park, she knows that no government handout is going to

---

*"A Tale of Two Moralities," *The New York Times*, January 13, 2011.

help her. She isn't even sure God will help her, though she cries out to Him and His Son, "Oh God. Help me, Lord!" and "I'm scared. . . . Holy Jeez!" She is tied by a rope to a guide above her and her husband below, but she can't seem to make progress on the rock. The guide gives her instructions, but she can't follow them. "I don't know what I'm going to hold on to here. . . . What about my legs? Where do I put 'em? . . . This may flippin' take me all day."

Forty-five minutes later (as a subtitle tells us) she is still clinging to the rock, helpless to take the next step up. "That's so much worse than I ever thought it would be," she groans. Finally, through a great effort of will, she manages to heave herself up to the pinnacle. "I don't think that I have been that scared or that challenged in a long time," she says, and we believe her. The episode has a realism not often seen in reality TV, and absent from most of the other episodes in which Palin, among other feats, shoots caribou, cuts down large trees, cuts up bloody fish, and even briefly slings hash in a diner. These segments are marked by the surrealism that is reality television's signature. Something always seems a little off in reality television. You don't believe that what you are seeing happened in the way it is shown to have happened, any more than you think that the man in the Magritte was born with an apple attached to his face.

Perhaps the most surreal episode of *Sarah Palin's Alaska* is the one in which the TV celebrity Kate Gosselin appears and shamelessly upstages Palin. Gosselin has eight children—a pair of twins and sextuplets—who are the raison d'être of the TLC reality series originally called *Jon & Kate Plus 8*, and renamed *Kate Plus 8* when the pair split up. Palin has invited Gosselin and her children to join her family on a camping trip to a mountain lake in a remote wilderness area that can only be reached by seaplane, and the role she assigns to herself is that of protectress: she will prevent bears from eating her guests. At Chimo Guns, as she selects her purchase, she tells the salesman about the "gal who's never camped before" who is "going to rely on *me* to protect her." But the minute we lay eyes on Gosselin, we know that Palin herself may need protection from this small, pretty, powerfully unsentimental blonde.

"Beautiful view," Gosselin says in a deadpan voice, as she and her eight enter the Palins' lakefront house in Wasilla, and adds, "There's a bear on the floor. Did anyone notice?" The kids throw themselves on the bear rug and toss about a tongue that has fallen out of its taxidermied head. After telling them to put the tongue back, Gosselin looks into the bear's glass eyes and says, "Is this really real? Like this was once walking outside?" Todd Palin says, "Yeah, Sarah's dad shot this a few years ago." Gosselin stares at the trophy with an expression of pain and disgust.

Palin quickly whisks her upstairs to see the office where she does what she calls her Fox News "hits" in front of a picture window or a stone fireplace; and then bundles her and her teenaged daughter Willow off to a survival school called Learn to Return. "I will die of a heart attack," Gosselin says as the instructor produces a map showing the large bear population of Alaska. Palin caresses her new firearm and patiently explains:

Even for those who may think maybe on a political level that they are anti-gun, they need to realize, if you are unarmed and you're out in the wilderness and perhaps you're with children camping, well you're putting yourself and your family in danger if you are not armed, if you are not prepared for a predator.

At the Learn to Return gun range, Palin, who never looks happier than when she is shooting, exhibits her powerful marksmanship; her bullet goes "right in the kill zone." After urging from the instructor, Gosselin picks up the rifle like a vampire agreeing to handle a crucifix, takes gingerly aim, and doesn't do too badly, either.

The morning of the camping trip arrives and it is a dismal day of pouring rain. As Gosselin disembarks from her seaplane (the Palins had come earlier in another plane), she says, "Are you kidding me? Doesn't the lodge sound much more exciting to you?"

What follows is like a scene in a dream—or piece of experimental theater—where disconnected things happen all at once, very fast *and* slow (such is the character of this genre), and anxiety covers everything like a sticky paste. As rain pelts the lake and the forest, Gosselin finds shelter under a small canopy, and begins a mesmerizing aria:

> I'm freezing to the bone. . . . I've been bitten about two hundred times already. This is horrible. . . . It just kills me that people like willingly do this. I can't get over it. I mean, that is so shocking to me.

Palin, in a yellow oilskin slicker and rain-splattered glasses, gestures toward the mist-shrouded mountains. "Look at how gorgeous this place is. . . . This is the beauty of Alaska."

Gosselin, entirely unmoved by the Sublime, continues her bitter lament:

> This is cruel and unusual punishment. This is where I'll be the whole time. Unparalyzed. . . . I'm standing in not-rain. That's what I'm doing. I have to admit, I wasn't terribly opposed to it, camping I mean, but in the rain? No way.

At the shore, the Palins—Sarah; her father, Chuck; Todd; Willow; the youngest daughter, Piper; and a brother of Sarah's also named Chuck—are working desperately to give the wet and somewhat confused-looking Gosselin kids a good time, teaching them how to fish, showing them natural curiosities like salmon teeth, and encouraging them to add twigs to a sprawling, weakly burning brush fire. Palin wanders about distractedly, saying things like "We're having a blast" and "Kids'll always have fun as they're being productive and helpful and pitching in." But she can't get purchase on the scene. It's as if she were back on the glacier helplessly looking for a foothold. No bears arrive to restore her to her rightful place in the series as its fearless heroine.

In a flash-forward monologue—a convention of reality TV that only adds to its atmosphere of oneiric unreality—a dry, pretty Palin sits under a tree reflecting that "Kate, she never felt more out of her element than there, camping," and permitting herself a single mean thought: "C'mon! It wasn't *that* bad." But there, camping, Gosselin lets us see just how bad it is:

> This is ridiculous. Why would you pretend to be homeless? I don't get it. I just don't get the concept. There's no paper towels. How do you make sandwiches for eight kids on your arm. I don't see a table. I don't see utensils. I don't see hand-cleansing materials. This is not ideal conditions. I am freezing to the bone. I have nineteen layers on. My hands are frigid. I held it together as long as I could and I'm done now. I'm hungry!

Someone brings Gosselin a hot dog, and she regards it suspiciously; when told it is made of moose meat, she takes a tiny bite and makes a face. Turning to her children, Gosselin asks if they want to stay or go and a few say they want to stay (s'mores are being distributed), and she says to them, "Goodbye, you're now a Palin, you're not a Gosselin," adding, "We're deciding who's a Palin and who's a Gosselin." Of course, when Kate heads down the path toward the seaplane that will take her away from the scene of suffering for no good reason, all eight children are with her. In parting, she says, "Sarah, all hail you, Amazon woman. This is where our likenesses end. Dead stop. . . . We're out of here. . . . We're going where there's warmth and dryness."

Palin looks after her and says, "I suppose if she took me to like New York City and some red-carpet event, I'd be the same way, like 'get me home.'" She is back in stride. With Kate gone, the episode draws an almost audible breath of relief. The family gathers around the fire—now burning brightly, with big logs in it that weren't there when Gosselin was casting her malign spell over the day—shrieking with laughter and horsing around as families do after difficult guests leave. It is no longer raining. The mountains have emerged from the mist. The Palins crawl into expensive blue tents and call cheerily back and forth to each other, their voices rising into the beautiful white night.

There is another passage in *Sarah Palin's Alaska* that stands out from the rest—this time not for weirdness, but for its emotional truth. It takes place in a native village called Eluk, where Todd Palin's Eskimo cousin Ina has set up a summer "fish camp" to which Palin, Willow, Piper, and Todd's sister Christina have flown. In Ina's kitchen, Sarah and Ina cut up fish and have an intimate women's talk. Both gave birth to Down's syndrome children—Ina's child, Matthew, is twelve and Trig Palin is two—and they compare their experiences. Palin asks Ina, a small, sympathetic woman who speaks with an accent, if she "knew" before the birth, and Ina says that she didn't. Palin says she herself did know and "had months to prepare—but still it was hard," though "a blessing." Ina says that her son "teaches our whole family about patience and love that is so deep."

In the next scene we see Matthew, a severely impaired child, who has climbed into the small plane that the Palins arrived in and is being approached with kindly curiosity by ten-year-old Piper. Then comes the unexpected moment. Palin sits on a hillside and burbles, "Well, getting to meet our little cousin there, Matthew, Ina's son, you know, kind of gives me maybe a look at ten years from now, Trig, and he's a beautiful child—" But what we see on her face belies her bright words. She is devastated by the look into the future that the impaired little cousin gives her. We see her breaking down and beginning to cry, and we cry with her. At this moment, she is not Sarah Palin the wicked witch of the right. She is a woman one pities and sympathizes with and, yes, even admires.

In her book *Going Rogue*, Palin writes of her initial refusal to believe that the baby she had conceived at the age of forty-three might have Down's syndrome. When an early sonogram reveals a possible fetal abnormality, "a whisper of fear tugged at my heart, but I brushed it away with a thought: *God would never give me anything I can't handle. And I don't think I could handle that.*" She adds, "*Unless He knows me better than I know myself. . . . God won't give me a special needs child.*" (The term "special needs" came into currency a few years ago—at about the time when everyone became "challenged" by something—and surely is an improvement over the callous "Mongolian Idiot" and "retarded" and "feeble-minded" labels that used to be applied to children with Down's syndrome, autism, and other genetic abnormalities, though it takes a little getting used to.)

After amniocentesis gives Palin proof of God's pesky unpredictability, she declines the option of abortion that 90 percent of women in her shoes take, but interestingly does not lord it over them with right-to-life rhetoric. Instead, she recalls the "fleeting thought" (of abortion) that came to her in 2007 in a New Orleans hotel room when she learned of her unplanned and seriously inconvenient pregnancy: *"I'm out of town. No one knows I'm pregnant. No one would ever have to know."* Now, in far greater distress ("How could God have done this? Obviously He knew Heather [Palin's sister] had a special needs child. Didn't He think that was enough challenge for one family?"), Palin feels "that fleeting thought descend[ing] on me again, not a consideration so much as a sudden understanding of why people would grasp at a quick 'solution,' a way to make the 'problem' just go away."

Palin cannot be faulted for choosing to bring the child to term—pro-choice means just that, after all—and, indeed, when he appears two years later in *Sarah Palin's Alaska*, we can only agree with Lee Siegel that "the entire staff of *The New York Review of Books* could not but melt when Todd picks up their son Trig, who has Down's syndrome, and the child laughs that self-devouring, self-delighted laugh of little boys as his father carries him into the house."* In *Going Rogue*, Palin quotes an arresting passage from a speech she gave during the 2008 presidential campaign whose purpose was "to present our policy on special needs issues":

> Every child is beautiful before God and dear to Him for their own sake. And the truest measure of any society is how it treats those who are most vulnerable.

The reader is arrested by the echo of left-wing rhetoric. How many times have we heard liberal politicians speak of the vulnerability—the special needs, you could

*"Dancing with the Scars," *The New York Observer*, November 30, 2010.

say—of people living in poverty, and society's obligation to help them? Conservative politicians rarely even
mention poor people—and then only to tell them to pull
up their socks. The right seems to be sinking deeper into
its fantasy of poverty as the result of character flaws and
of the governmental safety net as an agent of spoiling.
Palin writes of the "dependent lifestyle" that "state and
federal intrusion" brought to Alaska's Native communi-
ties as the coddled young "abandoned the strong work
ethic of their elders." Was the filming of Kate Gosselin's
meltdown some sort of screwball homage to the right's
vision of the whining and complaining underclass that
refuses to warm itself at the fire of capitalism and perversely
clings to its place on the margins? In which case: Kate,
all hail you, world-class kvetch and rising comic star.

The New York Review of Books, 2011

COMEDY CENTRAL ON THE MALL

On October 31, Peter Clothier, a seventy-four-year-old author and retired professor, posted an entry on his blog, called *The Buddha Diaries*, about the wonderful day he and his wife, Ellie, had spent at the Jon Stewart and Stephen Colbert Rally to Restore Sanity and/or Fear on October 30 at the Mall in Washington, D.C., between noon and 3:00 p.m. "We stood there trapped for a good two hours, surrounded by people who, like us, had showed up. We saw nothing, heard nothing of what was happening on the stage. It was great!" Clothier writes. He and Ellie had risen at 5:30 a.m. to catch a 6:45 Amtrak train from New York, which should have gotten them to the rally in time to not see and not hear for the full three hours. But they were detained by a horrendous and dangerous crush of people in the Washington Metro.

"The Metro system was utterly unprepared for the invasion," Clothier writes. The station was "a mob scene." "People were waiting in lines ten deep to board" and train after train went by "so full that not one single person could squeeze aboard." However, with the exception of one angry man, who was "quelled by fellow passengers," everyone kept his frustration in check and no one behaved badly.

Joseph Ward, a student at the University of Illinois, had been on a bus all night when he entered the little hell in the Washington Metro. And yet—as he wrote in the *Daily Illini*, where he is an assistant news editor—"I could not muster up the courage to get pissed at my situation. How could anyone not be positive?" He went on to describe the crowd of "young, old, black, white, hippies, yuppies and ex-servicemen pushing their comrades in wheelchairs" who "understood why they were there." When Ward finally boarded a train it was

> packed beyond belief to the point where the conductor would come over the loud speaker and remind people not to panic, push or get on a car that was already at maximum capacity. I felt like telling the conductor that his points were moot, that this was the sanest population in the western world he was addressing and that we would not buy into his Colbertian fear mongering.

After he got off the train Ward revised his opinion of the conductor's "points" ("Turns out, he may have been on to something"). "I feared for my life when the crowds uncontrollably pushed me to within six inches of the train as it began to speed away from the station." At the rally, Ward, like the Clothiers—and almost everyone else there—couldn't see or hear what was going on onstage. (There were a few, but hardly enough, TV monitors on the Mall.) For a moment his determination to be positive even if it killed him faltered. ("Uneasiness began to settle

over the crowd, which was virtually stuck in its position.") But he ended his story on a cheerful note, prais-
ing the musical numbers and comedy skits he had not
seen or heard.

I did not take the test of character in the Metro—I
had come to Washington the night before and had time
to make my way to the rally on foot. And I flunked the
endurance test on the Mall. After a few minutes of standing in radical proximity to the sanest people in the Western world, I managed to make my way back to the street
and then joined the people who were sitting on the steps
of the National Gallery. From there one could see the
phalanx of battleship-gray portable toilets that lined the
Mall, and, beyond them, the Mall itself colorfully glis-
tening with trapped people.

Everyone I talked to during and after the rally said it
was great. It was as if the sunny Stewart had sprayed the
place with his aura. Not seeing or hearing didn't matter.
What mattered was being there and, proleptically, having
been there: several people characterized the event as a
"historical" occasion. Evidently over two hundred thousand people came.

In the final minutes of the show Stewart gave a speech
(I saw it on C-SPAN the next day)—"I thought we might
have a moment, however brief, for some sincerity, if that's
okay"—in which he explained the point of the rally, in
case anyone had missed it. Stewart confirmed that we
had all come to Washington in order to congratulate ourselves on our decency and rationality. We were at a giant
preen-in.

To illustrate our collective fineness, Stewart used the
image of cars entering a tunnel under a river one by one,
and of drivers politely deferring to each other: "You go.

Then I'll go. You go. Then I'll go." "Sure, at some point there will be a selfish jerk who zips up the shoulder and cuts in." But he—like the angry man in the Metro station—"is rare and scorned." The rest of us are made of the right stuff:

> We know instinctively as a people that if we are to get through the darkness and back into light we have to work together. And the truth is, there will always be darkness. And sometimes the light at the end of the tunnel isn't the Promised Land. Sometimes it's just New Jersey.

Nice line. But what is he talking about? How do you work together in a car in a tunnel?

Stewart's and Colbert's following is largely liberal, but their rally was nonpartisan. "Most Americans don't live their lives as only Democrats or Republicans or liberals or conservatives," Stewart said.

> Americans live their lives more as people that are just a little bit late for something they have to do, often something they do not want to do. But they do it. Impossible things every day that are only made possible through the little reasonable compromises we all make.

What compromises? (Didn't this kind of blurry apoliticality give us George W. Bush via Ralph Nader in 2000?)

Stewart made no mention of the coming elections, nor did he blame the right for the darkness we live in now. He blamed the press—"the country's twenty-four-hour politico pundit perpetual panic conflictinator"—for making things look worse than they are. "If we amplify everything, we hear nothing," he said, and went on,

> There are terrorists and racists and Stalinists and theocrats, but those are titles that must be earned, you must have the résumé. Not being able to distinguish between real racists and tea baggers or real bigots and Juan Williams or Rick Sanchez is an insult, not only to those people but to the racists themselves who have put in the exhausting effort it takes to hate.

David Carr, after quoting these words in *The New York Times* of November 1, told a brutal truth: "All due respect to Mr. Williams and Mr. Sanchez, not many people know or care who they are." Carr further pointed out that

> Most Americans don't watch or pay attention to cable television. In even a good news night, about five million people take a seat on the cable wars, which is less than 2 percent of all Americans. People are scared of what they see in their pay envelopes and neighborhoods, not because of what Keith Olbermann said last night or how Bill O'Reilly came back at him.

Of course, the two hundred thousand people who came to the Rally to Restore Sanity and/or Fear are among the 5 million who do watch cable TV—specifically, *The Daily Show* and *The Colbert Report*. The scriptwriters assumed this was the case, and the rally skits were filled with references and allusions that only watchers of these shows would grasp. Who but a watcher of his show would know what Colbert was supposed to represent as he crazily pranced around the stage? Stewart's bland rally persona similarly drew on the resonance of his sharper *Daily Show* image. No doubt it was an accident of organization that required most of the people at the rally to defer their enjoyment of the stage show until they could watch it at home on a screen. But it couldn't have been a more fitting accident. The world of TV is the world that Stewart and Colbert inhabit. To have seen them in real life, or even on a live video monitor, might have felt inauthentic, perhaps even transgressional.

"An incredible gathering here in the Mall today," Stewart said after showing clips of "real stories of momentary unreasonableness," such as that of the irate flight attendant who got off his plane on an exit chute after a passenger dissed him. Stewart beamed at the crowd and went on, "But I think we all know that it doesn't matter what we all say and do here today. It matters what is reported about what we said and did here today."

On their late-night shows, Stewart and Colbert brilliantly satirize TV news and news commentary. At the rally they had to struggle with the lack of a subject to satirize. There was some fun with the Colbert character as an embodiment of irrational fear (Stewart: "FDR once said, 'The only thing we have to fear is fear itself.'" Colbert: "Yes. But just twelve years later he was dead.") But mostly there was more gesturing toward comedy than comedy itself.

If there is one thing that liberal Americans can legitimately pride themselves on it is their talent for creating irreverent signs. Who will forget, from the peace rallies of yesteryear, WHEN CLINTON LIED NO ONE DIED or THE ONLY BUSH I TRUST IS MY OWN? Here are a few examples from the Rally for Sanity and/or Fear:

> WE HAVE NOTHING TO FEAR BUT FEAR ITSELF
>   AND SPIDERS
> MODERATION OR DEATH
> JEW AGAINST INVOKING HITLER FOR
>   POLITICAL POINTS
> ATHEISTS FOR MASTURBATION
> GAY MALAYSIAN MUSLIMS FOR SARAH PALIN
> YOU KNOW WHO ELSE WAS A WHITE SOX FAN?
>   HITLER
> SUPPORT SEPARATION OF HEAD FROM ASS

On October 2, I'd attended the One Nation Working Together rally at the Lincoln Memorial, sponsored by, among others, the NAACP, the AFL-CIO, and the Sierra Club, and supported by groups that included the National Urban League, the National Baptist Convention, the Gay and Lesbian Task Force, and the Communist Party USA. The signs there had a different character:

> GOOD JOBS NOW
> STOP CORPORATE GREED
> GAY, LESBIAN, BISEXUAL AND TRANSGENDER
>   EQUALITY
> I WANT SINGLE PAYER HEALTH CARE
> GET OUT AND VOTE FOR DEMOCRATS

The October 2 rally was a sober affair. The crowd wasn't very large. (I noticed many minority and working-class families with children.) Most of the speakers (visible and audible on large TV monitors) were earnest and un-practiced. They were teachers and unionists and secretaries and veterans and carpenters and students and waitresses, as well as a few politicians like Al Sharpton, who spoke well. But when he exhorted the audience to vote—"We better get ready for the midterm exam"—there was only tepid applause.

Walking back to the train station on Constitution Avenue, my spirits lifted when I saw a man in an elaborate Colonial costume. I went up to him and asked him what his role in the rally had been. He gave me one of the most incredulous looks anyone has ever given me in my life. Then he stiffly informed me that he was the leader of a guided tour of Washington.

The New York Review of Books (NYR Daily), 2010

PANDORA'S CLICK

To say that *Send: The Essential Guide to Email for Office and Home* is more a users' manual than a book is not to belittle it. Email is like an appliance that we have been helplessly misusing because it arrived without instructions. Thanks to David Shipley and Will Schwalbe, our blind blunderings are over. With Shipley and Schwalbe's excellent instructions in hand we can email as confidently as we load the dishwasher and turn on the microwave.

Shipley and Schwalbe are not exaggerating when they say that their guide is essential. For, in truth, email is more like a dangerous power tool than like a harmless kitchen appliance. The more skillful (or lucky) among us have escaped serious injury, but many, perhaps most, of us have suffered the equivalent of burns, lost fingers, electric shocks, and bone fractures. Incautious emailing has cost jobs, ruined friendships, threatened marriages, subverted projects, even led to jail time. "On email, people aren't quite themselves," Shipley and Schwalbe write. "They are angrier, less sympathetic, less aware, more eas-

---

Send: The Essential Guide to Email for Office and Home, by David Shipley and Will Schwalbe

ily wounded, even more gossipy and duplicitous. Email has a tendency to encourage the lesser angels of our nature." It also has the capacity for instant retribution. In one of their cautionary illustrations, Shipley and Schwalbe hold up an email exchange between an executive and a secretary at a large American company in China. The executive nastily wrote:

> You locked me out of my office this evening because you assume I have my office key on my person. With immediate effect, you do not leave the office until you have checked with all the managers you support.

The secretary wrote back:

> I locked the door because the office has been burgled in the past. Even though I'm your subordinate, please pay attention to politeness when you speak. This is the most basic human courtesy. You have your own keys. You forgot to bring them, but you still want to say it's someone else's fault.

She then performed the two-click operation that sent copies of her and her boss's emails to the entire staff of the company. Before long the exchange appeared in the Chinese press and led to the executive's resignation.

Another anecdote that Shipley and Schwalbe tell to illustrate email's special killer combination of winking at our bad behavior and horribly punishing us for it also involves a boss and secretary. In this case, the secretary spilled ketchup on the boss's trousers, and he wrote an email asking for the £4 it cost to have the trousers cleaned (the company was a British law firm). Receiving no reply, he pursued the matter. Finally he—and hundreds of people at the firm—received this email:

> Subject: Re: Ketchup trousers
> With reference to the email below, I must apologize for not getting back to you straight away but due to my mother's sudden illness, death and funeral I have had more pressing issues than your £4.
> I apologize again for accidentally getting a few splashes of ketchup on your trousers. Obviously your financial need as a senior associate is greater than mine as a mere secretary.
> Having already spoken to and shown your email . . . to various partners, lawyers and trainees . . . , they kindly offered to do a collection to raise the £4.
> I however declined their kind offer but should you feel the urgent need for the £4, it will be on my desk this afternoon. Jenny.

Again, the exchange found its way into the press— and thus into *Send*. But Shipley and Schwalbe hardly needed to scour newspaper archives for examples of email's destructive power. How many of us have—among other self-immolations—badmouthed someone in an email, only to make the fatal mis-click that sends the email to the very person we have betrayed? And what can we do to repair the damage? Anything?

"The email era has made necessary a special type of apology," Shipley and Schwalbe write,

the kind you have to make when you are the
bonehead who fired off a ridiculously intemper-
ate email or who accidentally sent an email to the
person you were covertly trashing. In situations
like these, our first inclination is to apologize via
the medium that got us into so much trouble in the
first place. Resist this inclination.

Instead, go see the person or telephone him, for "the
graver the email sin, the more the email apology trivial-
izes it." "Just because we have email we shouldn't use it
for everything," Shipley and Schwalbe write, introducing
a notion that younger readers may find too radical to take
seriously. The generation that has grown up with email—
that has never done such a thing as mail a letter or walk
down the hall to a colleague's office to ask a question—
will derive different benefits from *Send*. The young make
different mistakes on email than the middle-aged and
old do. College students who send outrageous email requests to their teachers (addressed "Hiya Professor!")
or college applicants who write long, self-satisfied emails
to admissions officers "seem painfully unaware that the
person they are writing to (and annoying) is the same
person who could be offering them a place in a freshman class or grading them at term's end." The poor
lambs don't know better, and *Send* is good at setting
them straight.

On the face of it, an email and a letter are the same thing:
a piece of writing addressed to one or several persons. But
letter writing was never the fraught activity that email
writing is. Shipley and Schwalbe believe that the trouble

derives from a fundamental flaw in email for which the user has to compensate:

> If you don't consciously insert tone into an email, a kind of universal default tone won't automatically be conveyed. Instead, the message written without regard to tone becomes a blank screen onto which the reader projects his own fears, prejudices and anxieties.

To counteract this perilous ambiguity, Shipley and Schwalbe suggest a program of unrelenting niceness. Keep letting your correspondent know how much you like and respect him, praise and flatter him, constantly demonstrate your puppyish friendliness, and stick in exclamation points (and sometimes even smiling-face icons) wherever possible. "The exclamation point is a lazy but effective way to combat email's essential lack of tone," Shipley and Schwalbe write. "'I'll see you at the conference' is a simple statement of fact. 'I'll see you at the conference!' lets your fellow conferee know that you're excited and pleased about the event." Shipley and Schwalbe then make an arresting remark:

> Sure, the better your word choice the less need you will have for this form of shorthand. But until we find more time in the day—and until email begins to convey affect—we will continue to sprinkle exclamation points liberally throughout our emails.

So this is the crux of the matter: email is a medium of bad writing. Poor word choice is the norm—as is tone deafness. The problem of tone is, of course, the problem of all writing. There is no "universal default tone." When people wrote letters they had the same blank screen to fill. And there were the same boneheads among them, who alienated correspondents with their ghastly oblivious prose. One has only to look at the letter-writing manuals of the nineteenth and twentieth centuries to see that most of the problems Shipley and Schwalbe deal with are not unique to email but common to the whole epistolary genre. They are writing problems. Some of us do find the time in the day to write a carefully worded, exclamation-point-free email when the occasion demands. Mostly, though, all of us who use email avail ourselves of its permission to write fast and sloppy. Shipley and Schwalbe's serene acceptance of the unwriterliness of email, of its function as an instrument of speedy, heedless communication, is correct, and their guide is helpful precisely because it doesn't pretend that the instrument is anything but what it is.

"We don't think of ourselves as old, but we recall when the phone was a big deal," the fortysomething authors write. It won't be long before email, too, stops being a big deal. The people who now use email to fire employees or propose marriage or disparage friends will realize that they were doing the equivalent of throwing fragile silks into the washing machine. As email's novelty wears off and its limitations become clearer, we will revert to the telephone when something complex, intimate, or low-minded needs to be communicated. We will use email for straightforward business and social arrangements. One takes away from *Send* a refreshing sense of the authors' dislike of the tool they are teaching us to use.

They may not be old, but they are old enough to see email in the perspective of life as it was lived before this Pandora's box appeared among us.

Interestingly, the models Shipley and Schwalbe choose to illustrate their section "How to Write a Perfect Email" were written by twelve-year-olds. The really young, evidently, don't need the help the rest of us do; like Blakean innocents, they are untouched by email's evil. Their harmless chatter ("OMG! I was playing yesterday, when this really CUTE boy rode up on his bike") is reminiscent of the notes we used to pass in class, which are, come to think of it, the precursors of email: hastily written, instantly delivered and replied to, and, if intercepted by the wrong person, mortifying. As the really young become merely young it will be interesting to see what happens. Will their childish babbling evolve into decent writing? Does writing a lot lead to writing well? Even (OMG!) on email?

The New York Review of Books, 2007

PART III

DREAMS AND ANNA KARENINA

We do not think of Tolstoy as a comic writer, but his genius permits him to write farce when it suits him. There is a wickedly funny scene in *Anna Karenina* that directly precedes the painful scenes leading to Anna's suicide. It takes place in the drawing room of the Countess Lydia Ivanovna, who, almost alone among the novel's characters, has no good, or even pretty good, qualities. She embodies the kind of hysterical and coldhearted religious piety that Tolstoy was especially allergic to. "As a very young and rhapsodical girl," he writes, she

> had been married to a wealthy man of high rank, a very good-natured, jovial, and extremely dissipated rake. Two months after marriage her husband abandoned her, and her impassioned protestations of affection he met with a sarcasm and even hostility that people knowing the count's good heart, and seeing no defects in the ecstatic Lydia, were at a loss to explain. Though they were not divorced, they lived apart, and whenever the husband met the wife, he invariably behaved to her with the

same venomous irony, the cause of which was incomprehensible.

Tolstoy, with his own venomous irony, makes the cause entirely comprehensible to the reader of *Anna Karenina*, as he shows Lydia Ivanovna fasten herself on Karenin after Anna leaves his house to go abroad with Vronsky, and preside over his degeneration into his worst self. She is an ugly and malevolent creature who coats her spite in a thick ooze of platitudes about Christian love and forgiveness. When Anna was on the verge of death after giving birth to Vronsky's daughter, Karenin experienced an electrifying spiritual transformation: his feelings of hatred and vengefulness toward Anna and Vronsky abruptly changed into feelings of love and forgiveness, and under the spell of this new "blissful spiritual condition" he offered Anna a divorce and the custody of her son— neither of which she chose to accept. Now, a year later, she wants the divorce, but Karenin is no longer of a mind to give it to her. The blissful spiritual condition has faded away like a rainbow, and Karenin, in thrall to the malignant Lydia Ivanovna, has reassumed his old, supinely rigid, and unfeeling self.

Anna's brother, Stepan Arkadyevich (Stiva) Oblonsky, has gone to Karenin to intercede for Anna, and Karenin has said he would think the matter over and give his answer in two days' time, but when the two days pass, instead of an answer, Oblonsky receives an evening invitation to the house of Lydia Ivanovna, where he finds her and Karenin and a French clairvoyant named Landau, who is to be somehow instrumental in Karenin's decision.

The comic scene that follows is filtered through Oblonsky's consciousness.

By now we know Oblonsky very well. Tolstoy has portrayed him as a person whom it is necessary to condemn—he is another dissipated rake—but impossible to dislike. He radiates affability; when he comes into a room people immediately cheer up. And when he appears on the page, the reader feels a similar delight. In the novel's moral hierarchy, Lydia Ivanovna and Karenin occupy the lowest rung; they sin against the human spirit, while Stiva only sins against his wife and children and creditors. Through his geniality, Oblonsky has been able to maintain a job in government for which he is in no way qualified, but now, because he needs more money, he is trying to get himself appointed to a higher-paying position in the civil service. Lydia Ivanovna has influence among the appointers, and Oblonsky figures he might as well use the occasion to charm her into helping him. Thus, while listening to Lydia Ivanovna and Karenin's odious religious palaver, he cravenly—but, he hopes, not too cravenly—hides his atheism:

> "Ah, if you knew the happiness we know, feeling His presence ever in our hearts!" said Countess Lydia Ivanovna with a rapturous smile.
>
> "But a man may feel himself unworthy sometimes to rise to that height," said Stepan Arkadyevich, conscious of hypocrisy in admitting this religious height, but at the same time unable to bring himself to acknowledge his freethinking views before a person who, by a single word to Pomorsky, might procure him the coveted appointment.

During all this Landau, "a short, thinnish man, very pale and handsome, with feminine hips, knock-kneed, with fine brilliant eyes and long hair" and a "moist, life-less" handshake, is sitting apart at a window. Karenin and Lydia Ivanovna look at each other and make cryptic remarks about him. A footman keeps coming into the room with letters for Lydia Ivanovna, to which she rap-idly scribbles answers or gives brief spoken answers ("Tomorrow at the Grand Duchess's," say), before re-suming her pieties, to which Karenin adds pieties of his own. Stiva feels increasingly baffled. Lydia Ivanovna suddenly asks him, "*Vous comprenez l'anglais?*" and when he says yes, she goes to her bookcase and takes down a tract called *Safe and Happy*, from which she proposes to read aloud. Stiva feels safe and happy at the chance to collect himself and not have to worry about putting a foot wrong. Lydia Ivanovna prefaces her reading with a story about a woman named Marie Sanim who lost her only child, but found God, and now thanks Him for the death of her child—"such is the happiness faith brings!" As he listens to Lydia Ivanovna read *Safe and Happy*,

> aware of the beautiful, artless—or perhaps artful, he could not decide which—eyes of Landau fixed upon him, Stepan Arkadyevich [begins] to be con-scious of a peculiar heaviness in his head.
>
> The most incongruous ideas were running through his mind. "Marie Sanim is glad her child's dead . . . How good a smoke would be now! . . . To be saved, one need only believe, and the monks don't know how the thing's to be done, but Countess Lydia Ivanovna does know . . . And

why is my head so heavy? Is it the cognac, or all this being so strange? Anyway, I think I've done nothing objectionable so far. But, even so, it won't do to ask her now. They say they make one say one's prayers. I only hope they won't make me! That'll be too absurd. And what nonsense she's reading! But she has a good accent. . . ."

Stiva fights the drowsiness that is overcoming him, but begins to helplessly succumb to it. On the point of snoring, he rouses himself, but too late. "He's asleep," he hears the countess saying. He has been caught out. The countess will never help him with the appointment. But no, the countess isn't talking about him. She is talking about the clairvoyant. He is lying back in his chair with his eyes closed and his hand twitching. He is in the trance Lydia Ivanovna and Karenin have been waiting for him to fall into. She instructs Karenin to give Landau his hand and he obeys, trying to move carefully, but stumbling on a table. Stiva watches the scene, not sure he isn't dreaming it. "It was all real," he concludes.

With his eyes closed, the clairvoyant speaks: "*Que la personne qui est arrivée la dernière, celle qui demande, qu'elle sorte! Qu'elle sorte!*" Let the person who was the last to come in, the one who asks questions, let him get out! Let him get out! Stiva, "forgetting the favor he had meant to ask of Lydia Ivanovna, and forgetting his sister's affairs, caring for nothing, but filled with the sole desire to get away as soon as possible, [goes] out on tiptoe and [runs] out into the street as though from a plague-stricken house." It takes him a long time to regain his equanimity. The next day he receives from Karenin a final refusal of the divorce and understands "that this decision was based on what the Frenchman had said in his real or pretended trance the evening before."

It was all real. There has been a great deal written about the preternatural realism of *Anna Karenina,* and about the novel's special status as a kind of criticism-proof text because of the reader's feeling that what he is reading is being effortlessly reported rather than laboriously made up. "We are not to take *Anna Karénine* as a work of art; we are to take it as a piece of life," Matthew Arnold wrote in 1887. "The author has not invented and combined it, he has seen it; it has all happened before his inward eye, and it was in this wise that it happened." In 1946 Philip Rahv elaborated on Arnold's idea:

> In the bracing Tolstoyan air, the critic, however addicted to analysis, cannot help doubting his own task, sensing that there is something presumptuous and even unnatural, which requires an almost artificial deliberateness of intention, in the attempt to dissect an art so wonderfully integrated. . . . Such is the astonishing immediacy with which he possesses his characters that he can dispense with manipulative techniques, as he dispenses with the belletristic devices of exaggeration, distortion, and dissimulation. . . . The conception of writing as of something calculated and constructed— . . . upon which literary culture has become more and more dependent—is entirely foreign to Tolstoy.

Tolstoy—one of literature's greatest masters of ma-
nipulative techniques—would smile at this. The book's
"astonishing immediacy" is nothing if not an object of the
exaggeration, distortion, and dissimulation through which
each scene is rendered. Rahv calls these devices belletris-
tic but long before anyone wrote belles lettres, everyone
who dreamed was practiced in their use. If the dream is
father to imaginative literature, Tolstoy may be the novelist who most closely hews to its deep structures. As we
read *Anna Karenina* we are under the same illusion of
authorlessness we are under as we follow the stories that
come to us at night and seem to derive from some ancient
hidden reality rather than from our own, so to speak,
pens. Tolstoy's understanding of the sly techniques of
dream-creation is at the heart of his novelist's enterprise.
Like the films shown in the movie houses of our sleeping
minds, Tolstoy's waking scenes draw on a vast repertory
of collective emotional memory for their urgency.

Take the famous ballroom scene at the beginning of
the novel in which Anna and Vronsky fall in love as if
forced to do so by a love potion in a room filled with tulle
and lace and music and scent. The scene has inscribed itself on our memories as one of the most vividly romantic
scenes in literature. Who can forget the sight of Anna in
her simple black gown that shows off her beauty rather
than its own and sets her apart from all the other women
in the room? As Tolstoy describes her—practically caress-
ing her as he does so—we fall in love with her ourselves.
How could Vronsky resist her?

But wait. It isn't Tolstoy who describes Anna—it is
through the eyes of Kitty Scherbetskaya that we see her.
The scene is written not as a romance but as a nightmare.

Kitty, who loves Vronsky, has come to the ball in the happy expectation that he will propose to her. As in our worst nightmares, when a horrified realization of disaster comes upon us and will not let go of us, Kitty's delight turns to horror as she watches Anna and Vronsky displaying the signs of people falling in love, and grasps the full extent of Vronsky's indifference to her. Kitty will hate Anna for the rest of her life, but Tolstoy—to render his effect of Anna's powerful sexual magnetism—captures the moment when Kitty is herself attracted to Anna. Tolstoy places or rather displaces the weight of Kitty's crushing mortification onto the mazurka that she assumed she would dance with Vronsky and for which she now finds herself without a partner. In writing the scene as an archetypal nightmare of jealousy—in refracting Anna and Vronsky's passion through the prism of Kitty's anguish—Tolstoy performs one of the hidden tours de force by which his novel is animated.

The horse race offers another example of Tolstoy's use of the archetypal nightmare as a literary structure. This time his model is the dream of lateness. In this dream, no matter what we do, no matter how desperately we struggle, we cannot get to the airport, or the play, or the final examination in time. Something holds us back and we struggle against it to no purpose. On the morning of the race Vronsky makes a visit to the mare he is going to ride (and kill). The English trainer asks him where he is planning to go after he leaves the stable, and when Vronsky tells him he is going to see a man named Bryansky, the Englishman—evidently not believing him, knowing, as others seem to know, that he is going to visit Anna—says, "The vital thing's to keep quiet before a race . . . don't get disturbed or upset about anything."

Vronsky drives out to Anna's summer house and becomes predictably disturbed and upset when she tells him she is pregnant. He leaves for Bryansky's house to give him some money—he wasn't lying to the trainer, just not telling the whole truth—and the nightmare proper of lateness begins. Only on the way to Bryansky does he look at his watch and see that it is much later than he thought and that he never should have started out. Should he turn back? No, he decides to keep going. He believes he will just make the race.

At this point, Tolstoy veers away from the classic dream of lateness in which the dreamer never arrives at his destination and allows Vronsky to make the race. But Vronsky is clearly not in the right state of mind. An unpleasant encounter with his brother, who wants him to end the affair with Anna, is another assault on the necessary condition of quiet. When disaster strikes, when Vronsky makes the wrong move that breaks the mare's back, it registers, as these things do when we dream them, as a terrifying inevitability.

All dreams are not nightmares, of course. As we sometimes awaken from a dream in tears, so a number of Tolstoy's scenes draw on the sentimentality—a sort of basic bathos—that is lodged in the hearts of all but the most high-minded among us. One such scene takes place the day after the ball, when her sister Dolly comes to the humiliated Kitty's room in her parents' house and finds her sitting and staring at a piece of rug. Kitty rejects Dolly's attempts to make her feel better, is cold and unpleasant to her, and finally silences her by spitefully flinging Stiva's philandering in her face. "I have some pride, and never, *never* would I do as you're doing—go back to a man who's deceived you, who has cared for another woman. I can't understand it. You may, but I can't!" Tolstoy continues:

> And saying these words, she glanced at her sister, and seeing that Dolly sat silent, her head mournfully bowed, Kitty, instead of running out of the room, as she had meant to do, sat down near the door and hid her face in her handkerchief.
>
> The silence lasted for a minute or two. Dolly was thinking of herself. That humiliation of which she was always conscious came back to her with a peculiar bitterness when her sister reminded her of it. She had not expected such cruelty from her sister, and she was angry with her. But suddenly she heard the rustle of a skirt, and with it the sound of heart-rending, smothered sobbing, and felt arms about her neck. Kitty was on her knees before her.
>
> "Dolinka, I am so, so wretched!" she whispered penitently. And the sweet face covered with tears hid itself in Darya Aleksandrovna's skirt.

The novel is filled with such passages (another is the scene in which Dolly comes upon her daughter Tanya and her son Grisha eating cake and crying over Tanya's kindheartedness in secretly sharing it with him after he had been forbidden dessert as a punishment) that do not advance its plot—almost seem to retard its forward motion—but heighten the sense of piercing reality Arnold and Rahv could find no words to account for.

The novel is also filled with accounts of actual dreams

experienced by characters that entirely lack the vividness of the scenes of waking life. They seem, in their various ways, flat, formulaic, even boring. When Anna dreams of sleeping with both Karenin and Vronsky, we get the point—and feel that Tolstoy is not being very subtle. On the morning after Dolly confronts Stiva with the evidence of his affair with a former governess, he awakens in the study to which he has been banished from this uninterestingly incomprehensible dream:

Alabin was giving a dinner at Darmstadt; no, not Darmstadt, but something American. Yes, but then, Darmstadt was in America. Yes, Alabin was giving a dinner on glass tables, and the tables sang *Il mio tesoro*—not *Il mio tesoro*, though, but something better, and there were some sort of little decanters on the table, and they were women, too.

"Yes, it was nice, very nice," Stiva recalls. "There was a great deal more that was delightful, only there's no putting it into words, or even expressing it in one's thoughts once awake." Tolstoy was obviously well acquainted with the guard who stops us at the border of sleep and awakening and confiscates the brilliant, dangerous spoils of our nighttime creations. The capacity to re-create these fictions in the unprotected light of day may be what we mean by literary genius. As the full realization of the mess he has made of his domestic life comes over Stiva, he reflects that "to forget himself in sleep was impossible now, at least till nighttime; he could not go back now to the music sung by the decanter women; so he must forget himself in the dream of daily life."

•

In January 1878, a professor of botany named S. A. Rachinsky wrote to Tolstoy about what he felt to be "a basic deficiency in the construction" of *Anna Karenina*, namely that "the book lacks architectonics." To which Tolstoy replied,

> Your opinion about *Anna Karenina* seems wrong to me. On the contrary, I take pride in the architectonics. The vaults are thrown up in such a way that one cannot notice where the link is. That is what I tried to do more than anything else. The unity in the structure is created not by action and not by relationships between the characters, but by an inner continuity.

One of these continuities—perhaps the most significant—is Tolstoy's keen, almost prying, interest in the sexuality of his characters and the hierarchy he has set in place that runs parallel to, though distinct from, his moral hierarchy. At the top he has set his sexually robust characters—Anna, Vronsky, Oblonsky, Levin, Kitty, and Dolly—and to the bottom he has consigned figures like the creepy Landau and Varenka, a sexless young woman Kitty meets at the spa to which she has been sent to cure her broken heart, and whose limp handshake is echoed a hundred pages later by Landau's flaccid grip. Levin's bloodless-intellectual half brother Sergey Ivanovich Koznishev, a kind of double of the bloodless-intellectual Karenin (as Lydia Ivanovna is a double of another dreadful pious woman named Madame Stahl—the novel is filled with doubles and doublenesses), is another member of the league of the sexually underpowered, though his portrait is a mere sketch in comparison to the full-blown case study of impotence that Tolstoy has fashioned out of his complicated cuckold.

He allows us to study Karenin both from the point of view of his sexually unfulfilled wife and, most interestingly, from his own sense of how he doesn't measure up to other men. At a court event, the flatfooted and wide-hipped Karenin keeps looking at the attractive, powerfully built court functionaries around him and asks himself

> whether they felt differently, did their loving and marrying differently, these Vronskys and Oblonskys . . . these fat-calved chamberlains . . . those juicy, vigorous, self-confident men who always and everywhere drew his inquisitive attention in spite of himself.

Anna is the special case of poetical sexual awakening turning into terrifying erotomania that reflects Tolstoy's own famous craziness about sex, which in some sense is what the novel is "about." The transformation of the wonderful Anna we first meet at the railway station—"the suppressed eagerness which played over her face . . . as though her nature was so brimming over with something that against her will it showed itself now in the flash of her eyes, and now in her smile"—into the psychotic who throws herself in front of a train is chronicled over the book's length, and doesn't add up.

Standard readings of the novel attribute Anna's descent into madness to the loss of her son and to her ostracism by society. But in fact, as Tolstoy unambiguously tells us, the situation is of her own making. She did not lose her son—she abandoned him when she left for Italy with Vronsky after her recovery from the puerperal fever that propelled Karenin into his "blissful spirituality." Under its influence, he was willing to give up his son and give Anna a divorce that would permit her to marry Vronsky and rejoin respectable society as, even in those days, divorced women were able to do. But as the novel goes on and Anna's life unravels, it is as if this opportunity had never arisen. We experience the novel, as we experience our dreams, undisturbed by its illogic. We accept Anna's disintegration without questioning it. Only later, when we analyze the work, does its illogic become apparent. But by then it is too late to reverse Tolstoy's spell.

The New York Review of Books, 2015

SOCKS

In *Anna Karenina*, the day after the fateful ball, resolved to forget Vronsky and resume her peaceful life with her son and husband ("my life will go on in the old way, all nice and as usual"), Anna settles herself in her compartment in the overnight train from Moscow to St. Petersburg, and takes out an uncut English novel, probably one by Trollope judging from references to fox hunting and Parliament. Tolstoy, of course, says nothing about a translation—educated Russians knew English as well as French. In contrast, very few educated English speakers have read the Russian classics in the original and, until recent years, they have largely depended on two translations, one by the Englishwoman Constance Garnett and the other by the English couple Louise and Aylmer Maude, made respectively in 1901 and 1912. The distinguished Slavic scholar and teacher Gary Saul Morson once wrote about the former:

> I love Constance Garnett, and wish I had a framed picture of her on my wall, since I have often thought that what I do for a living is teach the

Collected Works of Constance Garnett. She has a fine sense of English, and, especially, the sort of English that appears in British fiction of the realist period, which makes her ideal for translating the Russian masterpieces. Tolstoy and Dostoevsky were constantly reading and learning from Dickens, Trollope, George Eliot and others. Every time someone else redoes one of these works, reviewers say that the new version replaces Garnett; and then another version comes out, which, apparently, replaces Garnett again, and so on. She must have done something right.

Morson wrote these words in 1997,* and would recall them bitterly. Since that time a sort of asteroid has hit the safe world of Russian literature in English translation. A couple named Richard Pevear and Larissa Volokhonsky have established an industry of taking everything they can get their hands on written in Russian and putting it into flat, awkward English. Surprisingly, these translations, far from being rejected by the critical establishment, have been embraced by it and have all but replaced Garnett, Maude, and other of the older translations. When you go to a bookstore to buy a work by Tolstoy, Dostoevsky, Gogol, or Chekhov, most of what you find is in translation by Pevear and Volokhonsky.

In an article in the July/August 2010 issue of *Commentary* entitled "The Pevearsion of Russian Literature," Morson used the word "tragedy" to express his sense of the disaster that has befallen Russian literature in English

---

*In correspondence with the writer.

translation since the P&V translations began to appear. To Morson "these are Potemkin translations—apparently definitive but actually flat and fake on closer inspection." Morson fears that "if students and more-general readers choose P&V . . . [they] are likely to presume that whatever made so many regard Russian literature with awe has gone stale with time or is lost to them."

In the summer of 2015 an interview with the rich and happy couple appeared in *The Paris Review*. The interviewer—referring to a comment Pevear had made to David Remnick in 2005—asked him: "You once said that one of your subliminal aims as a translator was 'to help energize English itself.' Can you explain what you mean?" Pevear was glad to do so:

> It seemed to me that American fiction had become very bland and mostly self-centered. I thought it needed to break out of that. One thing I love about translating is the possibility it gives me to do things that you might not ordinarily do in English. I think it's a very important part of translating. The good effect of translating is this cross-pollination of languages. Sometimes we get criticized—this is too literal, this is a Russianism— but I don't mind that. Let's have a little Russianism. Let's use things like inversions. Why should they be eliminated? I guess if you're a contemporary writer, you're not supposed to do it, but as a translator I can. I love this freedom of movement between the two languages. I think it's the most

important thing for me—that it should enrich my language, the English language.

This bizarre idea of the translator's task only strengthens one's sense of the difficulty teachers of Russian literature in translation face when their students are forced to read the Russian classics in Pevear's "energized" English. I first heard of P&V in 2007 when I received an email from the writer Anna Shapiro:

> I finished the Pevear/Volokhonsky translation of Anna Karenina a few weeks ago and I'm still more or less stewing about it. It leaves such a bad taste; it's so wrong, and so oddly wrong, turning nourishment into wood. I wouldn't have thought it possible. I've always maintained that Tolstoy was unruinable, because he's such a simple writer, words piled like bricks, that it couldn't matter; that he's a transparent writer, so you can't really get the flavor wrong, because in many ways he tries to have none. But they have, they've added some bad flavor, whereas even when Garnett makes sentences like "Vronsky eschewed farinaceous foods" it does no harm. . . . I imagine Pevear thinking he's CORRECTING Tolstoy; that he's really the much better writer.

When I leafed through the P&V translation of *Anna Karenina* I understood what Anna Shapiro was stewing about. The contrast to Garnett glared out at me. Garnett's fine English, her urgent forward-moving sentences, her feeling for words—all this was gone, replaced by writing that is like singing or piano playing by someone who is not musical. For example:

Garnett: All his efforts to draw her into open discussion she confronted with a barrier that he could not penetrate, made up of a sort of amused perplexity.

P&V: To all his attempts at drawing her into an explanation she opposed the impenetrable wall of some cheerful perplexity.

Or:

Garnett: After taking leave of her guests, Anna did not sit down, but began walking up and down the room. She had unconsciously the whole evening done her utmost to arouse in Levin a feeling of love—as of late she had fallen into doing with all young men—and she knew she had attained her aim, as far as was possible in one evening, with a married and honorable man. She liked him very much, and, in spite of the striking difference, from the masculine point of view, between Vronsky and Levin, as a woman she saw something they had in common, which had made Kitty able to love both. Yet as soon as he was out of the room, she ceased to think of him.

P&V: After seeing her guests off, Anna began pacing up and down the room without sitting down. Though for the whole evening (lately she had acted the same way towards all young men) she had unconsciously done everything she could to arouse a feeling of love for her in Levin, and though she knew that she had succeeded in it, as far as one could with regard to an honest, married man in one evening, and though she liked him very much (despite the sharp contrast, from a man's point of view, between Levin and Vronsky, as a woman she saw what they had in common, for which Kitty, too, had loved them both), as soon as he left the room, she stopped thinking about him.

If these examples are not convincing, let me try to demonstrate Garnett's brilliance as a translator with a passage in chapter 8 of book 3 of *Anna Karenina*. We are at Dolly Oblonsky's country estate where she is spending the spring and summer with her six children, while the philandering Stiva remains in Moscow. Dolly is taking the children to the village church for a Sunday mass. During the previous week she had been preoccupied with the making or alteration of the children's clothes for the service. Now the coach is at the door, the beautifully dressed children are sitting on the steps of the house, but their mother is still inside, primping. After she finally appears, dressed in a white muslin gown, Tolstoy pauses to explain the careworn, self-sacrificing Dolly's uncharacteristic concern with her appearance. Garnett's translation of the passage reads:

> Darya Aleksandrovna had done her hair, and dressed with care and excitement. In the old days she had dressed for her own sake to look pretty and be admired. Later on, as she got older, dressing up

became more and more distasteful to her. She saw that she was losing her good looks. But now she began to feel pleasure and interest in dressing up again. Now she did not dress for her own sake, not for the sake of her own beauty, but simply so that as the mother of those exquisite creatures she might not spoil the general effect. And looking at herself for the last time in the mirror, she was satisfied with herself. She looked nice. Not nice as she would have wished to look nice in old days at a ball, but nice for the object she now had in view.

Here is P&V:

Darya Alexandrovna had done her hair and dressed with care and excitement. Once she used to dress for herself, to be beautiful and admired; then, the older she became, the more unpleasant it was for her to dress; she saw that she had lost her good looks. But now she again dressed with pleasure and excitement. Now she dressed not for herself, not for her own beauty, but so that, being the mother of these lovely things, she would not spoil the general impression. And taking a last look in the mirror, she remained satisfied with herself. She was pretty. Not as pretty as she had once wanted to be at a ball, but pretty enough for the purpose she now had in mind.

The key Russian words here are *krasivaya* and *khorosha*.* Tolstoy uses the first, meaning "beautiful" or "pretty,"

---

*The reader should not be misled into thinking that I know Russian. A Russian speaker kindly supplied these words.

in the sentence referring to the old days when Dolly dressed to be admired. He uses the second, meaning "good" or "fine," in writing of Dolly's present selfless purpose. Garnett's "She looked nice" conveys the sense of the passage as no other translator of *Anna Karenina* into English has conveyed it. Louise and Aylmer Maude (some readers prefer their version of the novel to Garnett's) write "She looked well," which is better than P&V's "She was pretty." But Garnett's "She looked nice" is inspired.

There is a popular conception of Garnett as a scatter-brained Edwardian lady who dashed off her translations at a mad pace, making huge mistakes in her haste, and writing in an outdated language that has necessitated the retranslations that have followed. A famous description of her by D. H. Lawrence established the sense of her hurry and carelessness. Lawrence recalled Garnett

> sitting out in the garden turning out reams of her marvelous translations from the Russian. She would finish a page, and throw it off on a pile on the floor without looking up, and start a new page. The pile would be this high . . . really almost up to her knees, and all magical.

You can feel the condescension. The garden setting, the impetuous flinging of the "marvelous" and "magical" pages. A serious translator would be indoors working with orderly deliberation. Garnett did make mistakes, but correctable ones, as an excellent revised edition by Leonard

Kent and Nina Berberova demonstrates.* As for the charge that Garnett writes in an outdated language, yes, here and there she uses words and phrases that no one uses today, but not many of them. We find the same sprinkling of outdated words and phrases in the novels of Trollope and Dickens and George Eliot. Should they, too, be rewritten for modern sensibilities? (Would u really want that?)

Another argument for putting Tolstoy into awkward contemporary-sounding English has been advanced by Pevear and Volokhonsky, and, more recently, by Marian Schwartz,† namely that Tolstoy himself wrote in awkward Russian and that when we read Garnett or Maude we are not reading the true Tolstoy. Arguably, Schwartz's attempt to "re-create Tolstoy's style in English" surpasses P&V's in ungainliness. Schwartz actually ruins one of the most moving scenes in the novel—when Kitty, fending off her sister's attempt to comfort her for Vronsky's rejection, lashes out and reminds her of her degraded position vis-à-vis the womanizing Stiva. After the outburst the sisters sit in silence. In Garnett's version:

> The silence lasted for a minute or two. Dolly was thinking of herself. That humiliation of which she was always conscious came back to her with a peculiar bitterness when her sister reminded her of it. She had not expected such cruelty from her sister, and she was angry with her. But suddenly

*Leo Tolstoy, *Anna Karenina*, introduction by Mona Simpson, translated by Constance Garnett, translation revised by Leonard J. Kent and Nina Berberova (Modern Library, 2000).
†Leo Tolstoy, *Anna Karenina*, translated by Marian Schwartz, edited and with an introduction by Gary Saul Morson (Yale University Press, 2014).

she heard the rustle of a skirt, and with it the sound of heart-rending, smothered sobbing, and felt arms about her neck.

Schwartz writes:

The silence lasted for a couple of minutes. Dolly was thinking about herself. Her humiliation, which was always with her, told especially painfully in her when her sister mentioned it. She had not anticipated such cruelty from her sister, and she was angry with her. Suddenly, however, she heard a dress and instead of the sound of sobs that had been held back too long, someone's hands embracing her around the neck from below.

Perhaps a slip of the copy editor's pen created this ungrammatical muddle. The following instance of Schwartz's obtrusive literalism was clearly deliberate. It occurs in an exchange between Stiva and his servant Matvey about the upset in the Oblonsky household following Dolly's discovery of his affair with the governess. Stiva wants Matvey's opinion of whether Dolly will take him back. Garnett writes:

"Eh, Matvey?" he said, shaking his head.
"It's all right sir; it will work out," said Matvey.
"Work out?"
"Yes, sir."

Schwartz writes:

"Eh, Matvei?" he said, shaking his head.

"It's all right, sir, things will shapify," said Matvei.

"Shapify?"

"I'm certain of it, sir."

The neologism "shapify" is Schwartz's attempt to render Tolstoy's neologism *obrazuetsia* (derived from the word *obraz*, meaning image or form). Tolstoy reintroduces his invention a few pages later. "Stepan Arkadyevich liked a good joke. 'And perhaps things will shapify! A fine turn of phrase: *shapify*,' he thought. 'I must repeat that one.'" But where the Russian neologism is funny, the English one is merely weird. It stops the reader in his tracks.

No other translator fell into the trap Schwartz fell into. The other translators—including Pevear and Volokhonsky—evidently understanding that the Slavic languages' capacity for playfulness (or what you could call playing-with-itself-fulness) is not innate to English, made no attempt to create an English neologism. (Rosamund Bartlett and P&V come closest to *obrazuetsia* with "things will shape up" and "it'll shape up.") Sometimes, of course, the attempt has to be made, as in Chekhov's story "Ionitch," where a character talks in "his extraordinary language, evolved in the course of prolonged practice in witticism and evidently now become a habit: 'Badsome,' 'Hugeous,' 'Thank you most dumbly,' and so on." But in the case of Matvey, whose language is not usually extraordinary, an elaborately badsome English neologism is uncalled for.

Or is it? What side are you on? Whose interests should the translator serve? Those of the reader of simple wants, who only asks of a translation that it advance rather than impede his pleasure and understanding? Or those of the more advanced (or masochistic) school who want to know what the original was "like"? I am speaking here of translations of fiction. Poetry and humor are untranslatable in the view of some readers. But surely novels can be successfully translated. The basic myths they transform into stories of their time belong to all cultures and can be retold in any number of languages. Let me give one more example of the point I have been belaboring on behalf of the reader of simple wants.

While the Kent/Berberova edition of *Anna Karenina* contains thousands of revisions, it essentially remains Garnett's translation. "That she made errors and that her heritage dictated pruderies which occasionally mute some of Tolstoy is certain," Kent and Berberova write, "but that her language and syntax almost always faithfully reproduce both the letter *and* the tone of the original is no less true; indeed, we remain as unconvinced as many others that her translation has ever been superseded." Kent and Berberova deftly change "he eschewed farinaceous and sweet dishes" to "he avoided starchy foods and desserts." They correct a truly serious error in the passage where Vronsky first lays eyes on Anna at the train station. Garnett writes that he "felt he must glance at her once more; not that she was very beautiful . . . ," which seems odd, since Anna's exceptional beauty is one of the novel's givens. In the corrected version "not that" becomes "not because," and all falls into place.

However, there are revisions that subvert, you could almost say Pevearise, the Garnett translation. In book 5, chapter 3, Tolstoy writes with delicious malice of the ridiculous young man Vassenka Vesselovsky's realization that his fancy new hunting outfit is wrong while the tatters Stiva wears are the height of chic. In the original Garnett version Stiva is dressed "in rough leggings and spats, in torn trousers and a short coat. On his head there was a wreck of a hat." Kent and Berberova properly remove "spats" but substitute some mystifying "linen bands wrapped around his feet." What are these bands? In their version, the Maudes solve the mystery for the reader: "Oblonsky was wearing raw hide shoes, bands of linen wound round his feet instead of socks, a pair of tattered trousers. . . ." There are no socks in the Tolstoy original. The Maudes just decided to help out the reader. Whether you think they were right or wrong to do so says something about where you stand in the current controversy about the translation of Russian fiction.

The New York Review of Books, 2016

THE MASTER WRITER OF THE CITY

In 1942 *The New Yorker* published Joseph Mitchell's profile of a homeless man in Greenwich Village named Joe Gould, whose claim to notice—the thing that separated him from other sad misfits—was "a formless, rather mysterious book" he was known to be writing called "An Oral History of Our Time," begun twenty-six years earlier and already, at nine million words, "eleven times as long as the Bible." Twenty-two years later, in 1964, the magazine published another piece by Mitchell called "Joe Gould's Secret" that ran in two parts, and that drew a rather less sympathetic and a good deal more interesting portrait of Gould.

Mitchell revealed what he had kept back in the profile—that Gould was a tiresome bore and cadger who attached himself to Mitchell like a leech, and finally forced upon him the realization that the "Oral History" did not exist. After confronting Gould with this knowledge, the famously kindhearted Mitchell regretted having done so:

Man in Profile: Joseph Mitchell of The New Yorker, by Thomas Kunkel

I have always deeply disliked seeing anyone shown up or found out or caught in a lie or caught red-handed doing anything, and now, with time to think things over, I began to feel ashamed of myself for the way I had lost my temper and pounced on Gould.

Mitchell went on to make a generous imaginative leap. "He very likely went around believing in some hazy, self-deceiving, self-protecting way that the Oral History did exist. . . . It might not exactly be down on paper, but he had it all in his head, and any day now he was going to start getting it down."

"It was easy for me to see how this could be," Mitchell continued in a remarkable turn, "for it reminded me of a novel that I had once intended to write." The novel, conceived "under the spell of Joyce's *Ulysses*, . . . was to be 'about' New York City" and to chronicle a day and a night in the life of a young reporter from the South who was no longer a believing Baptist but is "still inclined to see things in religious terms" and whose early exposure to fundamentalist evangelists has

left him with a lasting liking for the cryptic and the ambiguous and the incantatory and the discon-nected and the extravagant and the oracular and the apocalyptic. . . . I had thought about this novel for over a year. Whenever I had nothing else to do, I would automatically start writing it in my mind. . . . But the truth is, I never actually wrote a word of it.

•

In fact, however, Mitchell did write—if not a novel exactly—a book about New York City that fully achieved his young self's large literary ambition. The book is *The Bottom of the Harbor*, published in 1959, a collection of six pieces that are nothing if not cryptic and ambiguous and incantatory and disconnected and extravagant and oracular and apocalyptic. The book was reprinted in the thick anthology of Mitchell's writings, *Up in the Old Hotel*, published in 1992, but it deserves to stand alone. The other books reprinted in the anthology—*McSorley's Wonderful Saloon*, *Mr. Old Flood*, and *Joe Gould's Secret*— are wonderful, but they are to *The Bottom of the Harbor* what *Tom Sawyer* and *A Connecticut Yankee in King Arthur's Court* are to *Huckleberry Finn*.

The opening piece, "Up in the Old Hotel" (from which the later anthology took its name), tells a minimal, almost nonexistent story. Mitchell goes for breakfast to Sloppy Louie's, a seafood restaurant in a decrepit old building on South Street in the Fulton Fish Market, and converses with its owner, Louis Morino, "a contemplative and generous and worldly-wise man in his middle sixties," a widower and father of two daughters, who immigrated to New York from a fishing village in Italy in 1905 at the age of seventeen, and worked as a waiter in restaurants in Manhattan and Brooklyn until 1930 when he bought his own restaurant.

Almost imperceptibly, Mitchell turns over the narration of the story to Louie, as he calls Morino, sliding into the long monologue that was once a commonplace of *New Yorker* nonfiction, and is a signature of Mitchell's mature work. Occasionally Mitchell breaks in to speak in his own voice, which is slightly different from Louie's, but in the same register, giving the effect of arias sung by alternating soloists in an oratorio.

Louie dilates on a change that has taken place in the clientele of his restaurant, which used to consist solely of fishmongers and fish buyers. Now, people from the financial district, the insurance district, and the coffee-roasting district are coming in at lunchtime, and on some days the lunch crowd is so great that latecomers have to wait for tables. "This gets on his nerves," Mitchell says of the too-successful restaurateur, who has reluctantly decided to put tables on the second floor to accommodate the overflow. His reluctance comes from the fact that his building, like the other South Street buildings that stand on filled-in river swamp, has no cellar, and he has to use the second floor to store supplies and equipment and as a changing room for his waiters. "I don't know what I'll do without it, only I got to make room someway," Louie says. "That ought to be easy," Mitchell says. "You've got four empty floors up above."

But it isn't easy. To get to the empty floors, whose windows are boarded up, it is necessary to enter a monstrous, uninspected elevator that has to be pulled up by hand, like a dumbwaiter. This is the pivot on which the story's slender plot turns. During all the twenty-two years he has rented the building, Louie has never dared to enter the elevator. Each time he has peered into it he has felt a primal dread:

> I just don't want to get in that cage by myself. I got a feeling about it, and that's the fact of the matter. It makes me uneasy—all closed in, and all that furry dust. It makes me think of a coffin, the

inside of a coffin. Either that or a cave, the mouth of a cave. If I could get somebody to go along with me, somebody to talk to, just so I wouldn't be all alone in there, I'd go.

"Louie suddenly leaned forward. 'What about you?' he asked. 'Maybe I could persuade you.'"

Mitchell agrees, but before the trip takes place, Louie launches into another aria in which he explains why he has remained in a building he was never keen on and always intended to move from. "It really doesn't make much sense. It's all mixed up with the name of a street in Brooklyn." The street was Schermerhorn Street near a restaurant Louie waited tables at, Joe's on Nevins Street, one of the great Brooklyn chophouses, where political bosses ate alongside rich old women of good family of whom Louie says: "They all had some peculiarity, and they all had one foot in the grave, and they all had big appetites." One of these trencherwomen was a widow named Mrs. Frelinghuysen: "She was very old and tiny and delicate, and she ate like a horse. . . . Everybody liked her, the way she hung on to life." She liked Louie in turn, and if his tables were filled would defer her meal until he was free to wait on her. While she ate, he observed her closely:

She'd always start off with one dozen oysters in winter or one dozen clams in summer, and she'd gobble them down and go on from there. She could get more out of a lobster than anybody I ever saw. You'd think she'd got everything she possibly could, and then she'd pull the little legs off that most people don't even bother with, and suck the juice out of them.

During his afternoon break, Louie's recitative continues, he would go over to Schermerhorn Street, a quiet back street, and sit on a bench under a tree and eat fruit he had bought at a nearby fancy-fruit store. One afternoon, it occurs to him to wonder, "Who the hell was Schermerhorn?" So that night at the restaurant he asks Mrs. Frelinghuysen and she tells him that the Schermerhorns are one of the oldest and best Dutch families in New York, and that she had known many of the descendants of the original seventeenth-century settler Jacob Schermerhorn, among them a girl who had died young and whose grave in Trinity Church cemetery in Washington Heights she had visited and "put some jonquils on."

Where the hell is this going? As in all of Mitchell's pieces everything is always going somewhere, though not necessarily so you'd notice. Mitchell is one of the great masters of the device of the plot twist disguised as a digression that seems pointless but that heightens the effect of unforced realism. Louie tells Mitchell of an incident that occurred a few years after he left Joe's. Mrs. Frelinghuysen had died and Louie had married and bought his restaurant and rented the building it was in. One afternoon a long black limousine pulled up in front of the building and a uniformed chauffeur came into the restaurant and said, "Mrs. Schermerhorn wanted to speak to me, and I looked at him and said, 'What do you mean—Mrs. Schermerhorn?' And he said, 'Mrs. Schermerhorn that owns this building.'" Louie is stunned to hear this. He had assumed the real estate company he paid his rent to was the owner. But no, the beautiful woman who gets out of the limousine, the recently widowed Mrs. Arthur F. Schermerhorn, owns the building. Louie asks her if she knows anything about its history, but she doesn't—she is just inspecting the properties she has inherited from her husband. She drives off and he never sees her again.

> I went back inside and stood there and thought it over, and the effect it had on me, the simple fact my building was an old Schermerhorn building, it may sound foolish, but it pleased me very much. The feeling I had, it connected me with the past. It connected me with Old New York.

Louie pursues city records and after many years and many dead ends learns that his building and the identical one next door had been put up in the 1870s by a descendant of Jacob Schermerhorn and combined to form a hotel called the Fulton Ferry Hotel after the ferry to Brooklyn that stood in front of it. From the mid- to late 1800s the hotel flourished. The ferry passengers crowded its saloon, and out-of-town passengers from the steamships docked in the East River along South Street filled its rooms.

But then one of those disasters occurred by which the life of the city is punctuated and defined, the disaster of change. The Brooklyn Bridge went up, followed by the Manhattan and Williamsburg Bridges, which ended the ferry traffic that gave the saloon its trade; then "the worst blow of all," the passenger lines left South Street for docks on the Hudson and the hotel declined into "one of those waterfront hotels that rummies hole up in, and old men on pensions, and old nuts, and sailors on the beach." What remained finally were two buildings with boarded-up top floors, one of them occupied by Sloppy Louie's and the other by a saloon no longer in business. Louie concludes his monologue: "Those are the bare bones of the matter. If I could get upstairs just once in that damned old elevator and scratch around in those hotel registers up there and whatever to hell else is stored up there, it might be possible I'd find out a whole lot more."

As Mitchell and Louie, wearing helmets and carrying flashlights, pull the rope and heave the ancient elevator up to the third floor, the story's lyrical music gives way to harsh new sounds. Louie is no longer the contemplative and generous and worldly-wise man of the monologues. He has become angry and almost hysterically agitated. In the pitch-dark, dust-laden room the elevator opens onto that had been the hotel's reading room and is now stacked with hotel furniture, Louie yanks (Mitchell's word) drawers out of a rolltop desk. "God damn it! I thought I'd find those hotel registers in here. There's nothing in here, only rusty paper clips." A mirror-topped bureau yields only a stray hairpin and comb and medicine bottle. Louie opens the medicine bottle and smells the colorless liquid in it and says disgustedly, "It's gone dead. . . . It doesn't smell like anything at all."

The men move on to the hotel bedrooms at the rear of the floor, all empty except for one with an iron bedstead and a placard tacked to the wall saying "The Wages of Sin is Death; but the Gift of God is Eternal Life through Jesus Christ our Lord." Louie has had enough and heads back toward the elevator. Mitchell wants to go up to the other floors but Louie says no. "There's nothing up there." In the elevator, Louie

was leaning against the side of the cage, and his shoulders were slumped and his eyes were tired. "I didn't learn much I didn't know before," he said.

"You learned that the wages of sin is death," I said, trying to say something cheerful.

Louie is not amused. The third floor and the place where there is nothing to look at or read or smell, toward which we are all headed, have evidently become fused in his imagination. He is desperate to get back down to the restaurant. "Come on, pull the rope faster! Pull it faster! Let's get out of this." Mitchell has circled back to his opening sentence: "Every now and then, seeking to rid my mind of thoughts of death and doom, I get up early and go down to Fulton Fish Market." The stands heaped with forty to sixty varieties of gleaming fish, "the smoky riverbank dawn, the racket the fish-mongers make, the seaweedy smell, and the sight of this plentifulness" give Mitchell a feeling of well-being, even of elation. But they hardly rid him of his existential anguish.

Mitchell often said that his favorite book was *Ulysses*, but it is another book—Ecclesiastes—that hovers over the pages of *The Bottom of the Harbor*. Like the preacher/narrator of Ecclesiastes, Mitchell is all over the place. He is at once an absurdist and a moralist and a hedonist. All is vanity, there is nothing new under the sun, eat, drink, and be merry. The rhetorical slyness of verse 9:10— "Whatsoever thy hand findeth to do, do it with thy might; for there is no work, nor device, nor knowledge, nor wisdom, in the grave, whither thou goest"—is almost uncannily consonant with the legerdemain Mitchell himself performs in *The Bottom of the Harbor*, as he celebrates, and describes in the most minute and interesting detail, the excellence of the work done by his subjects—a series of men connected in one way or another to the New York waterfront—while helplessly murmuring about the probable pointlessness of it all.

"The Rivermen," the final and arguably strongest piece in the volume, is its most explicit memento mori. It is set in Edgewater, New Jersey, a small town on the Hudson across from the Upper West Side of Manhattan, first settled in the seventeenth century by Dutch and Huguenot farmers. By the time of Mitchell's visit in 1950, most of the farms are gone, replaced by factories, which are themselves declining. A ferry between Edgewater and Manhattan had just been discontinued; like the Fulton Ferry it fell victim to its natural enemy the bridge, in this case the George Washington.

As he was with Louis Morino, Mitchell is a little in love with Harry Lyons, a retired fireman who fishes for shad in the polluted waters of the Hudson during the season of their upriver journey to spawn. "He has an old Roman face," Mitchell writes. "It is strong-jawed and prominent-nosed and bushy-eyebrowed and friendly and reasonable and sagacious and elusively piratical." As if this wasn't enough, when Mitchell runs into Lyons on his way to (what else?) a funeral in his Sunday best, "I was surprised at how distinguished he looked; he looked worldly and cultivated and illustrious."

An ignorant visitor to Lyons's barge becomes the audience for an exquisitely detailed lecture on the art of shad fishing in the Hudson. And once again Mitchell doesn't do the telling himself, but allows his central character to hold forth in a monologue that goes on for many pages. But this time it isn't the main but a secondary character who delivers Mitchell's message of death and doom. He is Joseph Hewitt, a man in his seventies, a former bookkeeper at the Fulton Fish Market, who has made money from real estate since his retirement, and shouldn't be complaining, but can't tear himself away from the handwriting on the wall:

> "Things have worked out very well for you, Joe,"
> I once heard another retired man remark to him
> one day . . . "and you ought to look at things a
> little more cheerful than you do." "I'm not so sure
> I have anything to be cheerful about," Mr. Hewitt
> replied. "I'm not so sure you have, either. I'm not
> so sure anybody has."

At the beginning of "Mr. Hunter's Grave," the best known of the pieces in *The Bottom of the Harbor*, Mitchell strolls through a cemetery on Staten Island and examines his feelings. "Invariably, for some reason I don't know and don't want to know, after I have spent an hour or so in one of these cemeteries, looking at gravestone designs and reading inscriptions and identifying wild flowers and scaring rabbits out of the weeds and reflecting on the end that awaits me and awaits us all, my spirits lift, I become quite cheerful. . . ."

Mitchell isn't the only one to find a visit to a graveyard a cheering rather than depressing experience. These places produce a kind of homeopathic effect on the visitor. They make him feel better by giving him a whiff—real or imagined—of the worst. The interconnectedness of what we have to feel cheerful about and what we don't is Mitchell's great subject. The image of old Mrs. Frelinghuysen sucking the juice out of lobster legs can hardly be surpassed as an emblem of the defiant life-force.

In "The Rivermen" Mitchell offers the quieter but no less powerful image of old men who have gathered on the banks of the river to see Harry Lyons bring in his catch and to accept from him the eucharistic gift of a roe shad that they wrap in newspapers and carry home in neatly folded paper bags. In the passage in "Joe Gould's Secret" about his own unwritten book, Mitchell quotes an old black street preacher that his young hero meets in Harlem:

> Like the Baptist preachers the young reporter had listened to and struggled to understand in his childhood, the old man sees meaning behind meanings, or thinks he does, and tries his best to tell what things "stand for." "Pomegranates are about the size and shape of large oranges or small grapefruits, only their skins are red," he says. . . . "They're filled . . . with juice as red as blood. When they get ripe, they're so swollen with those juicy red seeds that they gap open and some of the seeds spill out. And now I'll tell you what pomegranates stand for. They stand for the resurrection. . . . All seeds stand for resurrection and all eggs stand for resurrection. The Easter egg stands for resurrection. So do the eggs in the English sparrow's nest up under the eaves in the 'L' station. So does

the egg you have for breakfast. So does the caviar the rich people eat. So does shad roe."

Images that "stand for something" recur throughout Mitchell's writing and reinforce the sense that we are reading a single metaphoric work about the city. That the author was a southerner only heightens its authority. As Robert Frank's European sensibility permitted him to see things as he traveled around America that had been invisible to the rest of us, so Mitchell's outsiderness gave him his own X-ray vision.

Thomas Kunkel's biography adds some telling details to what Mitchell's readers already know about his childhood as the eldest son of a prosperous cotton and tobacco grower in North Carolina.* Perhaps the most striking of these is Mitchell's trouble with arithmetic—he couldn't add, subtract, or multiply to save his soul—to which handicap we may owe the fact that he became a writer rather than a farmer. As Mitchell recalled late in life:

> You know you have to be extremely good at arithmetic. You have to be able to figure, as my father said, to deal with cotton futures, and to buy cotton. You're in competition with a group of men who will cut your throat at any moment, if they can see the value of a bale of cotton closer than you. I couldn't do it, so I had to leave.

*See the posthumous "Days in the Branch," *The New Yorker*, December 1, 2014, part of an unfinished memoir.

Mitchell studied at the University of North Carolina without graduating and came to New York in 1929, at the age of twenty-one. Kunkel traces the young exile's rapid rise from copy boy on the *New York World* to reporter on the *Herald Tribune* and feature writer on *The World Telegram*. In 1933 St. Clair McKelway, the managing editor of the eight-year-old *New Yorker*, noticed Mitchell's newspaper work and invited him to write for the magazine; in 1938 the editor, Harold Ross, hired him. In 1931 Mitchell married a lovely woman of Scandinavian background named Therese Jacobson, a fellow reporter, who left journalism to become a fine though largely unknown portrait and street photographer. She and Mitchell lived in a small apartment in Greenwich Village and raised two daughters, Nora and Elizabeth. Kunkel's biography is sympathetic and admiring and discreet. If any of the erotic secrets that frequently turn up in the nets of biographers turned up in Kunkel's, he does not reveal them. He has other fish to gut.

From reporting notes, journals, and correspondence, and from three interviews Mitchell gave late in life to a professor of journalism named Norman Sims, Kunkel extracts a picture of Mitchell's journalistic practice that he doesn't know quite what to do with. On the one hand, he doesn't regard it as a pretty picture; he uses terms like "license," "latitude," "dubious technique," "tactics," and "bent journalistic rules" to describe it. On the other, he reveres Mitchell's writing, and doesn't want to say anything critical of it even while he is saying it. So a kind of weird embarrassed atmosphere hangs over the passages in which Kunkel reveals Mitchell's radical departures from factuality.

It is already known that the central character of the

book *Old Mr. Flood*, a ninety-three-year-old man named Hugh G. Flood, who intended to live to the age of 115 by eating only fish and shellfish, did not exist, but was a "composite," i.e., an invention. Mitchell was forced to characterize him as such after readers of the *New Yorker* pieces from which the book was derived tried to find the man. "Mr. Flood is not one man," Mitchell wrote in an author's note to the book, and went on, "Combined in him are aspects of several old men who work or hang out in Fulton Fish Market, or who did in the past." In the *Up in the Old Hotel* collection he simply reclassified the work as fiction.

Now Kunkel reveals that another Mitchell character—a gypsy king named Cockeye Johnny Nikanov, the subject of a *New Yorker* profile published in 1942—was also an invention. How Kunkel found this out is rather funny. He came upon a letter that Mitchell wrote in 1961 to *The New Yorker*'s lawyer, Milton Greenstein, asking Greenstein for legal advice on how to stop a writer named Sidney Sheldon from producing a musical about gypsy life based on Mitchell's profile of Nikanov and a subsequent piece about the scams of gypsy women. Mitchell was himself working on a musical adaptation of his gypsy pieces—it eventually became the show *Bajour*, named after one of the gypsy women's cruelest scams, that came to Broadway in 1964 and ran for around six months—and was worried about Sheldon's competing script.

"Cockeye Johnny Nikanov does not exist in real life, and never did," Mitchell told Greenstein. Therefore "no matter how true to life Cockeye Johnny happens to be, he is a fictional character, and I invented him, and he is not in 'the public domain,' he is mine." Mitchell's Gilbertian logic evidently prevailed—Sheldon gave up his musical. But the secret of Johnny Nikanov's wobbly ontological status—though Greenstein kept quiet about it—had passed out of Mitchell's possession. It now belonged to tattling posterity, the biographer's best friend.

What Kunkel found in Mitchell's reporting notes for his famous piece "Mr. Hunter's Grave" made him even more nervous. It now appears that that great work of nonfiction is also in some part a work of fiction. The piece opens with an encounter in the St. Luke's cemetery on Staten Island between Mitchell and a minister named Raymond E. Brock, who tells him about a remarkable black man named Mr. Hunter, and sets in motion the events that bring Mitchell to Hunter's house a week later. But the notes show that the encounter in the cemetery never took place. In actuality, it was a man sitting on his front porch named James McCoy (who never appears in the piece) who told Mitchell about Mr. Hunter years before Mitchell met him; and when Mitchell did meet Hunter it was in a church and not at his house.

This and other instances in the reporting notes about Mitchell's tamperings with actuality cause Kunkel to ask: "Should the reputation of 'Mr. Hunter's Grave' suffer for the license Mitchell employed in telling it?" He adds primly: "As with any aspect of art, that is up to the appraiser."

The obvious answer to Kunkel's question—the one that most journalists, editors, and professors of journalism would give—is yes, of course, the reputation of "Mr. Hunter's Grave" should suffer now that we know that

Mitchell cheated. He has betrayed the reader's trust that what he is reading is what actually happened. He has mixed up nonfiction with fiction. He has made an unwholesome, almost toxic brew out of the two genres. It is too bad he is dead and can't be pilloried. Or perhaps it is all right that he is dead, because he is suffering the torments of hell for his sins against the spirit of fact. And so on.

As a former journalist and professor of journalism (he is now president of St. Norbert College in De Pere, Wisconsin), Kunkel might be expected to share these dire views; but as Mitchell's biographer, he can't bring himself to express them. He clearly disapproves of Mitchell's "tactics," but he venerates Mitchell and hates to show him up as Mitchell hated showing up Joe Gould. His own tactic is to invoke the pieties of journalism. "Of course, today's *New Yorker*, or any mainstream publication, would never knowingly permit such liberties with quotation; they would take a dimmer-yet view of composites being billed as 'non-fiction.'" And: "The dubious technique would not really disappear from the print media's bag of tricks until the general elevation of journalistic standards several decades later."

Kunkel magnanimously excuses Mitchell and other of the early *New Yorker* writers for their subprime practices because they didn't know any better. Of course, Mitchell and his *New Yorker* colleagues such as A. J. Liebling knew very well what they were doing. On October 14, 1988, Mitchell told Norman Sims:

My desire is to get the reader, well, first of all to read it. That story ["The Bottom of the Harbor"] was hard to write because I had to wonder how long can I keep developing it before the reader's going to get tired of this. Here and there, as I think a fiction writer would, I put things that I know— even the remark the tugboat men make, that you could bottle this water and sell it for poison— that are going to keep the reader going. I can lure him or her into the story I want to tell. I can't tell the story I want to tell until I've got you into the pasture and down where the sheep are. Where the shepherd is. He's going to tell the story, but I've got to get you past the ditch and through these bushes.

Every writer of nonfiction who has struggled with the ditch and the bushes knows what Mitchell is talking about, but few of us have gone as far as Mitchell in bending actuality to our artistic will. This is not because we are more virtuous than Mitchell. It is because we are less gifted than Mitchell. The idea that reporters are constantly resisting the temptation to invent is a laughable one. Reporters don't invent because they don't know how to. This is why they are journalists rather than novelists or short-story writers. They depend on the kindness of the strangers they actually meet for the characters in their stories. There are no fictional characters lurking in their imaginations. They couldn't create a character like Mr. Flood or Cockeye Johnny if you held a gun to their heads. Mitchell's travels across the line that separates fiction and nonfiction are his singular feat. His impatience with the annoying, boring bits of actuality, his slashings through the underbrush of unreadable facticity, give his pieces their electric force, are why they're so much more exciting to read than the work of other nonfiction writers of ambition.

In the title piece of *The Bottom of the Harbor*, a short work of great subtlety about the ability of fish and shellfish to survive in polluted water, Mitchell mentions a small area of the New York waterfront where, in contrast to the general foulness, "clean, sparkling, steel-blue water" can be found. This image of purity in the midst of contamination could serve as an emblem of Mitchell's journalistic exceptionalism. He has filtered out the impurities other journalists helplessly accept as the defining condition of their genre. Mitchell's genre is some kind of hybrid, as yet to be named.

Kunkel pauses to shake his head about "a strain of perfectionism" in Mitchell, "an obsession for his writing to be just so." "Mitchell would patiently cast and recast sentences, sometimes dozens of times, changing just a word or two with each iteration until an entire paragraph came together and seemed right," Kunkel wonderingly writes, and adds, "All this fussing was exceedingly time-consuming, even for a magazine writer." Kunkel's naïveté about writing is evident, but his picture of Mitchell at work only confirms and amplifies our sense of his artistry.

Much has been made of the fact that after "Joe Gould's Secret" Mitchell published nothing in *The New Yorker*, though he came to the office regularly, and colleagues passing his door could hear him typing. I was a colleague and friend, and I always assumed that the reason he wasn't publishing was because he wasn't satisfied with what he was writing: he had been producing work of increasing beauty and profundity, and now the standard he had set for himself was too high. Mitchell spoke of James Joyce,

Mark Twain, Herman Melville, Ivan Turgenev, D. H. Lawrence, and T. S. Eliot as writers he read and reread. This was the company he was in behind his closed door. We should respect his inhibiting reverence for literary transcendence and be grateful for the work that got past his censor.

The New York Review of Books, 2015

WOMEN AT WAR:
A CASE OF SEXUAL HARASSMENT

The First Stone, by Helen Garner, is a work of personal journalism that can be likened to a novel with an unreliable narrator. It is the story of the author's thwarted attempt to write a "quiet, thoughtful account" of a case of sexual harassment in Melbourne, Australia, and of the remarkable, almost vertiginously turbulent narrative she was forced by her frustration to produce instead. Two young women have filed complaints of indecent assault against the Master of Ormond College, a residential college of Melbourne University, where they are students. One woman, pseudonymously named Nicole Stewart, says that, six months earlier, the Master, while dancing with her at a student party, put his hand on her left breast; and the second, pseudonymously named Elizabeth Rosen, says that during the same party he made indecent suggestions to her in his locked office (and felt her up as well).

When Helen Garner, who is an Australian novelist, screenwriter, and journalist, reads about the first woman's complaint in the newspaper (she reads about the second

The First Stone: Some Questions About Sex and Power, by Helen Garner

woman's complaint a few weeks later), she is stunned. Garner came of age in the early years of the women's movement and is possessed of a finely tuned feminist consciousness. But this case seems to her a very betrayal of feminism and its claims to good faith. Has the world come to this? she thinks. He touched her breast and she went to the *cops*? Impulsively, she dashes off a letter to the accused, a middle-aged man she calls Colin Shepherd:

> Dear Dr. Shepherd,
>   I read in today's paper about your troubles and I'm writing to say how upset I am and how terribly sorry about what has happened to you. I don't know you, or the young woman; I've heard no rumours and I have no line to run. What I want to say is that it's heartbreaking, for a feminist of nearly fifty like me, to see our ideals of so many years distorted into this ghastly punitiveness. I expect I will never know what 'really happened', but I certainly know that if there was an incident, as alleged, this has been the most appallingly destructive, priggish and pitiless way of dealing with it. I want you to know that there are plenty of women out here who step back in dismay from the kind of treatment you have received, and who still hope that men and women, for all our foolishness and mistakes, can behave towards one another with kindness rather than being engaged in this kind of warfare.

The sending of this letter is the act that fuels the book's plot—it is the mistake whose consequences we watch the author helplessly struggle to undo for two hundred pages. After Shepherd is acquitted in court of both women's charges (for lack of proof) but is predictably ejected from the university, to which he is no longer of use as a "good father" figure, Garner decides to write about the case and "its wider meanings." Although sympathetic to Shepherd, she is hardly convinced of his innocence. She has lived in the world long enough to know that men are beasts and that the probability is strong that Shepherd forgot himself at the party. She happily sets about her journalist's task of interviewing both sides, getting each antagonist's version of what happened, and then writing her "truthful, calm, and balanced" account. But it is too late: she has shot herself in the foot with her letter to Shepherd. She did what a journalist must never do—she showed her hand too early—and Nicole Stewart and Elizabeth Rosen, who have read the letter (Shepherd couldn't resist circulating it), naturally refuse to speak to her. Garner's increasingly desperate and hysterical efforts to interview the young women are the action of the book.

As Garner pursues the young women, we see that more is at stake than the fate of a piece of journalism, that something beyond journalistic zeal impels her, and that her dilemma as a reporter reflects dilemmas of more fundamental kinds. In her attempt to shatter the Cordelia-like silence of Nicole Stewart and Elizabeth Rosen, Garner seeks out their young feminist supporters, abjectly pleading with them to intervene for her; but she is met at every turn with coldness and condescension. During a particularly humiliating interview with one of these chilly interlocutresses, an officer of the university Student Union,

Garner begins to twig to the "wider meaning" of her quest:

> Her seat was slightly higher than mine; she was looking down at me, and the light from the high north-facing window behind her was so strong that I had to keep blinking and turning away to rest my eyes. I felt terrifically at a disadvantage, as if I were importuning her. In fact, this sense of being out of date, irrelevant, reminded me painfully of certain days when I have visited my daughter and she had gone about her business in the house as if I weren't there. So this is about middle-aged mothers and daughters then.

Garner goes to a feminist of her own age for comfort:

> I related to my friend my pathetic bravado in the presence of the fierce young Women's officer from the Student Union. "I practically pleaded for her respect," I said. "I talked about abortion law reform, demos and police and so on—I said, 'We put our bodies on the line'—but she just looked at me coldly—she didn't give a shit about our *magnificent heroism.*"
>
> We sat at the table howling with laughter. "It's a dialogue between generations," said Angela Z—, wiping away her tears.
>
> "It's not a dialogue," I said, blowing my nose. "It's a fucking *war.*"

•

The war between the generations is a peculiar war, un-like a war between nations. One of the sides—the older generation—is in love with as well as threatened by the other. The old try to warm themselves at the fire of the young. *King Lear* is about (among all the other things it is about) a man trying to escape death through inces-tuous sex. A middle-aged teacher sexually harassing a student is an actor trying to remain in a play where he has no lines. What makes *The First Stone* such an ex-traordinary book, a book unlike any other study of sex-ual harassment, is Garner's enactment—in her obsessive pursuit of Nicole Stewart and Elizabeth Rosen—of the very misdemeanor she has set out to investigate. Al-though her purported goal is "balance," it is as a very unbalanced person that she represents herself. "I wanted to find Elizabeth Rosen and Nicole Stewart and *shake them until their teeth rattled*," she writes upon receiving another rebuff from the young women. "I gnashed my teeth so hard I saw stars," she writes on hearing they have agreed to give interviews to a writer from *Vogue*. "*Vogue!*" These are not the reactions of a seasoned jour-nalist but the ravings of a rejected lover. "I felt so much sympathy for the man in this story and so little for the women," Garner had wonderingly written at the begin-ning of her account, worrying that "my feminism and my ethics were speeding towards a head-on smash." Now she is in the grip of something to which feminist theory and ethical belief are irrelevant, and which has degraded the original object of her interest to the status of worthless money. Garner's interview with the ruined Master is a perfunctory affair. She listens to his denials politely but indifferently. Only the interviews she can't get excite her.

In the end, Garner all but "knows" that Shepherd did it, not because she has discovered any evidence of his guilt but because of her experience as a woman. If she cannot wrest the young women's version of what happened from them, she will supply an equivalent from the store of her own memories of being importuned. She recalls an incident from her youth: she was sitting in an empty train compartment, contentedly reading, when a loutish middle-aged man, who had been drinking, came in and engaged her in an unwelcome and tedious conversation, from which she felt helpless to extricate herself, and then asked her for a kiss, which she helplessly gave him. Garner meditates on the "strange passivity" that overcomes women in these situations:

> What was my state, that allowed me to accept his unattractive advances without protest? I was just *putting up with him.* I felt myself to be luckier, cleverer, younger than he was. I felt sorry for him. I went on putting up with him long past the point at which I should have told him to back off. *Should have?* What *should* is this? What I mean is *would have liked to. Wanted to but lacked the ... the ...* Lacked the what?

Another shaming memory—this one of more recent vintage, involving a male masseur who kissed the back of her neck and then her mouth while she lay near-naked on the massage table, and whose importunities she once again accepted without protest (she even paid for the massage!)—gives her further empathetic understanding of Nicole and Elizabeth's behavior: of why they had accepted the Master's unattractive advances without remonstrance, and only much later lodged their complaints against him. She writes:

> What woman would not feel a shot of rage at the QC's question to Nicole Stewart: "Why didn't you slap 'im?"
>
> We all know why.
>
> Because, as Nicole's friend said angrily in court, all we want to do when a man makes a sleazy, cloddish pass is "to be polite and get away."

But Garner cannot sustain her feminist's rage. In spite of "these sharp flashes of empathy with the girls . . . something in me, every time, slams on the brakes. . . . I invent and discard a dozen fantasies of less destructive responses to such an incident. . . . I see myself marching into some man's office and saying, 'I don't know what you tried on my daughter. This time I'm prepared to let it pass. But I'm warning you—if anything like this ever happens again, you can expect big trouble.'" Garner's fantasy of the "less destructive response" gives her away, of course. "This time I'm prepared to let it pass." This isn't good enough. This is closing ranks with the abuser. This is paying for the massage. Sexual harassment isn't sexual abuse— exactly. It lies on the border between a crime and a mistake. It is a minor offense with major associations. Garner's oscillating identifications with harasser and harassed, her lurchings between generations and genders, her alternating states of delusion and perception invite comparison with the coded messages of patients in psychotherapy. In the unconscious we are children and parents, old and young, victim and aggressor, gay and straight all at once.

In an afterword [to the later American edition of *The First Stone*] Garner unnecessarily defends her book against the criticism it has received from feminists in Australia. It no more needs defending than our dreams do, with which there is no arguing, and which are always true.

The New Yorker, 1997

IT HAPPENED IN MILWAUKEE

Halfway through this remarkable and peculiar book, the feminist academic Jane Gallop tells a story about two dazzlingly brilliant male professors who were on her dissertation committee when she was in graduate school in the mid-seventies, and whom "I did my utmost to seduce." The men were reluctant at first: "Both of them turned me down, more than once." However, "over the years, I did what I could to sway them. Trying not to be too obnoxious, I watched for opportunities that might present themselves, prepared to take advantage and press my suit." Finally, both men bowed to the fate better than a poke in the eye with a sharp stick. "I had sex but once with each of them," Gallop reports. "Neither of these became a 'relationship.' It was just what is called 'casual sex.'" She adds, "To be honest, I think I wanted to get them into bed in order to make them more human, more vulnerable. . . . I was bowled over by their brilliance; they seemed so superior. I wanted to see them naked, to see them as like other men." And, most important of all,

---

Feminist Accused of Sexual Harassment, by Jane Gallop

Screwing these guys definitely did not keep me from taking myself seriously as a student. In fact, it seemed to make it easier for me to write. Seducing them made me feel kind of cocky and that allowed me to presume I had something to say worth saying.

The occasion for this reminiscence—and for the writing of *Feminist Accused of Sexual Harassment* itself—was a scandal at the University of Wisconsin at Milwaukee in 1992. Two women graduate students filed charges of sexual harassment against Gallop, claiming that she had tried to seduce them and, when she failed to do so, had retaliated by harshly criticizing the work of one and refusing to write letters of recommendation for the other. Gallop denied the charges and was eventually cleared of them. After a long investigation, the university found no evidence that Gallop had attempted to get the students into bed with her or that she had dealt with their work unfairly. But in the case of one of the women the university found Gallop guilty of violating a rule forbidding "consensual amorous relations" between professors and students and put a black mark on her record.

Gallop, as may be gathered from her encounter with the two professors, is not one to meekly accept defeat. As she wore down the professors' resistance, she gamely goes to work on the reader to whom the merits of her idea of pedagogy as a sort of sixties love-in may not be immediately apparent. "I sexualize the atmosphere in which I work," Gallop writes with the matter-of-factness with which another teacher might speak of charts and slides. Further, she calmly tells us, she habitually forms intense, sexy, even sexual relationships with certain of her students. Her extracurricular activities with students have ranged from shopping for clothes to going to bed. Although she actually stopped sleeping with students in 1982, when, rather inconveniently, she fell "madly in love with the man I'm still happily with today," she has continued to be available to favorite students for kissing, fondling, and talking dirty. This is her teaching style. When we put down her book (such is its dogged seductiveness), we are almost persuaded that any other style is unthinkably stuffy.

Gallop was named Distinguished Professor of English and Comparative Literature at Wisconsin in 1992 and is one of the ornaments of the poststructuralist school. Her writings on Freud, Lacan, Sade, Barthes, and French feminist theory are famously witty; she has taken the technique of close reading to hitherto untried extremes of playfulness. Here is an example of her wit, which appears in a paper called "The Student Body," first published in 1982 in *Yale French Studies* and later reprinted in a book called *Thinking Through the Body*:

> One of Sade's contributions to pedagogical technique may be the institution, alongside the traditional oral examination, of an anal examination. The Sadian libertines have a technical term for such an examination; they use the verb *socratiser* (to socratize), meaning to stick a finger up the anus. This association between the great philosopher/ teacher and this form of anal penetration recalls the Greek link between pedagogy and pederasty. . . .
>   Pederasty is undoubtedly a useful paradigm for

classic European pedagogy. A greater man pene-
trates a lesser man with his knowledge.

The passage touches on one of Gallop's dominant
preoccupations—relations between "greater" and "lesser"
figures—an interest that has led to some of her most arresting strokes. In an essay on Freud's Dora case, called
"Keys to Dora" (it appears in her book *The Daughter's Seduction*), she compares the relationship of Freud and Dora
(and by extension of every analyst and patient) to the relationship between a servant and a master—Freud being
the servant and Dora the master. (Her starting point is the
passage in Freud's text where Dora says she is quitting the
analysis and Freud asks her when she had decided to do so.
"A fortnight ago," she replies. Freud remarks, "That sounds
just like a maidservant or a governess—a fortnight's warning." The remark has traditionally been read to mean that
a servant is giving notice; Gallop opts—plausibly, when
you think of it—for the reading that it is the employer giving the employee two weeks' notice of dismissal.) In *Feminist Accused of Sexual Harassment* Gallop offers the equally
novel view of professor/student sex as a transaction that
reduces rather than increases the power of the putative
"greater man." We have seen the student Gallop reduce her
intimidatingly brilliant professors to a couple of contempt-
ibly naked guys; and we see the obverse as well: the professor Gallop so reduced. She writes of her seduction early in
her teaching career by a student named Micki, who came
to her lecture afterward, "bursting with the sense of
having possessed me but a few hours earlier," and looking
"like the proverbial cat who'd eaten the canary"; and of
her fling with a student named Scott, a sort of volunteer

worker, who kindly offered to sleep with her when her boy-friend (another student) left her, and paid a house call on her birthday because "in view of the occasion, he wanted to make sure I got laid." With the lightheartedness—you could almost say the dippiness—of these anecdotes Gallop underscores the heaviness and unpleasantness of the nar-rative of the two graduate students for whom it wasn't enough to see their brilliant teacher naked (so to speak), but who needed to see her pilloried as well.

In the light story of the two professors and the heavy story of the two graduate students we may read the sad pass things have come to during the two decades that separate them. In one respect, however, the polarity isn't quite as neat as it should be. Where Gallop could keep the professors indistinguishable from each other (like a brace of game), she is obliged to differentiate between the two graduate students: the charges of one of the women were so insubstantial that her case was quickly dismissed. So it is actually only one graduate student who figures in the heavy story. This glitch, like that of the inconvenient lasting love, points up the schematic, unreal character of the text. This is hardly a work of confessional autobiography; in its taut stylization it more resembles a work of pornography (though the content is PG-rated). Gallop has represented herself not as a real person but as the precision instrument of an argument. She reveals noth-ing about herself that doesn't serve her polemic. She gets laid or flirts or engages in "sexual banter" because this is the job her character has been assigned to do to propel the book's argument along. This functionalism gives the character its interesting and curious chasteness. We are never embarrassed by Gallop. We are sometimes aston-ished by her, and we sometimes find her absurd, but she never makes us cringe, because she never invades her own privacy. Her subjects are sex and pedagogy, and every story about herself is a single-minded fable constructed to demonstrate the essential connection between the two.

Gallop's opening story is like the introduction of an opera's leitmotif. She writes about herself as a freshman in college in 1970 sunk into a typical freshman's malaise: she was uninterested in her work, cut classes, watched late-night TV, and got poor grades. Her love life was just as impoverished: "As a good soldier in the sexual revolution, I had sex often, but with little pleasure and no orgasms. Although I fervently wished that all these young men I bedded would fall in love with me, all my wishing and hoping wasn't really desire." All this changed in Gallop's sophomore year, when she came under the influence of feminism. She learned to masturbate (Simone de Beauvoir's *The Second Sex* introduced her to the sport) and to experience desire for women:

> I had the hots for so many of the energetic young women who went to the same meetings as I. While I actually slept with very few of them, these attractions introduced me to the feel of desire. Whereas my adolescent boy-craziness had filled me with romantic fantasies of love, when I thought about the women at the meetings I burned to touch their bodies. I walked around that year constantly in heat. . . .

She simultaneously became a good student: "One and the same change made me both an engaged, productive student and a sexually energized, confident woman." Gallop writes of an unforgettable women-only dance, which a group of men tried unsuccessfully to crash; the women threw their bodies against the door and repelled the invaders, and to celebrate their triumph flung off their shirts and danced bare-breasted. The breasts of a woman named Becca—"the most beautiful breasts I had ever seen"—linger in Gallop's memory.

But more memorable yet was the spectacular arrival of a famous feminist professor with a beautiful senior on her arm: "The teacher was wearing a dress, the student a man's suit; their carefully staged entrance publicly declared their affair." The impressionable Gallop was blown away: "I thought the two of them were just the hottest thing I'd ever seen." But she also took careful note of what the pair's costumes denoted: "It was crucial to this feminist spectacle that the student was the one wearing men's clothing. This seemed a role reversal. Her suit hinted that the connection made it possible for this student to take on power with the teacher." We have seen Gallop take the hint and run away with it. The image of the teacher in the dress and the student in the suit hovers over the book as a kind of pictograph of its thesis that professor/student sex gives the student power over the professor.

The power to get a teacher into trouble, if not fired from her job, was a power hardly anticipated by Gallop, and one she blames on "the chill winds of the current climate" rather than on what she ought to have recognized (she writes that she is "at heart a Freudian") as the sirocco of the oedipal universe. Her ability to see that the love affair between the generations is also a struggle for power that the "lesser man" cannot lose is accompanied by a refusal—like her refusal to take no for an answer from the reluctant professors—to accept the tragic dimension of the story. Gallop's vision is a comic one. She is a clown, an exhibitionist, a person who, as she tells us, likes to make a spectacle of herself, and who has an activist's optimistic belief that things can be worked out if you work at them hard enough. But in the case of the graduate student things could not be worked out.

The story begins, in Gallop's account, as the story all over again of an ambitious, eager student with a crush on a brilliant teacher ("She was . . . enamored of my work even before she met me") and of the teacher's helpless surrender to the student's desire. As we know, after 1982 Gallop was not available, as the two professors had been, for going all the way, but she was up for the "intensely personal and personally intense" relationship that developed almost immediately between herself and the graduate student. The woman had come up to Gallop after an evening class, insisted on an immediate conference, pressed to be taken on as a dissertation advisee, and, when Gallop agreed, still not satisfied, persuaded her to accompany her to a bar across the street for talk into the night. This new version of her pushy young self could not but enchant Gallop. The student further endeared herself by sharing Gallop's love of being outrageous. Thus, at a gathering of graduate students in a bar during an event at the university called the First Annual Graduate Student Gay and Lesbian Conference, Gallop saw no reason not to take part in a long, passionate kiss with her advisee ("I don't actually know who started it," she writes) as the other graduate students watched in awe. She saw it as just another piece of amusing showing-off of the kind she and the advisee were devoted to. She did not see it as the kiss that mafia figures bestow on the guy they are going to kill. A year and a half later the kiss turned up in the graduate student's sexual harassment complaint, along with another piece of naughtiness Gallop permitted herself at the gay and lesbian conference, in the innocent belief that she was among young friends rather than ancient enemies.

Gallop was entranced by the conference. There was so much sex in the air she thought she was back in the hot seventies. (A graduate student "complimented me on my legs, and asked if I wanted to go back to her hotel room with her. I was flattered but graciously declined.") And "everyone seemed so clever and sassy; I wanted to rise to the occasion." Gallop did so while formulating a question for one of the speakers ("a really good-looking woman from out of town"); before she knew it she had said "graduate students are my sexual preference." "The statement was meant to be a joke," she explains, a trifle leadenly. It "was playing with these two identities, trying loosely to suggest that 'graduate student' was somehow like 'gay and lesbian.'" But no one got it, least of all the sexual harassment complainants, who were in the audience. In their complaint they said they understood Gallop to be publicly announcing that she slept with graduate students and privately signaling that she wanted to sleep with them.

Gallop's relationship with the pushy graduate student went sour when Gallop began criticizing her work. "More than once I told [her] her work was not satisfactory." Here is where the story diverges from the story of the two professors who, after sleeping with Gallop, "continued to serve on my dissertation committee [and] continued to serve me well" and who "did not treat my work any differently than before we had sex." In *Thinking Through the Body*, Gallop recalls a meeting with one of the seduced professors (as we now know him) to discuss a chapter of her thesis on Barthes's reading of Sade, and writes that "we tore the chapter to shreds, while I laughed hysterically at the stupidity of my reading of Barthes." Sixteen years later, Gallop's student did not laugh hysterically when *her* stupidity was pointed out to her. She "felt let down, became outraged, and charged me with sexual harassment."

Gallop cannot help but allow some of her reciprocal disappointment and anger to surface. But she reserves her bitterest reflections for the university that rapped her on the knuckles for "consensual amorous relations" and, in effect, found her guilty of "something like 'fourth-degree harassment.'" She points out that sexual harassment has to do with *unwanted* sexual attentions. She reminds us that in all the stories she has told about herself as a student or teacher lover, it was always the student who was the instigator. And she holds up the policies that forbid consensual sex and romance between professors and students as a threat to pedagogy:

> At its most intense—and, I would argue, its most productive—the pedagogical relation between teacher and student is, in fact, "a consensual amorous relation." And if schools decide to prohibit not only sex but "amorous relations" between teacher and student, the "consensual amorous relation" that will be banned from our campuses might just be teaching itself.

Modern American pedagogy is poised on the fiction that there is no "greater man" or "lesser man" in the teacher/

student dyad. Although the socratizing lecture course is still offered, the action in American higher (no less than lower) education is in the democratizing discussion class. Here any idiotic thing the student says is listened to as if it was brilliant, and here our national vice of talking for the sake of hearing ourselves talk is cultivated as if it was a virtue. A good teacher is someone who can somehow transform this discouraging gathering of babblers into an inspiriting community of minds working together. That an erotic current (a transference, to use the psychoanalytic term) is the fulcrum of this transformation is unquestionable. The students begin to speak the teacher's language and to ape his thought, like lovers under the illusion that they are alike. Gallop is a good teacher who is also a dedicated bad girl. Her transgressive after-class relationships with students are evidently a condition of the sparkle and zest of her performance as a teacher. Teachers like her— larger-than-life characters with quirky minds—are the teachers one remembers best from college. They are a precious resource, there aren't many of them, and colleges know their worth and compete for them. Gallop has offered a persuasive argument for the harmlessness (to the student) of a teacher who is a pushover. (She never addresses the obviously more fraught question of the teacher who is a seducer.) But her book has not convinced me that the unpleasantness she has been subjected to has put her teaching at risk. The book itself is a testament to the prod that unpleasantness can provide to a restless spirit. The new repression can only spur the irrepressible Gallop to new audacities.

The New York Review of Books, 1997

SISTERS, LOVERS, TARTS, AND FRIENDS

This book opens with a confession of defeat. "There was a time, not so long ago, when I thought that it would be agreeable to write my own life. After three failures I have changed my mind," Quentin Bell writes. "Therefore the main body of this work is devoted, not to me, but to my elders and betters, a term I have used to describe my parents, their friends and acquaintances." His parents were the painter Vanessa Bell and the critic Clive Bell; their friends and acquaintances were, among others, Duncan Grant, Roger Fry, Lytton Strachey, Maynard Keynes, E. M. Forster, and Ottoline Morrell.

Now in his mid-eighties, Bell evidently could not change the habits of a lifetime of literary self-effacement; he continues to feel comfortable in the position of the observer and uncomfortable as the observed. Knowing that the subject of an autobiography is no less at the mercy of the writer than the subject of a biography, he has prudently declined the blandishments of his writing self, and retreated to his accustomed safe place at the periphery. In his extraordinary biography of his aunt Virginia

---

Bloomsbury Recalled, by Quentin Bell

Woolf, published in 1972, Bell emerged as a writer of rare perspicacity and moral authority. It was he who first made public the painful family secret of Virginia's sexual molestation by her half brothers Gerald and George Duckworth (Gerald examined her private parts when she was five, and George would come into her bedroom and paw her when she was a teenager) and excoriated the miscreants with a contemptuous force that no subsequent writer has matched. It was he, too, who brought to light a flirtation between his father and Virginia, which took place two years before his own birth in 1910, when his mother was preoccupied with her firstborn baby, Julian— this time passing judgment on Virginia herself, as well as on Clive, for bringing what seemed to him gratuitous unhappiness to Vanessa.

Virginia Woolf belongs to the elect body of biographies whose authors have been close to and fond of their subjects—works such as Boswell's life of Johnson and Jones's life of Freud—which gives them a conviction that biographies by strangers never achieve. But where Boswell and Jones write as sons, Bell writes as a nephew, one whose affection for his subject is never in doubt but whose primary loyalty to his immediate family is always implicit. Thus while Bell faithfully fulfills his contract to write a life of Virginia (he was asked to do so by Leonard Woolf), he allows us to feel the constraint that he feels when narrating family history strictly in relation to the consciousness of his aunt. Throughout the biography, we feel the presence of other consciousnesses (most notably the consciousness of Vanessa Bell) and sense other ways in which the story could be told. The episode of the flirtation between Clive and Virginia is only one of many passages where this perspectival tension flashes out of the narrative. Another is a passage dealing with the death of Julian Bell in the Spanish Civil War, at the age of thirty. "The matter concerns us only in as much as it concerned Virginia," Bell remarks, as if to assure the reader that he is not being solicited for more sympathy than he, as the purchaser of a book about Virginia Woolf, is required to extend to the family of her sister. The reader, however, as he follows Bell's account of Virginia's tender ministrations to Vanessa, who had collapsed under the pressure of the unendurable and lay in bed for several weeks in "an unreal state," cannot but find himself concerned about the matter far beyond the limits set by the punctilious biographer.

In *Bloomsbury Recalled*, free of the constraints of his nephew-biographer role, Bell returns to this and to other critical moments in his family's history. But much water has gone over the dam since the publication of *Virginia Woolf*. In 1983, Frances Spalding's biography of Vanessa Bell was published, followed by Bell's half sister Angelica Garnett's memoir *Deceived with Kindness: A Bloomsbury Childhood* (1985); Jane Dunn's comparative study of Virginia and Vanessa, *A Very Close Conspiracy* (1991); and Regina Marler's *Selected Letters of Vanessa Bell* (1993). Bell need no longer apologize for writing about his mother in her own right; she has become a full-fledged character in the intertextual novel of Bloomsbury that has arisen from these and other publications by and about Bloomsbury figures, which the success of *Virginia Woolf* (and that of its predecessors, Michael Holroyd's life of Lytton Strachey and Leonard Woolf's autobiography) emboldened publishers to issue. The restoration and opening to the public of Charleston farmhouse, Bell's childhood country home, was a kind of crowning moment of the diversion to Vanessa of the public's exclusive interest in

Virginia. "As you have the children, the fame by rights belongs to me," Virginia once playfully wrote to Vanessa. But Vanessa now has the fame, too, less for her art (which belongs among the distinguished but non-innovative examples of Post-Impressionism) than for her remarkable, unconventional life. Ms. Spalding was the first to fully explore the almost comical unruliness of the household in which Quentin Bell grew up, a sort of single-parent household with explanations. The father, Clive, was absent—he and Vanessa had (amicably) split up in 1916, when the boys were six and eight—and yet he was present much of the time, often accompanied by a current mistress. The mother's lover, the painter Duncan Grant, was present—he had moved in with Vanessa in 1916—and yet he was absent in a very fundamental sense, since he preferred to sleep with men. However, in 1918, Duncan fathered a child by Vanessa—Angelica—who grew up believing that Clive was her father and wasn't disabused of the notion until she was eighteen. In Ms. Spalding's version, Vanessa was the calm mistress of the situation, presiding over the family with a beautiful dignity and simplicity, exemplifying a life of enviable artistic and domestic fulfillment. Angelica Garnett's memoir offered a different view, and sounded a different note—one that had never before been heard in the annals of Bloomsbury. Whereas the characteristic tone of Bloomsbury is soft, oblique, offhand, ironic, *Deceived with Kindness* is loud and direct, a cry of rage and resentment. The book reveals that Angelica had never been easy or happy in her bohemian family; she would have much preferred growing up in a regular bourgeois household, and she cannot forgive her parents for the lie they made her live under. She writes of her mother not as a magnificent but as a pathetic woman, forced by her passion for the charming, selfish, homosexual Grant into a sexless gray existence. Garnett herself emerges from the book—as many writers of victim autobiographies, beginning with Rousseau, have done—as a person rather short on humor.

Whether Quentin Bell's failure of nerve in writing his autobiography was shaped by the example of his sister's book we cannot presume to know, of course. But the cheerful and amiable book he did write could not contrast more sharply with Garnett's dark, accusing memoir. Bell is not entirely uncritical of his elders and betters. He writes contemptuously of his father's pro-Fascist leanings ("I for my part never found Clive great fun after the advent of Hitler. Taking an interest in politics, and feeling, as I do, that the Jews are the salt of the earth, it was too difficult"); he expresses his distaste for some elements of the gay society around Duncan Grant ("They were the most unappetizing male tarts I ever saw, filthy with a dirt which was moral rather than physical"); he complains about Leonard Woolf's marmoset, Mitz. ("Marmosets are very small monkeys which I believe inhabit trees; in aspect they bear a certain resemblance to the late Dr. Goebbels." Mitz "seemed to be in a perpetual state of vicious fury; ugly at all times, it became hideous when it vented its spite at the world. It was deeply in love with Leonard and would spit out its jealousy upon the rest of humanity. Perhaps it was showing its affection when it crouched upon his arm and defecated upon him; this was so much its favorite occupation that Leonard had to have waterproofing upon the sleeves of his jacket.") But, significantly, Bell never complains about the adults vis-à-vis himself; he insists on his role of detached observer; he keeps his child's griefs to himself.

This has resulted in a certain sacrifice of tautness in Bell's narrative. Without the rudder of an engaged consciousness, the anecdotes and observations of *Bloomsbury Observed* bob about somewhat aimlessly. Bell accepts the trade-off. With his characteristic modesty, he is content to offer a text that is a kind of extended footnote to the work of other chroniclers of Bloomsbury (including that of his younger self), correcting where he feels correction is required, clarifying, amplifying, modulating. He is no longer as exercised as he once was over the Duckworth brothers' malefactions; he is more anxious now to reprove the writers who have gone beyond the evidence to claim that Virginia (and Vanessa, who had also suffered from George's attentions) had been raped. "I must pause to state the proven facts of the case," he writes, and goes on to say of Gerald's inspection of Virginia's genitals that "it was a horrid act, but we may doubt whether he was the first schoolboy to do such a thing; it is not a misdemeanor which justifies us in suspecting the offender of anything more serious." As for George and his "kissing, fondling, toying," he "was certainly guilty of stupid and inconsiderate behavior. . . . But it remains unclear exactly what happened and when." Because "we have every reason to think that both Vanessa and Virginia were virgins when they married," and because "according to his brother-in-law J. W. Hills, George himself was a virgin when he married," Bell considers it highly improbable "that copulation took place."

Analyzing a "lasting antipathy" between Clive and Leonard, which he believes derived from mutual jealousy over Virginia, Bell writes: "To Clive it seemed that Leonard was too austere, too political, too critical of that which he considered frivolous or worldly. He missed all

the jolly and decorative side of life; this made him censorious and puritanical and limited his appreciation of the
arts. In short he was a 'kill-joy.' Clive never quite forgave
Leonard for having been an Apostle while he, Clive, was
not. Leonard thought Clive an intellectual lightweight
whose views on politics and life in general were those of a
timid, spoilt and selfish man; as a critic he was superficial,
as a man fussy, snobbish and frequently ridiculous." Bell
goes on to extend the opposition between his father and
uncle to his brother and himself. He writes that in the
period 1926 to 1933 "I was charmed by Clive's worldly
panache, his urbanity and his sense of fun, while Julian,
serious, sometimes ruthlessly serious, a member of the
Labor Party, an Apostle, unworldly, interested in poetry
and at times displaying a kind of intellectual puritanism,
was probably at that time Leonard's favorite nephew. . . .
I was regarded . . . as a very precious, affected young man."
However, the novelistic polarity of the frivolous, apolitical
younger brother versus the dour, politically correct elder
one falls apart almost immediately, since Quentin himself, as he tells us, became involved in politics—politics
that were far to the left of Julian's—as the 1930s progressed.
Bell never tells us how he felt about his brother. He indi-
cates and hints but he never comes out and says—as he
never comes out and says what he thinks of his sister's
book. We must read between the lines. "Of the three of
us I was the least precious," he writes, as if stating an
obvious and mildly irksome fact. He goes on to tell the
following astonishing anecdote, set in 1937 when Julian
was deciding whether or not to go fight in Spain. "There
was a meal at Charleston eaten by Vanessa, we three
children and, I think, Duncan. Vanessa served a pudding; she gave half to Julian, the rest of us divided what

remained. Vanessa herself realized that there was something more than a little absurd about this method of displaying affection and said something like: 'You see, I have to.' My own feeling was: 'how hideously embarrassing for Julian.' Luckily he liked the pudding and ate it all up with an unembarrassed grin."

One can't but feel that Bell's telling of this incident, which has lingered in his memory for nearly sixty years, has undergone some of the softening changes that his account of Gerald's and George's horrid acts has undergone. When he was younger, Bell's innate geniality (he writes of "my flattering pencil") could give way if the provocation was severe enough. Some prods—like that of the unspeakable Mitz or those of certain impertinent revisionist writers about Virginia Woolf ("I cannot feel much charity for those imbeciles who have . . . maintained," he writes, that Leonard "did not love Virginia")—will evidently never lose their electrical charge. But in general Bell allows the laid-back, Clivish parts of his nature, the parts drawn to the jolly and decorative side of life, to override, if not to entirely eradicate, the austere and censorious aspects of himself he associates with his uncle. In a letter of 1907 (it appears in Regina Marler's selection), Vanessa drew a remarkable sketch of her husband—one in which her younger son might well recognize himself today: "I see that Clive has taken up the only possible attitude. . . . One ought to go one's own way without argument or fuss and without attempting to make the stupid see one's point of view, and when asked to do things one does not want to do one ought to give a half jocular refusal and stick to it, which is the only way of baffling them."

"A VERY SADISTIC MAN"

On page 313 of his biography of Ted Hughes, Jonathan Bate paraphrases a racy passage from the journal Sylvia Plath kept in the last months of her life:

> On the day that she found Yeats's house in Fitz-roy Road, she rushed round in a fever of excitement to tell Al [Alvarez]. That evening, she noted in her journal with her usual acerbic wit, they were engaged in a certain activity when the telephone rang. She put her foot over his penis so that, as she phrased it, he was appropriately attired to receive the call.

We assume that Bate is paraphrasing rather than quoting Plath's entry because of the copyright law prohibiting quotation of unpublished writing without permission of the writer or of his or her estate. As Bate wrote in *The Guardian* in April 2014, in an angry article entitled "How the Actions of the Ted Hughes Estate Will Change My Biography," the estate had abruptly withdrawn permission

---

Ted Hughes: The Unauthorised Life, by Jonathan Bate

to quote after initially enthusiastically approving "my plan for what I called 'a literary life.'"

But in fact, the action of the estate was not the reason for Bate's resort to paraphrase. As readers familiar with the Hughes/Plath legend will realize or have already realized, Bate was paraphrasing words he could not possibly have read since Plath's last journal was destroyed by Hughes soon after her suicide. ("I did not want her children to have to read it," Hughes explained when he revealed his act of destruction in the introduction to a volume of Plath's earlier journals.) What Bate was paraphrasing, he tells us, was Olwyn Hughes's *memory* of what she had read in the journal before her brother destroyed it.

In the introduction to his book, Bate—who is a professor of English literature at Oxford and the author of numerous books on Shakespeare, along with a biography of John Clare—offers a "cardinal rule" of literary biography: "The work and how it came into being is what is worth writing about, what is to be respected. The life is invoked in order to illuminate the work; the biographical impulse must be at one with the literary-critical." And: "The task of the literary biographer is not so much to enumerate all the available facts as to select those outer circumstances and transformative moments that shape the inner life in significant ways." But these fine words—are just fine words. The revelation, if that's what it is, of sex between Plath and Alvarez (in his autobiographical writings Alvarez indicated that there had never been any) illuminates neither Hughes's work nor his inner life. It only makes plain, along with his prurience, Bate's dislike of Alvarez. "At the time of Sylvia's death, a contemporary noted that Alvarez had a 'hangdog adoration of T.H.' and expressed the opinion that he was 'stuck in Freudianism like an American teenager,'" Bate writes, and, as if this wasn't mean enough, adds: "Alvarez could make or break a poet, but his own poetry was thin gruel." Bate's malice is the glue that holds his incoherent book together— malice directed at other peripheral characters but chiefly directed at its subject. Bate wants to cut Hughes down to size and does so, interestingly, by blowing him up into a kind of extra-large sex maniac.

He starts the book with a chapter called "The Deposition." In 1986 a psychiatrist named Jane Anderson, a friend of Plath's on whom a character in *The Bell Jar* had been based, sued the makers of a film version of the novel, along with Hughes (who held the copyright of the book), for portraying her as a lesbian. The lawsuit was settled. It was a nuisance and expense for Hughes, but hardly a seminal event that merits the opening chapter of his biography. The purpose of the chapter is to introduce this piece of Anderson's testimony:

> [Sylvia] said that she had met a man who was a poet, with whom she was very much in love. She went on to say that this person, whom she described as a very sadistic man, was someone she cared about a great deal. . . . She also said that she thought she could manage him, manage his sadistic characteristics.
>
> Q. Was she saying that he was sadistic towards her?
>
> A. My recollection is she described him as someone who was very sadistic.

The stage is now set for the examples of Hughes's sadism that give Bate's book the sensational character that caused the estate to withdraw from it in horror. The most shocking of these examples is a scene of sex in a London hotel between Hughes and Assia Wevill, the beautiful woman with whom he began an affair in the last year of his marriage to Plath, and who killed herself and her four-year-old daughter with Hughes (by gas, presumably in imitation of Plath, after living with him intermittently for five years). At the hotel, Bate writes, Hughes's "lovemaking was 'so violent and animal' that he ruptured her." Bate's source is a diary kept by Nathaniel Tarn, a poet, anthropologist, and psychoanalyst in whom, unbeknownst to each other, Assia and her husband David Wevill confided.

Tarn would write down what they said to him and his papers, including the diary, found their way to an archive at Stanford University, where anyone can read them. Bate was not the first to do so. The scene of the violent and animal sex appeared in a biography of Assia Wevill, *A Lover of Unreason*, by Yehuda Koren and Eilat Negev. Bate writes condescendingly of Koren and Negev as "touchingly literalistic" in their interpretation of a poem of Hughes about Assia, but he is not above quoting from their interview with David Wevill in which he told them that Assia told him that Sylvia caught Hughes kissing her in the kitchen of his and Plath's Devon house during their first visit to the couple.

Like the evidence of Olwyn's memory, the evidence of Tarn's diary or of David Wevill's interview is not evidence of the highest order of trustworthiness. The standing that the blabbings of contemporaries have in biographical narratives is surely one of the genre's most problematic conventions. People can say anything they want about a dead person. The dead cannot sue. This may be the least of their troubles, but it can be excruciating for spouses and offspring to read what they know to be untrue and not be able to do anything about it except issue complaints that fall upon uninterested ears.

Hughes's widow Carol recently issued such a complaint, in the form of a press release written by the estate's lawyer, Damon Parker, citing eighteen factual errors in the sixteen pages of the book she had been able to bring herself to read. The "most offensive" of these errors concerned Bate's account of the car trip Carol Hughes and Plath and Hughes's son Nicholas made from London to Devon with the hearse carrying Ted Hughes's coffin: "The body was returned to Devon, the accompanying party stopping, as Ted the gastronome would have wanted, for a good lunch on the way." Parker quotes an outraged Carol Hughes: "The idea that Nicholas and I would be enjoying a 'good lunch' while Ted lay dead in the hearse outside is a slur suggesting utter disrespect, and one I consider to be in extremely poor taste."

If poor taste is uncongenial to Mrs. Hughes, she will do well to continue not reading Bate's biography. Among the specimens of tastelessness lodged in the book like the threepenny coins in a Christmas pudding, none may surpass Bate's quotation from Erica Jong in her book *Seducing the Demon: Writing for My Life*, about meeting Hughes in New York and resisting his advances ("He was fiercely sexy, with a vampirish, warlock appeal. . . . He did the wildman-from-the-moors thing on me full force"), after which "I taxied home to my husband on the West Side, my head full of the hottest fantasies. Of course we f—— our brains out with me imagining Ted."

But beyond tastelessness there is Bate's cluelessness about what you can and cannot do if you want to be regarded as an honest and serious writer. Here is what he does with an article in the *Daily Mail* called "Ted Hughes, My Secret Lover" by a woman from Australia named Jill Barber. Barber wrote: "His first act of love was to hold me tenderly, mopping my brow with a wet flannel as I threw up the cheap champagne into his sink. . . . He lay me on the bed and tenderly unbuttoned and unzipped me and gazed admiringly at me. . . . He was rough, passionate and forceful." Bate writes: "He mopped her brow with a wet flannel as she threw up the cheap champagne into his sink, then he tenderly unbuttoned and unzipped her, gazed admiringly at her body and made forceful love to her."

In 2000 Bate came to Faber and Faber, which acts as agent for the Ted Hughes estate, proposing to write an authorized biography of Hughes, who was "the obvious choice for my next literary biography after I had done with two of his favourite poets, Shakespeare and John Clare." He was told that Hughes had left instructions opposing an authorized biography, so that was that. But in 2009, emboldened by Carol Hughes's sale to the British Library of documents that Hughes had held back when he sold his papers to Emory University in Atlanta, and by the publication of a book of his letters, Bate approached Faber and Faber again and proposed to write not a biography, but a work of literary criticism in which the life would merely figure.

This time the estate accepted. In his *Guardian* piece Bate recalled a delightful initial lunch with an editor from Faber and Faber and Carol (who "expressed herself 'totally happy with my idea of using the life to illuminate the work'") at a restaurant "in, of all places, Rugby Street—where Ted first made love to Sylvia Plath. I took this to be my symbolic anointing." After the deal hideously unraveled, Damon Parker wrote in *The Guardian*:

> At the risk of disillusioning him, there was no significance to the restaurant or the street chosen for a lunch with Mrs. Hughes and the poetry editor. The restaurant just happened to be a favourite haunt of Faber & Faber executives at that time. Nor was there any "symbolic anointing" of him in anyone's mind other than his own.

The estate and Faber and Faber had begun to smell a rat early on. "The tone and style of a draft article Professor Bate wanted to submit to a respected literary magazine here soon after he was commissioned, based on his initial researches, led to concerns that he seemed to be straying from his agreed remit," Damon Parker wrote in reply to my inquiry about what had got their wind up. (He could say nothing further about the article.) Also

> despite what had been previously agreed Professor Bate then resisted repeated requests to see some of his work in progress, from that time in 2010

right up until the Estate withdrew support for his book in late 2013. . . . The Estate could no longer cooperate once it seemed increasingly likely that his book would be rather different in tone and content from the work of serious scholarship which he had initially proposed.

Bate and Faber and Faber parted company and Harper Collins became the book's publisher.

Bate's claim that withdrawal of permission to quote forced him to write the distasteful book he has written is hard to credit. In "How the Actions of the Ted Hughes Estate Will Change My Biography," he writes of the "pages and pages of detailed analysis of the multiple drafts of the poems" that will now "have to go," and of how "the new version will be much more biographical." What Bate writes about Hughes's poetry in the HarperCollins text is of staggering superficiality. He tells you what he does and doesn't like. When he likes a poem he uses terms like "aching beauty" and "achingly sad." When he dislikes a poem he will talk of Hughes "operating on auto-pilot, writing nature notes instead of penetrating to the forces behind nature and in himself."

It is odd to read that last awkward phrase. Bate should be the last person to complain about the absence of unseen forces. For the mystical and mythic influences that inform Hughes's understanding of imaginative literature and shape his poetic practice, Bate has only contempt, writing of his "sometimes bonkers ideas about astrology and the occult; his use of ancient ideas and obscure literary sources as a way of explaining, even justifying, what most reasonable people would simply describe as bad behavior."

In a letter of 1989 to his friend Lucas Myers, published in *Letters of Ted Hughes*, Hughes writes about how "pitifully little" he is producing and goes on to

> wonder sometimes if things might have gone differently without the events of 63 & 69 [the years of Plath's and Wevill's suicides]. I have an idea of those two episodes as giant steel doors shutting down over great parts of myself, leaving me that much less, just what was left, to live on. No doubt a more resolute artist would have penetrated the steel doors—but I believe big physical changes happen at those times, big self-anaesthesias. Maybe life isn't long enough to wake up from them.

Hughes's feeling of not writing enough is common among writers, sometimes even among the most prolific. In Hughes's case it was certainly delusory. The posthumous volume of Hughes's collected poems is over a thousand pages long and there are five volumes of prose and seven volumes of translations. But without question Hughes suffered blows greater than those it is given to most writers to suffer. His life had been ruined not just once, but twice. It has the character not of actual human existence but of a dark fable about a hero born under a malign star.

That it was Bate of all people who was chosen to write Hughes's biography only heightens our sense of Hughes's preternatural unluckiness; though the choice might not have surprised him. Ancient stories about innocents delivered into the hands of enemies disguised as friends were well known to him, as was *The Aspern Papers.* He emerges from his letters as a man blessed with a brilliant mind and a warm and open nature, who seemed to take a deeper interest in other people's feelings and wishes than the rest of us are able to do and who never said anything trite or obvious or pious or self-serving. Of course, this is Hughes's epistolary persona, the persona he created the way novelists create characters. The question of what he was "really" like remains unanswered, as it should. If anything is our own business, it is our pathetic native self. Biographers, in their pride, think otherwise. Readers, in their curiosity, encourage them in their impertinence. Surely Hughes's family, if not his shade, deserve better than Bate's squalid findings about Hughes's sex life and priggish theories about his psychology.

The New York Review of Books, 2016

REMEMBER THE LADIES

Among the many oddities of Alexander McCall Smith's
No. 1 Ladies' Detective Agency series is its unabashed
sexism. McCall Smith treats the weaker sex—men—with
pitying condescension. "Boys, men. They're all the same,"
a woman Sunday school teacher says when she learns that
a boy has been exposing himself to a girl in the next seat.
"They think that this thing is something special and
they're all so proud of it. They do not know how ridiculous it is." Another female character dryly observes, in
another context: "We are all human. Men particularly."
She is Precious Ramotswe (known as Mma Ramotswe),
the regally fat, brilliantly sensible, and preternaturally
good and kind private detective around whom the series,
set in the young republic of Botswana, revolves. "The Miss
Marple of Botswana," a book jacket quote says of her. But
this is wrong. Mma Ramotswe resembles Christie's character as little as the books resemble Christie's mysteries.
The No. 1 Ladies' Detective Agency books aren't really
mysteries at all. There are no murders in them and little
suspense. When asked about what the agency does, Mma

In the Company of Cheerful Ladies, by Alexander McCall Smith

Makutsi, Mma Ramotswe's assistant, replies (as a psychoanalyst might), "Most of the time we are just helping people to find out things they already know."

The Sunday school teacher admonishes the boy who exhibits his penis by creeping up behind him and hitting him over the head with a Bible. McCall Smith similarly uses the Bible to fix the reader's attention. The laconic, fast-paced stories of the Old Testament are the ur-texts for Mma Ramotswe's clean-edged cases, whose solutions have an air of mythic inevitability. In his classic study *The Art of Biblical Narrative*, Robert Alter identifies the "type-scenes" of the Hebrew Bible—notably, the betrothal that takes place at a well—and the No. 1 Ladies' Detective Agency series is ordered by a similar repertoire of set pieces.

One of the most charged of these occurs at a rural orphanage and involves a fruitcake. Mma Potokwane, the bossy head of the orphanage, serves the cake to people from whom she wishes to extract favors; no one who eats the cake can refuse her. In the fifth book of the series, *The Full Cupboard of Life*, McCall Smith spells out the reference that has obscurely hovered over the scene: "Just as Eve had used an apple to trap Adam, so Mma Potokwane used fruitcake. Fruitcake, apples; it made no difference really. Oh foolish, weak men!"

But lest it appear that McCall Smith is himself a foolish and weak author, writing heavy-handed parables, he pushes the scene to an extreme that illustrates the quality that is perhaps the chief reason for the appeal of these books: his playfulness. In the sixth and latest book, *In the Company of Cheerful Ladies*, McCall Smith moves the cake scene to the waiting room of a famous Johannesburg surgeon to whom Mma Potokwane has brought—

with no appointment—an orphan with a clubfoot. When the surgeon appears, Mma Potokwane whisks the primal fruitcake out of her bag and thrusts it into "the astonished man's hands"—and he, of course, after accepting his second slice, can do nothing but helplessly agree to operate on the orphan. At the end of the tall tale, Mma Potokwane reports that "he did not charge anything either. He said that the fruitcake was payment enough."

Good comedy requires villains—they give the game its high stakes—and McCall Smith provides his feminist comedy with an especially chilling one in the form of Note Mokoti, a sociopathic trumpet player, whom Mma Ramotswe as a very young woman makes the terrible mistake of marrying. This man is not weak and foolish; he is strong and evil. He regularly hits Mma Ramotswe, sometimes so hard that she has to go to the hospital for stitches. He abandons her after the death of their newborn baby and disappears from her life—and from the series. But he remains a sinister background presence, the touchstone of the capacity men have for reducing women to primitive fear and helplessness. In the new book, he reappears and threatens to destroy Mma Ramotswe's successful career and happy second marriage.

Of course, Note is routed in the end (I will not say how), but his reappearance has deepened our sense of the seriousness of these light books and strengthened our bond with its heroine. She is the only daughter of Obed Ramotswe, a man of exquisite virtue—there are deviants from the weak and foolish majority on the good as well as on the evil side—from whom she inherits her own moral poise and also the means to set up her detective agency. McCall Smith does not render her realistically. Although he repeatedly cites her fatness (traditional build, he calls it) and the tiny white van she drives and the bush tea she drinks, we see her more at the majestic distance from which we view characters in the Bible rather than in intimate novelistic closeup. However, in contrast to the Bible's rather bloodthirsty feminist heroines (Judith and Jael, for example) Mma Ramotswe is an entirely benign instrument of justice. She exacts no revenge from the errant men (and the occasional errant woman) she catches out. Her impulse is always to spare the sinner and find some kindhearted way of exacting retribution.

"She was a good detective, and a good woman," McCall Smith writes of his heroine in the first book, and adds: "A good woman in a good country." The goodness of Botswana is crucial to McCall Smith's enterprise, and the source of much of its comic inspiration. McCall Smith follows the satiric literary tradition in which a "primitive" culture is held up to show the laughable backwardness of Western society. But, as McCall Smith is aware, the goodness of Botswana, a former British protectorate that gained its independence in 1966, has a hybrid character. The country's unspoiled natural beauty and the unhurried, kindly ways of its people are only a part of what makes Botswana the paradise of Africa. After independence, Botswana rapidly became one of the most prosperous and progressive—and Westernized—countries in Africa. (The prosperity is a result largely of the discovery of diamonds.)

McCall Smith gamely takes on the task of distinguishing between the good and the bad things that have come to Botswana from the West. Among the unarguably good things, for example, are the antidepressants that rescue Mr. J.L.B. Matekoni, a gifted automobile mechanic and the transcendently kind husband-to-be of Mma Ramotswe, from incapacitating clinical depression; and among the unarguably bad things is the fashion for thinness that is telling ladies of traditional build that a slice of Mma Potokwane's fruitcake has seven hundred calories. To illustrate the brilliant evenhandedness with which McCall Smith plays the two cultures against each other, here is a conversation between Mma Potokwane and Mr. J.L.B. Matekoni that takes place in *Tears of the Giraffe*, the second book of the series. Mma Potokwane has been on the telephone with a grocer who took an irritatingly long time to agree to donate some cooking oil to the orphanage.

"Some people are slow to give," she observes, and continues, "It is something to do with how their mothers brought them up. I have read all about this problem in a book. There is a doctor called Dr Freud who is very famous and has written many books about such people."

"Is he in Johannesburg?" asked Mr J.L.B. Matekoni.

"I do not think so," said Mma Potokwane. "It is a book from London. But it is very interesting. He says that all boys are in love with their mother."

"That is natural," said Mr J.L.B. Matekoni. "Of course boys love their mothers. Why should they not do so?"

Mma Potokwane shrugged. "I agree with you. I cannot see what is wrong with a boy loving his mother."

"Then why is Dr Freud worried about this?" went on Mr. J.L.B. Matekoni. "Surely he should be worried if they did *not* love their mothers."

Mma Potokwane looked thoughtful. "Yes. But he was still very worried about these boys and I think he tried to stop them."

"That is ridiculous," said Mr J.L.B. Matekoni.
"Surely he had better things to do with his time."

The passage is a tour de force of double-edged irony.
McCall Smith's gentle mockery falls equally on African
innocence and Western knowingness. Mma Potokwane's
"I do not think so" is worthy of Twain.

In the new book, Arcadia is showing signs of decline.
In the opening scene, Mma Ramotswe sits in an outdoor
café in the capital city of Gaborone and witnesses, in
rapid succession, three instances of flagrant antisocial behavior. First she sees a woman who is parking her car
scrape another car and drive away. Next she sees a woman
steal a bangle from an outdoor peddler while his back is
turned. And finally she herself is ripped off: as she runs
out of the café to try to stop the jewelry thief, she is
stopped by a waitress, who accuses her of trying to leave
without paying her check and demands money as a bribe
for not calling the police. Gaborone as Gomorrah.

After the incident of the scraped car, Mma Ramotswe
reflects that "it was not true that such a thing could not
have happened in the old Botswana—it could—but it was
undoubtedly true that this was much more likely to happen today." Her reverie continues: "This was what happened when towns became bigger and people became
strangers to one another; she knew, too, that this was a
consequence of increasing prosperity, which, curiously
enough, just seemed to bring out greed and selfishness."
A few pages later, in a scene in a church, we are recalled
to another threat to the African paradise. The minister
speaks of "this cruel sickness that stalks Africa"—that,
in fact, stalks Botswana more cruelly than almost any
other country: Botswana has one of the highest H.I.V.

infection rates in the world, roughly 40 percent of the adult population.

I get this statistic not from McCall Smith's series but from an article by Helen Epstein in the February 2004 issue of *Discover* magazine. The "cruel sickness" is not an overt theme of the No. 1 Ladies' Detective Agency books. McCall Smith does not even give the scourge its name. On some subterranean level, however, his sexual comedy and the tragedy of AIDS intersect. The sexual activity by which the H.I.V. infection is spread is the activity by which the books themselves are driven. Sex is everywhere in them.

A large percentage of the clients of the No. 1 Ladies' Detective Agency are women who want to know if their husbands are cheating on them. (They invariably are.) When Mma Ramotswe interviews one such client, "there flowed between them a brief current of understanding. All women in Botswana were the victims of the fecklessness of men. There were virtually no men these days who would marry a woman and settle down to look after her children; men like that seemed to be a thing of the past." The case takes a characteristically comic turn. After Mma Ramotswe personally entraps the husband and presents the client with the conclusive evidence of a photograph in which he is kissing the detective on her sofa, the client is beside herself. "You fat tart! You think you're a detective! You're just man hungry, like all those bar girls!" But the comedy only underscores the unfunniness of the priapism by which McCall Smith's Botswana is gripped.

McCall Smith does not connect the dots. He never talks explicitly about how "the cruel sickness" is transmitted. But one has only to look at the real Botswana (where McCall Smith has lived) to see what he must be gesturing toward. In a second article on the subject in *The New York Times Magazine*, Epstein writes chillingly about the promiscuity that is the agent of the AIDS epidemic in Africa. She attributes Botswana's especially high H.I.V. rate to a special sort of promiscuity: the concurrent long-term sexual relationships with more than one partner, largely male-orchestrated, that are a fixture of the country's life. She notes that a program of "partner reduction" or "increased faithfulness" in Uganda, where such relationships had also been commonplace, brought about a marked change in the H.I.V. infection rate; so far Botswana has not established such a program.

McCall Smith's major characters—Mma Ramotswe, Obed Ramotswe, J.L.B. Matekoni, Mma Makutsi, Mma Potokwane—are hardly in need of partner reduction. McCall Smith writes so compellingly of their goodness that we don't immediately notice their sexlessness. But there is a sort of chastity enveloping them that is in conspicuous contrast to the hypersexuality of the society at large. In the first book of the series, Mma Ramotswe articulates what is to become implicit. She has refused the first proposal of J.L.B. Matekoni, and worries about losing him as a good friend. "Why did love—and sex—complicate life so much? It would be far simpler for us not to have to worry about them. Sex played no part in her life now and she found that a great relief. . . . How terrible to be a man, and to have sex on one's mind all the time, as men are supposed to do. She had read in one of her magazines that the average man thought about sex over sixty times a day!" Mma Ramotswe later accepts the transcendently kind mechanic, and eventually marries him, but we don't get the feeling that sex has much to do with it. The sexual magnetism of the sociopathic trumpeter brought her nothing but suffering. Matekoni, clearly not a man who thinks about sex sixty times a day, if at all, brings her fatherly companionship. She is satisfied with it.

In a reprise of the cake scene, Mma Ramotswe and Mma Potokwane give the allegory of transgression yet another comedic tweak. As they sit in Mma Potokwane's office eating the magical confection, Mma Ramotswe asks her friend if she eats too much cake, and Mma Potokwane responds:

> "No, I do not. I do not eat too much cake." She paused and looked wistfully at her now emptying plate. "Sometimes I would like to eat too much cake. That is certainly true. Sometimes I am tempted."
>
> Mma Ramotswe sighed. "We are all tempted, Mma. We are all tempted when it comes to cake."
>
> "That is true," said Mma Potokwane sadly. "There are many temptations in this life, but cake is probably one of the biggest of them."

The No. 1 Ladies' Detective Agency series is a literary confection of such gossamer deliciousness that one feels it can only be good for one. Fortunately, since texts aren't cakes, there is no end to the pleasure that may be extracted from these six books.

The New York Times Book Review, 2005

"I SHOULD HAVE MADE HIM
FOR A DENTIST"

Norman Podhoretz's memoir *Making It* was almost universally disliked when it came out in 1967. It struck a chord of hostility in the mid-twentieth-century literary world that was out of all proportion to the literary sins it may or may not have committed. The reviews were not just negative, but mean. In what may have been the meanest review of all, Wilfred Sheed, a prominent critic and novelist of the time, wrote:

> In this mixture of complacency and agitation, he has written a book of no literary distinction whatever, pockmarked by clichés and little mock modesties and a woefully pedestrian tone. . . . Mediocrities from coast to coast will no doubt take *Making It* to their hearts and will use it for their own justification. . . . In the present condition of our society and the world, I cannot imagine a more feckless, silly book.

Making It, by Norman Podhoretz, with an introduction by Terry Teachout

Even before the book was published it was an object of derision. Podhoretz's friends urged him not to publish it, and his publisher shrank from it after reading the manuscript. Another publisher gamely took the book, but his gamble did not pay off. Word had spread throughout literary Manhattan about the god-awfulness of what Podhoretz had wrought. This and the reviews sealed the book's fate. It was a total humiliating failure.

Making It was reissued last year by New York Review Books as one of its Classics, and the literary world—perhaps because it no longer exists—remained calm. Bookish people didn't call each other up to exclaim about the scandal. Not many reviews appeared. And yet among those that did were some that in their nastiness might have been written in 1967. James Wolcott's review in the *London Review of Books* was the longest and nastiest. It began with a quote from an entry in Alfred Kazin's journal of 1963, in which Kazin wrote of a party he attended at the offices of *Commentary* magazine, of which Podhoretz was editor:

> Struck by the oafishness of Norman Pod, drunkenly clowning in the entrance to the elevator. That lovely, blond girl (wife of the publisher of the *NY Review?*) looked really offended, and I couldn't blame her.

Wolcott's decision to begin his put-down of *Making It* with an image of its author as a boorish jerk, taken from a text written years before the book's publication, may help answer the question of its original outlandish unpopularity. It illustrates a glaring problem of the autobiographical genre, namely its susceptibility to influences outside the text. At the time of the memoir's first publication Podhoretz was a well known if not universally well thought of figure in the New York literary establishment. He had been writing for *Commentary, Partisan Review,* and *The New Yorker* since the 1950s, when he was still in his twenties, and had become editor of *Commentary* in 1960 at the age of thirty. He was a kind of magnet for malice. A famous mischievous story going around was what Lauren Bacall was supposed to have said when he introduced himself to her at a cocktail party: "Fuck off, boy."

What was Edwin Frank, the editor of New York Review Books, thinking when he decided to reprint *Making It?* Had he seen virtues in the book that the fog of schadenfreude had obscured in 1967? Would a new audience see them, too? In his chapter on serving in the army, Podhoretz recalls that he got along extremely well with uneducated boys from the South. "I was puzzled as to what they saw in me, and my curiosity drove me once to ask one of them why he liked me. 'Because,' he answered in a thick Mississippi drawl, 'you *talk* so good.'"

Today's reader of *Making It* will immediately see that Podhoretz writes no less good than he talks. The 1967 reviewers were simply wrong when they added bad writing to their list of offenses. Writing as lucid and vital as Podhoretz's is not often encountered and should have been acknowledged. But the original critics were evidently too irked with the boy wonder to give him an inch. Perhaps more to the point, they could not distinguish between the book's narrator and its author. When we read a novel narrated in the first person we do not make that mistake. We know that Humbert Humbert and Vladimir Nabokov are not the same person. In the case of autobiography, because author and narrator share a name, we are only too prone to forget that the latter is a literary construct.

The "I" of *Making It* is a character we have never exactly met before. The outlines of his story are familiar: a precocious, poetry-writing boy, the son of poor, Yiddish-speaking immigrants in Brownsville, Brooklyn, rises above his origins and becomes a person to be reckoned with in the larger culture. But the particulars are unusual, a little mysterious. Norman—as I will call him to distinguish him from his creator, Podhoretz—is not the conventional changeling who doesn't belong with the Muggles he has been set down among. He is content with his lot. He is bookish and precocious, yes, but being the smartest boy in the class doesn't ruin his life. "By the age of thirteen I had made it into the neighborhood big time, otherwise known as the Cherokees, S.A.C. [social athletic club]," he says with modest pride, and adds:

> It had by no means been easy for me, as a mediocre athlete and a notoriously good student, to win acceptance from a gang which prided itself mainly on its masculinity and its contempt for authority, but once this had been accomplished, down the drain went any reason I might earlier have had for thinking that life could be better in any other place.

Once this had been accomplished. Norman doesn't explain how he negotiated this improbable feat, before which getting published in *Partisan Review* or becoming editor of *Commentary* pales. He simply tells us that the gang's uniform, a red satin jacket with white lettering stitched across the back saying "Cherokee," was his proudest possession, and that he wore it to school every day.

He was hardly waiting for a Princess Casamassima; but one came to him anyway in the form of a snobbish teacher at his high school named Mrs. K., who made him her pet and proposed to rid him of "the disgusting ways they had taught me at home and on the streets" and thus turn him into a plausible candidate for a Harvard scholarship. Norman's resistance to her three-year-long attempt to make him over comes to a dramatic head in a scene in which she takes him to de Pinna, a classy clothing store on Fifth Avenue, and tries to buy him a suit to wear to the Harvard interview. "Even at fifteen I understood what a fantastic act of aggression she was planning to commit against my parents and asking me to participate in," Norman recalls.

> Oh no, I said in a panic (suddenly realizing that I *wanted* her to buy me that suit), I can't, my mother wouldn't like it. "You can tell her it's a birthday present. Or else I will tell her. If I tell her, I'm sure she won't object." The idea of Mrs. K. meeting my mother was more than I could bear: my mother, who spoke with a Yiddish accent and of whom, until that sickening moment, I had never known I was ashamed and so ready to betray.

Norman somehow slides away from the betrayal; the suit is not bought. He later reflects:

Looking back now at the story of my relationship with Mrs. K. . . . what strikes me most sharply is the astonishing rudeness of this woman to whom "manners" were of such overriding concern. . . . Were her "good" manners derived from or conducive to a greater moral sensitivity than the "bad" manners I had learned at home and on the streets of Brownsville? I rather doubt it. The "crude" behavior of my own parents, for example, was then and is still marked by a tactfulness and a delicacy that K. simply could not have approached.

That is very handsomely said. But the seeds of class-consciousness that Mrs. K. had planted were well sprouted by the time Norman arrived at college. What she couldn't achieve with her obnoxious corrections, higher education achieved with its subtler admonishments. (He had received the Harvard scholarship—at the interview he wore a suit handed down from an uncle—but went to Columbia instead because it offered a more generous scholarship; the family could not afford the extra expenses of the Harvard offer.) While at Columbia Norman lived at home, traveling more than two hours by subway daily, and "I was, to all appearances, the same kid I had been before entering Columbia." Yet

we all knew that things were not the same. . . . I knew that the neighborhood voices were beginning to sound coarse and raucous; I knew that our apartment was beginning to look tasteless and tawdry; I knew that the girls in quest of whom my friends and I hornily roamed the streets

were beginning to strike me as too elaborately
made up, too shrill in their laughter, too crude in
their dress. . . . It was the lower-classness of
Brownsville to which I was responding with irri-
tation. . . . What did it matter that I genuinely
loved my family and my friends, when not even
love had the power to protect them from the
ruthless judgments of my newly delicate, oh-so-
delicate, sensibilities? What did it matter that I
was still naïve enough and cowardly enough and
even decent enough to pretend that my conver-
sion to "culture" had nothing to do with class
when I had already traveled so far along the road
Mrs. K. had predicted I would.

"I should have made him for a dentist," Norman's mother
murmurs to herself at a moment of special incomprehension of her boy's new ways.

It was at Columbia that Norman was bitten by the crazy
ambitiousness that was to become a sort of signature. For
the first time he was not automatically the smartest boy
in the class. In his freshman year he had to struggle just
to keep up, and then he had to claw his way to being first.
He attributes the excesses of his competitiveness to a
realization:

My hunger for success as a student, which was
great enough in itself but might yet have yielded
to discipline, became absolutely uncontrollable
when I began to realize that I would never make

the grade as a poet. . . . The truth was that I could not bear the idea of not being great.

Norman won his way to the academic top by being weirdly energized by exams and by an equally uncanny ability to write papers in the styles of the professors for whom they were written. Not only A's but A+'s poured in as a result of these aptitudes. He was not liked by a lot of his fellow students, but he didn't care. He cared only that the professors liked him. In his final year he took a course with Lionel Trilling, who was determined not to be taken in by this famous know-it-all. But Trilling was won over by the exceptional quality of Norman's academic performance. He, too, gave him an A+.

Trilling and his wife, Diana, became friends of Norman's after his graduation, and Trilling was to provide an important link to the literary world outside the academy by introducing him to Elliot Cohen, the editor of *Commentary*. But Norman's entrance into that world was delayed by another academic triumph. After graduation from Columbia he went to England, as the recipient of the Kellett Fellowship to Clare College at Cambridge University. Getting the coveted Kellett did not further endear Norman to his classmates, as he unrepentantly notes.

He recalls the pleasures of a room of his own, with early morning tea brought by a servant. He notes that this was the first time in his life he had the leisure to read for the sake of the work rather than to show someone how clever he was. In the English system the tutor for whom he wrote a weekly paper had no influence on the outcome of the exam he would take at the end of two years. Sucking up to him served no purpose.

[He] was the best possible antidote I could have found to the frenetic pursuit of "brilliance" to which I had become habituated at Columbia and whose imperatives constituted a more fearful tyranny, being largely internal, than any that could conceivably have been imposed upon me from the outside.

However:

There was, as usual, another side to the story. Worlds apart from the Cambridge of Clare was the Cambridge of Downing College, and if the fires within me were banked at Clare, to Downing I came, burning, burning, even more hotly than before: burning to learn, burning to impress, burning to succeed. . . . Downing was the college of F.R. Leavis, the greatest critic in England . . . the editor of the country's most formidable critical review, the terrifying *Scrutiny*.

Norman wins the heart of the fanatical Leavis as he had won those of his predecessors at Columbia. He is older (twenty-one) and "no longer so unformed as to be capable of an effortless imitation of the master's style in the papers I wrote." But his more subtle fawning succeeds beyond his dreams: Leavis invites him to write for *Scrutiny*, and prints the piece.

Norman can't help being Norman. Here as throughout the book Podhoretz writes about his hero with a finely judged mixture of affection and mockery. He knows as well as his critics that Norman's ambitiousness verges on the insane. But such is the power of Podhoretz's storytelling that we continue to want to follow the fortunes of his peculiar hero even as our sense of his peculiarity grows.

To complicate matters, Podhoretz has encased the story of Norman's feverish strivings—the way chocolate encases the soft center of a bonbon—in a rather puzzling polemic about a social problem that not many readers will recognize as such, much less want to carry on about. His idea is that American culture is dominated by a doctrine of "anti-success" that keeps successful people in a perpetual state of nervous guilt over the "corruption of spirit" that underlies their power, riches, and fame. "On the one hand," he writes, "our culture teaches us to shape our lives in accordance with the hunger for worldly things; on the other hand, it spitefully contrives to make us ashamed of the presence of those hungers in ourselves and to deprive us as far as possible of any pleasure in their satisfaction."

This said—and how well he says it—Podhoretz goes on to describe his hero's conquest of literary New York as anything but the angst-ridden experience we would expect it to be, given his thesis. We follow Norman's campaign to gain acceptance into "the family"—the mostly but by no means exclusively Jewish intellectuals associated with *Partisan Review*—with the sort of interest we reserve for favorite sports teams. We are rooting for him even as (with Podhoretz's good-natured permission) we are laughing at him. *Commentary* gave him his start, assigning him monthly book reviews. "What I wanted was to see my name in print, to be praised, and above all to attract attention." But it was the attention of the family I most dreamed of arousing. . . . There was nothing I loved better than to sit around with [Robert] Warshow or [Clement] Greenberg and listen (my wide-eyed worshipful fascination egging them on) to tales of the patriarchal past: how "Mary" had left "Philip" to marry Edmund Wilson . . . how "Dwight" had once organized nude swimming parties at the Cape, how "William" had really felt about "Delmore," and how "Isaac" really felt about "Saul." Oh to be granted the right to say "William" and "Philip" and "Dwight," as I could already say "Bob" and "Clem" and "Nat."

The right was granted in due course. When Norman's negative review of Saul Bellow's *The Adventures of Augie March* appeared in *Commentary*, the *Partisan Review* people took special notice. His dislike of the book, against the prevalent view that it was great, turned out to be the view that a lot of the family secretly held. There is a mordant account of a party at Philip Rahv's apartment that Norman characterized as the bar mitzvah ceremony that admitted him into the family. He got very drunk. "I remember hearing my voice pronounce an incredulous, 'You mean Alfred *Kazin*?' or 'You mean Dwight *Macdonald*?' or 'You mean Mary *McCarthy*?' as Rahv and a woman who was present treated me to my first horrified experience of true family-style gossip." After the party Norman stood out on the street violently throwing up. "And yet in the very midst of all that misery, I knew that I had never been so happy in my life."

A few months later Norman was drafted into the army and didn't enjoy basic training, but it was only after his release from the army that he became "more unhappy than I had ever been in my life" in a job as an editor at *Commentary* that had been promised to him by Elliot Cohen before he left for Fort Dix. By the time Norman came to claim the job, *Commentary* was no longer the place he had known when he had hung out with the editors and heard about Dwight's nude swimming parties. Cohen had had a nervous collapse and was in a mental institution. All of its former subeditors were gone except for two men who now jointly ran the journal and did not welcome Norman into their midst. They undermined and bullied him.

Podhoretz does not name the men but combines them into a character called "The Boss." "One of the reasons I was so miserable at *Commentary* during my time there under The Boss was that it had become practically the only place in the world where the sun still failed to shine on my fortunate young head," Norman reflects. His book reviews—in *Partisan Review, Commentary*, and *The New Yorker*—had made him into what he calls a "minor literary celebrity." At *Commentary*, under "The Boss," he was made to feel like a pathetic incompetent.

Finally he couldn't take it anymore and quit the job, but not before stopping into the offices of the American Jewish Council—the organization that owned *Commentary*—and telling the head of its personnel department why he was quitting. The result was a great upheaval that ended the autocratic reign of "The Boss" and allowed Norman to continue in the job as one of three equal editors. Norman asks himself: "In thus committing the prime crime of American boyhood, snitching to the authorities, did I feel guilty? A little, but mostly I felt pleased with myself for having acted so selflessly, so nobly." Here as elsewhere Norman keeps the reader on his side by telling the story on himself. He has no illusions about the dirtiness of what he did. We helplessly admire his honesty, as the women in his childhood

> marveled at my cleverness, quoting my bright sayings to one another and even back to me ("You remember what you said that time when I was here last? Let me hear you say it again."). They called me adorable, they called me delicious, they called me a genius, and predicted a great future for me: a doctor at the very least I would be.

They probably would not have predicted his politics. Soon after writing *Making It* Podhoretz veered sharply right (until then he was a regular lefty like most of the rest of the family) and has grown ever more firmly committed to right-wing causes. He has written numerous books about his extreme conservative beliefs. Perhaps more than any other of the leakages from life that give autobiography its wobbly ontological status, Podhoretz's radical post-publication politics hover over the book he wrote when he was an innocuous liberal. My attempt to seal it off from its author's later career, and to write as if I didn't know what I know—and what everyone who hears the name Norman Podhoretz knows—was made in the name of the New Critical ideal of textual fidelity: don't muddy the waters with stuff surrounding the text. In the case of *Making It*, however, the mud clinging to the tale of the strange ambitious boy may be crucial to its discreet charm.

The New York Review of Books, 2018

A NOTE ABOUT THE AUTHOR

Janet Malcolm is the author of many books, including *In the Freud Archives*; *The Journalist and the Murderer*; *Two Lives: Gertrude and Alice*, which won the 2008 PEN/Bograd Weld Prize for Biography; and *Forty-One False Starts*, which was a *New York Times Book Review* Notable Book and a finalist for the 2013 National Book Critics Circle Award for Criticism. She is a frequent contributor to *The New Yorker* and *The New York Review of Books*. In 2017, Malcolm received the Gold Medal for Belles Lettres and Criticism from the American Academy of Arts and Letters.